JOHN HIRST

JOHN HIRST

Selected Writings

Edited by
Chris Feik

Published by La Trobe University Press in conjunction with Black Inc.
Wurundjeri Country
22–24 Northumberland Street
Collingwood VIC 3066, Australia
enquiries@blackincbooks.com
www.blackincbooks.com
www.latrobeuniversitypress.com.au

La Trobe University plays an integral role in Australia's public intellectual life, and is recognised globally for its research excellence and commitment to ideas and debate. La Trobe University Press publishes books of high intellectual quality, aimed at general readers. Titles range across the humanities and sciences, and are written by distinguished and innovative scholars. La Trobe University Press books are produced in conjunction with Black Inc., an independent Australian publishing house. The members of the LTUP Editorial Board are Vice-Chancellor's Fellows Emeritus Professor Robert Manne and Dr Elizabeth Finkel, and Morry Schwartz and Chris Feik of Black Inc.

9781760645748 (paperback)
9781743824146 (ebook)

 A catalogue record for this work is available from the National Library of Australia

Cover design by Aira Pimping
Text design by Peter Long
Typesetting by Marilyn de Castro
Index by Diane Lowther

Every effort has been made to trace copyright holders and obtain their permission for the use of copyright material. The publisher apologises for any errors or omissions and would be grateful if notified of any corrections that should be incorporated in future reprints or editions of this book.

CONTENTS

ON THE SELECTION

F OR THIS VOLUME, I HAVE SELECTED FROM JOHN HIRST'S work as a historian of Australia and not of Europe (in one free-standing book, *The Shortest History of Europe*, that has enjoyed international success), nor as a commentator on social policy (such as in the Quarterly Essay *'Kangaroo Court': Family Law in Australia*).

I worked with John as editor and publisher on five of his books. Two of them represented his own choice of essays to reprint, so the ground was well prepared for a book of this kind. The chief editing task was to work out which piece to take when he had several excellent ones on the same topic. John's own piece 'Changing My Mind' describes his political evolution nicely.

I have retained the language used by John in the original publications even where, especially in matters of Indigenous history, it no longer conforms with the expectations or conventions of scholarly or public discourse. John's judgements and style were necessarily those of an Australian historian of his generation and politics, writing at a particular time in the development of his country and his discipline of history. Much that he wrote retains its force, but he would expect later generations to offer their own differing interpretations.

For their comments and suggestions, I am very grateful to Frank Bongiorno, Alex McDermott and Cathy Hirst. I am also grateful to Alex McDermott and Robert Manne for their support. Responsibility for the selection is, of course, mine.

Chris Feik

THREE VIEWS OF
JOHN HIRST

I

——

Frank Bongiorno

THERE WAS A PERSISTENT THEME, ESPECIALLY AMONG younger historians, in the tributes that appeared on social media to the eminent historian John Hirst on the news of his untimely death in early 2016: although they did not agree with everything he ever said or wrote, they admired and respected him.

Hirst might have found the idea that anyone was likely to agree with everything that anyone else said as amusing as his sudden prominence on social media. He would certainly have found the implication that anyone could agree with everything that *he* had to say a most peculiar one. For Hirst prided himself on his resistance to the current of fashionable opinion, and he was above all else a fiercely independent intellectual.

I've thought long and hard about why Hirst evoked this kind of response. He evoked it in me, too, and in many others I know. Apart from his personal generosity and kindness, I think it was because he wasn't afraid to argue a case – historical or political – from a set of premises he knew to be debatable. Even if you could not accept those premises – for instance, that border protection was not thoroughly entangled in Australia's distinctive and resilient politics of race – it was hard not to admire the passion, the fluency and the consistency with which Hirst would then prosecute his argument. The value was really in the case itself which, in his hands, would take flight with wings of its own.

Hirst was not really a historian of the 'look at this startling new document I found today' type, although he was certainly no slouch among the dusty archive boxes. He ranged widely but I believe was at his best in writing about colonial Australia – the sharpest of his historical articles and essays on the nineteenth century disclose a raw intellectual power decades after they were first published. He never seemed quite as comfortable when venturing far into the twentieth century. A South Australian by birth and education, his doctoral research culminated in a fine study, *Adelaide and the Country, 1870–1917: Their Social and Political Relationship* (1973), that remains the standard work on its subject. But it was the appearance of his *Convict Society and Its Enemies* a decade later that announced the arrival of a historian of real originality.

In effect, Hirst founded a school of historical writing about convict Australia that is usually – if somewhat simplistically – referred to as the 'normalisers'. The convict system, he argued, had suffered bad press in being presented as a form of slavery. Those who had wanted to end transportation had portrayed it as a brutal system dominated by chains and floggings, one that debased master and convict alike. He argued that this was essentially political rhetoric put about by enemies of the convict system; it did not correspond with a more prosaic reality. Colonial New South Wales, he said, 'was not a society which had to become free; its freedoms were well established from the earliest times'. Even Robert Hughes, who would later write a bestseller indebted to the very image of convict society Hirst had tried to overturn, could not but admire the persuasiveness of his argument.

Hirst was not afraid to take up some of the big controversies and puzzles in Australian historical writing – as in *Australian History in 7 Questions* (2014) – or to challenge the orthodoxies created by the profession's biggest names. So Geoffrey Blainey thought distance shaped Australia? Hirst was doubtful, and he outlined his case to his colleagues with characteristic eloquence in their premier professional journal, *Historical Studies*, in 1975. Russel Ward reckoned that the noble bushman, the pastoral worker, was the typical Australian? What about the pioneer, asked Hirst in the same journal in 1978; the conservative and patriotic small farmer who was also widely noticed and frequently celebrated? The federation of the Australian colonies was a mere business deal? Hirst wrote a whole book, and a very good one, *The Sentimental Nation: The Making of the Australian Commonwealth* (2000), putting that one to rest, presenting it instead as the fruit of nationalist idealism.

Hirst understood that nationalist idealism particularly well because he felt it so strongly himself. But I also sensed disappointment here; Australia never quite lived up to his ambitions for it. In these matters, he sometimes seemed like a talented bowler stuck on a pitch – his home turf, no less – offering precious little encouragement.

Hirst did not shy away from the fundamentally political and contemporary nature of historical writing, including his own. But his politics were much harder to pin down than the predictable 2016 headline in the *Australian* proclaiming him a 'culture warrior' might lead one to imagine. He was an active and principled supporter of public education but became a critic of what he regarded as some of the sloppier, levelling versions of progressive pedagogy. He believed in economic redistribution but came to worry about welfare dependence. He thought Australia's immigration program a great success but was a sceptic about some versions of multicultural ideology. He was an ALP voter by instinct and practice – he had been greatly angered by the dismissal of the Whitlam government – but he increasingly presented as a disappointed Labor man. At one point during the Howard era he declared in an op-ed piece that he was a social democrat and therefore a supporter of John Howard!

He was out of sympathy with the libertarianism of the 1970s, a period that coincided with his work on *Convict Society and Its Enemies*; by his own account, working on that book changed his 'bedrock assumptions about the world'. Hirst often found himself sympathising not with the convicts – which would have been a familiar enough stand for someone of the left – but with the masters and others in authority. His understanding, he recalled, was influenced by dealing with a 'very rebellious teenager' at home: 'I was under siege myself as I watched masters trying to control convicts'; an unusual insight into the relationship between this – or perhaps any – private man and public historian.

Other distinguished books followed: in 1988, the year of the Bicentenary, there was *The Strange Birth of Colonial Democracy: New South Wales 1848–1884*; perhaps less successful than the startling *Convict Society and Its Enemies* but all the same an important contribution to our understanding of the development of Australian political culture and one I still use in my own teaching and research. Hirst puzzled over how democracy seemed to have come into being 'almost without a struggle' – a claim that has been hotly contested by others in the years since he wrote – and somewhat in the manner of E.M. Forster he seemed to want to offer only two cheers for the results. 'But why should we care what [democracy] was like?', Hirst asked at the beginning of the book, then answering his own question: 'because in many fundamentals this is the political world we still inhabit.'

Hirst did not jump on and off bandwagons. A republican out of historical expertise and political conviction, he threw himself into the cause with passion and energy. He served as the Australian Republican Movement's (ARM) first Victorian convener and was also appointed by the Keating government to its Republic Advisory Committee. He did not commit himself to republicanism because it was flavour of the month, but rather out of a belief that Australian democracy would be incomplete for as long as its people owed allegiance to the British monarchy. As he made clear in *A Republican Manifesto* (1994), Hirst did not see a republican Australia as a break with our British past but rather as completing a decolonising and democratising process he had traced through his major works of Australian history since the 1970s. ARM's weakness for glitzy celebrities, however, ensured that the country's leading republican intellectual would have no place at the table when a convention finally met in Canberra to devise a model for a referendum. The occasion and the nation were the poorer for it.

There were perhaps some complex issues on which he might have been well advised not to tread – the area of family law and fathers' rights springs to mind – but it was hard not to see the usual Hirst traits in this business; his compassion for a student in distress; the embrace of a cause and a case he considered right; his concern with political and legal authority; his belief that historians should be public intellectuals grappling with difficult things that mattered. Hirst was a frequent contributor to newspaper opinion pages not because he particularly enjoyed the limelight – I never sensed any desire for fame – but because it was part of his ideal of engaged citizenship. Hirst set a high bar for himself in such matters. There was a fierce intensity to many of his contributions to the media. These were invariably delivered in his spare but compelling prose.

The public saw a creative historian capable of engaging a wide audience, as well as a public intellectual who delighted, infuriated and provoked. Hirst's colleagues in academia knew this John Hirst, but also a generous colleague and decent man. He spent a long career at La Trobe

University in Melbourne, contributing to making its history program one of the strongest in the country. He was a committed teacher as well as a highly successful supervisor of postgraduate theses on a bewildering array of topics. Several of his students are now successful history professors in their own right, often with historical interests and political opinions diametrically opposed to Hirst's, yet grateful for the guidance and support he offered them as young scholars. He also edited the nation's leading academic history journal, *Historical Studies* (now *Australian Historical Studies*). And the large number of tributes that appeared on the web in the weeks following Hirst's passing attest to the boards and committees on which Hirst served, even during a busy retirement. Governments from both sides of politics felt able to call on his skills, judgment and expertise. After his work for the Keating government, the Howard government asked him to chair the Civics Education Group and advise on a history curriculum. Meanwhile, a new generation of postgraduate history students at the University of Sydney learned from him the craft of historical writing, just as new readers of his work in several countries can enjoy his bestselling *The Shortest History of Europe*, published like most of Hirst's later work by Black Inc., which was a surprising late season fruit of his teaching at La Trobe. It was translated into Chinese, something about which he was justly proud when I last saw him.

I cannot claim to have known John well but our acquaintanceship went back over twenty years, and he was a generous supporter of my career at critical junctures. In later years, I visited him at his home in Coburg occasionally, where we would have a coffee either in a nearby shop or in his and Christine's front room. I always enjoyed these brief moments in his company. We last exchanged emails just a few weeks before his death: he wrote to congratulate me on my book on the 1980s, which he'd just read. Having encountered a passage in it on Nick Cave's 'The Mercy Seat', he had looked up YouTube to see what all the fuss was about. Couldn't hear a word of it, John reported, but it spoke of his intellectual openness that he had bothered looking. I suggested he try the Johnny Cash cover version.

Alex McDermott

THE PUBLICATION IN 2005 OF JOHN HIRST'S COLLECTION of essays, *Sense & Nonsense in Australian History*, marked a watershed in both Hirst's own trajectory as public intellectual and the national conversation.

Hirst had been (in his own words) 'quarrelling' with the prevailing left-leaning historical orthodoxies in various journals, symposia and assorted forums. Now these challenges were brought together for a wider public.

Hirst challenged conventional wisdom on several fronts. He questioned the unalloyed goodness of multiculturalism and diversity, suggesting that its best quality – mutual tolerance – arose from the previously denigrated assimilationist era. He urged a reassessment of self-determination as the only viable approach to Indigenous social policy. He even dared to question the necessity of constant apologies for past injustices.

The feminist retelling of the Australian story received a vigorous riposte. So too did a cluster of general assumptions – convicts were badly oppressed, Federation was a pragmatic business deal, twentieth-century anti-communism was politically weaponised propaganda, Australians are natural rebels and rule-breakers who barely tolerate authority, and so on. The 'gadfly of Australian history, stinging and provocative', in friend and colleague Stuart Macintyre's phrase, was more than making his presence felt.

For the general public engaged in the ongoing 'history wars' whose 'starting pistol' had been fired by Paul Keating in the early 1990s, the book was undeniably captivating. Even more remarkable was that Hirst continued to be read by the very left-liberal intelligentsia he so often disagreed with – a feat unmatched by any comparable figure in Australian public life.

Yet the 'gadfly' thing, the image of the born provocateur, can be overdone. And it is simply wrong to sharply demarcate Hirst's views on current issues from his rightly celebrated scholarly work. Hirst himself had little patience for such compartmentalisation and viewed his project as more than mere provocation. Rather, his contributions to contemporary debate stemmed directly from his historically nuanced understanding of national life and character, developed through studies spanning the entirety of Australian history.

His public commentaries and campaign involvements are of a piece with his history. Taken seamlessly together they confirm Aristotle's view of 'man the political animal' – a creature who thrives only in a polis, a political community which every citizen actively participates in shaping through debate, discussion and governance.

The tight mesh connecting Hirst's explorations of the past with his interventions in the present was exemplified by his contribution to the multiculturalism debate of the 1990s and 2000s. While critical of the policy of multiculturalism's shortcomings – its emphasis on difference and diversity while neglecting common identity and mutual allegiance – he situated its successes within a larger historical context. He argued that the Australian approach to difference had evolved in the nineteenth century among settlers of diverse, often conflicting, ethno-sectarian origins (Catholic Irish, Protestant English and Scottish), a dynamic that carried into the post–World War II policy of assimilation.

Multiculturalism's relative success, therefore, stemmed from the continuation of a pre-existing dynamic rooted in practices established over a century earlier, when people dealt with difference by quarantining ethno-sectarian conflict in politics and religion from community life. They sought – and created – common ground, ensuring that shared local organisations included representatives of all faiths and backgrounds.

The social origins of Australia's 'national style' also had a long prehistory before it was fixed by Anzac diggers as 'casual, egalitarian and disrespectful'. Distinctions between rough and respectable behaviour – less a reflection of class divisions than the difference between men with each other and men with women and children – were blurred when rough, unruly and irresponsible manhood achieved apotheosis as national heroism in war, their values enshrined as the quintessence not the outriders of Australian experience.

The feel of Australian society today, whereby people interacting largely continue to pretend that the differences do not matter, is a perfected egalitarianism which dominates the social sphere, if not its social, economic or political structures. This tendency to treat one another as equals, despite obvious differences – Hirst's 'democracy of manners' – also had its roots in the early foundational decades.

A main reason for the consistency of view informing his entire career lay in the fact that Hirst was a profoundly democratic thinker. This was evident in his civic practice – leading the development of the Discovering Democracy education project under education minister David Kemp in the Howard government (still the stand-out civics curriculum project of the last fifty years) and advocating for a republic – and in what Robert Manne once called his magnum opus, the history of Australia's federation movement, *The Sentimental Nation.*

Hirst's democratic ethos was deeply rooted in his affinity for ordinary Australians and his suspicion of elites. He excavated the roots of their experience, even as he deftly interrogated key protagonists at the levers of power – Bourke, Wentworth, Parkes, Deakin, Hughes, Curtin and others – whose decisions had such impact on the course of national life.

Convict society's enemies, for example, were the ultimate nineteenth-century elite – influential evangelical social reformers located in London, the metropolitan centre of Britain's empire. Here Hirst preferred, and took more seriously, the observations and opinions of ordinary settlers, both convict and free. He clearly relished, too, documenting the cataclysmic crash in public esteem for politicians once the democratic franchise was secured from the 1850s.

His heroes of Federation are 'the 422,788 YES voters who have no other memorial'. He excoriated the NSW government's Federation monument, opened in 1988, for its failure even to mention Federation, seeing it as emblematic of the degree to which multicultural Australia could not agree on what to celebrate. His closing pages of *The Sentimental Nation* feature a close description of the monument's domed ceiling, devoted to a post-colonial artwork which denounced Australia as abjectly provincial and a genocidal national project. 'What sort of nation is it that makes this the monument to its democratic foundations?' he asked pointedly, concluding that once it's torn down we'll know that Australian democratic history 'has begun to matter'.

While the new establishment feels the edge of his despairing rage here, Hirst maintained a wry affection for Australia's total uninterest in its democratic history. He knew where it came from. The nation's commitment to social equality (the democracy of manners) and key liberal freedoms predated its development of political equality. Its rapid achievement of high living standards, leisure and personal independence, exceeding the dreams of ordinary workers in Britain and Europe, well before the right to vote, perhaps made inevitable its fixation on avowedly apolitical national heroes: a bushranger, a racehorse and a cricketer.

Yet Hirst's democratic passion endured. He 'parted company' with Donald Horne's argument that Australia could be held together by a civic faith composed solely of 'tolerance, fairness, a commitment to parliamentary democracy, respect for due process, minority interests and diversity'. These civic virtues alone made a thin gruel. 'It does not meet the human need for warmth and belonging,' Hirst wrote. He needed something more than this 'cold and cerebral formula'.

This need for something more drove his commitment to republicanism, which he reckoned a continuation, not a repudiation, of Australia's past. 'Our predecessors are not the republicans,' he declared in his *Republican Manifesto*. 'We are the people who demanded self-government from the British. We are the people who made the Commonwealth out of six colonies. We are the people who adopted our own flag and our own national anthem. Now we ask for an Australian head of state, the last step to our independence.'

In the republic he sought, 'the sacred object' would not be the president but 'the bond which unites the citizens'. He hoped a republic would 'revive our civic culture', arguing that while suspicion of politicians might be healthy, suspicion of politics itself was dangerous for a free people.

This civic vision of republicanism was so compelling that it induced him to work in the 1990s with the Sydney elites who led the Australian Republican Movement (ARM). He acknowledged the ARM as 'a movement from within the new establishment of Sydney' – business leaders, professionals, media figures and successful artists. He described the 'fish and chardonnay lunch where the plot to form the ARM was hatched', the decision to establish it as a company with shareholders, and its invitation-only launch at a five-star Sydney hotel.

This approach, however, ensured the group's support for a minimalist republican model, with a president mirroring the governor-general in almost all particulars, including their nomination by the prime minister. While Hirst sympathised with the popular resentment against politicians and the new establishment, he diverged on the issue of a popularly elected president. He believed this would jeopardise his vision of achieving a republic which was 'the culmination of the nation-building which our ancestors began'. Nonetheless it was this 'great gulf' between 'elite opinion-makers' and the rest which doomed the push for a republic.

Hirst's position on the republic reveals a central paradox in his thinking. While his writing style possessed the forceful directness of Thomas Paine's *Common Sense*, his vision was closer to that of Paine's great antagonist, Edmund Burke. His Burkean republic – a culmination of the constructive work of previous generations – underscores this, but it permeates Hirst's entire work. He combined Burkean respect for habits, social traditions and established order while his style and fundamentally democratic values reverberated with Paine's egalitarian, plain-speaking approach.

This paradox points to a deeper puzzle Hirst grappled with throughout his career: the problem of sustaining authority in an egalitarian democracy – a local manifestation of the broader question of generating order in a free society.

To a surprising degree for one of Australia's greatest political historians, Hirst delighted in the 'feel' of his society – its 'mores', Tocqueville would have said – far more than he focused on its formal institutions. He savoured the idiosyncratic and wilfully individual in human nature, in people, and in the democratic nation he both studied and participated in.

Yet Hirst also harboured what he described as an 'instinctive respect for authority', recognising its necessity for human flourishing. This was more than simple emphasis on the need for freedom under law as against free-for-all. It extended to sympathy for the difficulties of leadership – running committees, organisations, companies, institutions and countries.

As Hirst explained in 'Changing My Mind', his introductory essay to *Sense & Nonsense*, this respect for authority stemmed from his early work on convict society. Here he found the 'commonly accepted formula for success with convicts' centred on the notion of the 'good master' who exercised power justly, combining kindness and firmness, exerting a clear authority, which other historians had overlooked.

This discovery informed his response to changes in Australia across his lifetime. Lacking 'the temperament of the liberationist', he found himself increasingly estranged from the emergent *mentalité* of the progressive left which began to achieve ascendancy from the 1970s. The danger, as Hirst saw it, was that 'democratic principles and rights were being applied to all subordinate institutions, which rendered them less able to do their job'. After all, 'a school that has so little control over its pupils that it has to call the police is a failed institution'.

The democratic republican concluded that there could be such a thing as too much democracy. His Quarterly Essay, *'Kangaroo Court'*, explored this idea in the context of the Family Court, established by the Whitlam government in 1975. Hirst rejected accusations that the Court was a feminist conspiracy, its judges 'heartless monsters'. He saw the problem as the catastrophic weakening of authority – of justice combined with power – due to well-intentioned progressive idealism. The Court's judges, he felt, were 'soft-headed about enforcing the Court's authority' and seemed 'to have no realisation of the extent of the social and human disaster over which they have presided'.

'The Court, as a child of the 1970s, reminds me of those schoolteachers who thought that if they were caring and understanding they would have no need to resort to disciplining their charges,' he wrote. It had 'yet to try how its troubled and angry clients would react to true authority. It is the absence of authority that makes them seem ungovernable ... Wild accusations fly around the court because ... the judges have abandoned any attempt to encourage the telling of the truth.'

Hirst endorsed reforms recommended by public inquiries – using a range of remedies to enforce order, with fines and imprisonment as a last resort. Above all, though, 'take enforcement seriously ... be firm and consistent'. Like a good master would, be 'both robust and deft'. Without abandoning discretion, judges needed to establish a regime where the people appearing before them kept themselves in order, hesitated to defy the Court or tell flagrant lies.

One final paradox helps explain why Hirst matters. He understood Australia's development as an adaptation of British institutions and social codes within an antipodean setting; as a 'dependent culture' deriving meaning from a broader context. However, the democratic polity with which he fundamentally identified had far deeper roots than Britain's. In his first book, *Adelaide and the Country* (1973), based on his PhD thesis, Hirst drew parallels between colonial society and the classical Greek and medieval city-states.

Adelaide, the city he'd grown up in, had become the undisputed political, economic and social centre of South Australia, with technology (trains, steamships, telegraphs) erasing distance. The defining characteristic of this seemingly vast colony was not separation but 'closeness'. South Australians treated the Adelaide-based central government as their 'local' government, choosing not to utilise district councils for education, police and poor relief – traditional responsibilities of local bodies. A highly mobile population, living in a new colony, shared a common assumption: 'that South Australia could be treated as one community.'

Functionally, Hirst argued, South Australia resembled a city-state, akin to the original Greek polities. He later expanded on this, emphasising the extraordinarily local nature of all colonial politics. Flourishing local voluntary organisations, filling the gap left by limited local government, would send deputations, introduced by their local MP, to the premier to address immediate grievances.

'The Greek ideal of a city-state was one in which all its citizens could gather in one place and know each other personally,' Hirst wrote. 'Deputations begging for the spending of public money was not a central part of Greek democracy, but the gathering of country people in Adelaide and the face-to-face encounters between governors and governed came closer to the Greek ideal.'

While many would hesitate before drawing a line between Periclean Athens and Australian colonial society, Hirst actively lived it, combining the seriousness of the scholar with the public responsibility of the intellectual.

Ultimately, Hirst's work is even more relevant today than when the first collection of his essays was published in 2005. If we truly want to understand Australia, and grasp what has gone wrong, what has gone right and what might be done, we have to understand John Hirst. His contribution to the great river of ideas and argument which shapes our national conversation leaves us permanently in his debt.

III

Robert Manne

CRITICAL OVERVIEWS OF THE WORK OF AUSTRALIAN HIS-torians, as opposed to discussions of particular books, seem to be relatively rare. Sometimes, when it happens, the impulse is plainly political, as in the volume edited by Andrew Markus and Merle Ricklefs, *Surrender Australia?*, following Geoffrey Blainey's mid-1980s intervention in the immigration debate or in the case of the volume I edited, *Whitewash: Keith Windschuttle's Fabrication of Aboriginal History*, following the enthusiastic neo-conservative reception accorded Keith Windschuttle's radical revisionist account of Aboriginal dispossession. I can think of only one book-length assessment of a major Australian historian not driven by political intent, the volume on Manning Clark, Carl Bridge (ed.), *Manning Clark: Essays on His Place in History*. Given all this, it is not surprising that, so far as I am aware, no general discussion of John Hirst's contribution to the study of Australian history exists. As I regard him as the one of the most illuminating Australian political historians, this absence strikes me, a latecomer to the area, as somewhat odd. To talk in general about the contribution of John Hirst feels not like entering but initiating a conversation.

If I were asked to explain why I have found the work of Hirst particularly illuminating, I would say that more than any historian since Keith Hancock he has been able to see Australia simultaneously through the eyes of an insider, intimate with the spirit of the country, and through the eyes of an outsider, able to think about Australia in relation to other countries and to identify what is genuinely distinctive about the Australian political culture. Outsiders easily miss the spirit of a place. Insiders take too much for granted. Hirst does neither. He is capable of being surprised and curious about what is to him utterly familiar. Even though he has written almost exclusively about Australia, for these reasons he is one of the least provincial or parochial of our historians. In addition, although he is not at all a theoriser he is a natural generaliser, possessed of a broad sociological imagination and an unusual capacity to see the forest and not merely the trees. I know of no Australian historian who has been able to provide a more interesting or plausible overview and interpretation of the habits of mind underlying the Australian political culture and of the many ways in which the patterns established in the nineteenth-century polity have persisted in new circumstances and helped to shape the present. What follows is a brief account of a part of the Hirstian interpretation of the Australian political culture, as I understand it.

Understanding of the Australian political culture begins for Hirst with the benefits and burdens of colonial dependency. One of the most original of his essays begins thus: 'Our task as Australian historians is to understand a dependent culture.' One half of the dependency is psychological, connected to the status tensions created in the colonial mind because of the presumed cultural pre-eminence of the imperial centre. The status anxiety of the colonial is used by Hirst to explain the oddity of the disastrous Gallipoli campaign becoming the symbolic birth of the nation. He begins his short essay on Gallipoli with the striking sentence: 'The history of the colonial psyche is the struggle to manage the disdain of the metropolis.' It was at Gallipoli that the colonial Australians finally proved themselves in the eyes of the imperial centre as satisfactory, even outstanding, human material. Hirst's interpretation of the role of Gallipoli in the national imagination seems to me far more convincing than the alternative Manning Clark view of the gloomy tendency of Australians to celebrate only their disasters and defeats. According to Hirst, the status anxieties of the colonials also help explain the enthusiasms of the federal party and thus of their surprising commitment to the creation of the Commonwealth. It was only by becoming the leaders of a proper nation that the Australian elite would cease to be despised colonials, in London's eyes and, thus, in their own. In addition the complexity of dependency in the Australian setting also explains for Hirst one of the most curious features of the Australian political culture – the near-entire absence of a psychologically felt negative nationalism. Following its North American policy failure, the imperial elite in London learned how to offer the settler colonies something no previous empire had considered necessary – political independence within the broad imperial frame. As Hirst has pointed out, Australians have no idea or, indeed, interest in establishing when precisely it was they became independent. He knows it to be pure myth that it was only the non-Labor side who felt loyalty to the Empire or Commonwealth. And he learned through his political advocacy for republicanism how feeble was the popular response to the nationalist call for a final symbolic act severing links with the Crown and establishing complete independence.

In Hirst's account of Australia's political culture, the second half of his dependency thesis concerns the strange fate of British social attitudes and institutions here. What he seems to me to argue, although he never puts it as inelegantly as this, is a theory of downward and upward stretch. One of the most illuminating of his gently revisionist essays concerns the question of egalitarianism in the colonial setting. What Hirst shows is that far from Australia being, at the point of the coincidental arrival in the 1850s of self-government and democracy, a naturally egalitarian place, the settlers were almost obsessed with questions of status. At this time the colonists did not at all dispense with an honours system or with the critical British social marker, the idea of the gentleman. Instead they demanded that imperial honours be distributed far more broadly than was possible at home, and so broadened the concept of the gentleman (to incorporate those involved in middling commerce or of middling wealth) as to render it, from the point of view of the metropolitan culture, unrecognisable and risible. This was the downward trajectory of the social stretch.

Perhaps even more interesting and fruitful is Hirst's account of the upward stretch, that is to say of the fate of distinctively working-class institutions, like the mechanics' institutes, the friendly societies and, most importantly, the Labor Party, in their journey from the United Kingdom to Australia. In the United Kingdom such institutions were part of a distinctively working-class culture. In the more fluid society of Australia they grew rapidly upwards in a different social soil, moving from institutions of the working class to institutions representing a rather different construct, the working people. Hirst's account of the upward stretch of working-class institutions in Australia helps explain in particular the astonishing pre–World War I success of the Labor Party, which is without parallel for the working-class parties of either the United Kingdom or Europe, and in general the less rigid class structure of Australian society at that time and also perhaps since.

In Australia the social distance between a gentleman and a member of a mechanics' institute or, to adopt another Hirst example, between a farmer who worked the soil and the labourers he employed, was far less great than in the equivalent relations in the United Kingdom. Although he doesn't make the link himself, in combination with the downward stretch of social attitudes, the upward stretch of institutions may help explain the emergence of one of the most enduring and distinctive features of the Australian political culture identified by Hirst, a peculiar kind of egalitarianism, not of outcomes or of opportunities but of manners, of the kind of society where incomes and opportunities may be hugely discrepant but where wealthy businessmen call themselves Nobby and feel obliged to sit in the front seats of taxis.

Hirst is always on the lookout for the ways like this that nineteenth-century peculiarities cast their shadows forwards. Nowhere is he more original than in his unromantic account of the success of the post–World War II mass non-British migration program. For reasons altogether unlike those who use the phrase in a pejorative way, Hirst accepts that, in a very specific sense, nineteenth- and early twentieth-century Australia was indeed 'more British than the British'. In the United Kingdom three nations – the English, the Scots and the Irish – and two religions – Protestants and Catholics – in general lived apart. In Australia, from the first, they were obliged to live alongside each other. Practices developed to ensure that the most basic contradiction – between the English Protestants and the Irish Catholics – did not disturb the social peace. It was not merely that the Church of England was not established here. Intricate social arrangements penetrated the institutions of civil society to ensure as far as possible that the Catholics did not feel too marginal or the Protestants behave in too domineering a manner. These institutional arrangements influenced daily life. In neighbourhoods, people did not enquire too deeply about each other's backgrounds. In workplaces, they agreed not to raise in conversation the topics of greatest human interest –

politics and religion. These practices and habits evolved for the management of the three nations–two religions diversity of the nineteenth and early twentieth century. After World War II they were deployed instinctively by the host society, Hirst argues, as a means of painlessly digesting into the anglomorph society an ever-expanding circle of ethnic outsiders. Hirst is not unaware of the costs of the process – general lack of curiosity about the experiences and the cultures of those who came here; unnecessary or overdeveloped fear regarding the formation of ethnic ghettos or the possible importation of old-world conflict to our shores. But as a political realist, when offered the choice between interesting times and dull social peace, he is not in doubt about what constitutes the prudent path to take.

In his writing although not in his thinking, Hirst came late to the most interesting question of Australian political history, the dispossession of the Indigenous peoples, most systematically in the essay written for the 2005 collection, *Sense & Nonsense in Australian History*. Hirst argues that those (like me) who dwell on the injustice but who have no intention of departing Australia are hypocrites. He is dismissive of the work of Keith Windschuttle in part for his naive faith in documents, more deeply for his failure to understand that the harm done the Aboriginal people lies in the destruction of their culture not in how many were intentionally killed. He does not accept that the arrival of the British can be justified in the way of Blainey, by pointing to the better use of the land. Hirst's case is, rather, that no justification is needed. At the time of the occupations Europe believed in imperial conquest. There is simply no room for moral judgment. As with most traditional historians, Hirst is a relativist. 'It would be easy to be a historian if all we had to discover was that people in the past did not share our outlook,' is the way he puts it in a different context. He is also a realist. He is contemptuous of those he calls liberal fantasists who think a treaty or greater kindness from the settlers could have prevented an inevitable tragedy. In the settlement of the British, bloody conflict, whose ultimate outcome was predetermined, was unavoidable.

In one of his essays Hirst writes: 'The expansion of Europe was a phenomenon of such magnitude with such a profound and irreversible effect on humankind that it might be thought that our moralising tendency would be silenced in the face of it.' This is a revealing sentence which takes me to the heart of my disagreement with Hirst. For me neither time nor success washes away the capacity and requirement for judgment. For almost two thousand years the Church condemned the Jews as the killers of God. The length of the condemnation does not change the fact that it was always wrong. Slavery is almost as old as civilisation. It is not only since the nineteenth century that it constitutes a grave injustice. The same can be said for conquest and genocide. Even if it is true that, for historians, understanding is the major task, historians are also human beings, for whom moral judgment is inescapable. I am no liberal fantasist, in Hirstian terms. Given the nature of European imperialism, I agree with him that the near-destruction of Aboriginal society was inevitable. But nor am I, like Hirst, a stoic realist. In that attempted destruction, in my view, a terrible wrong was done. Liberals seek to wriggle away from the first thought; conservatives from the second. Among Australian conservatives there is no one who has argued the case more honestly than my colleague and friend John Hirst. In someone as persuasive and incisive as him this blind spot, which is connected to an exaggerated fear for the legitimacy of this country, deeply interests me, as does almost everything in John Hirst's writing.

CHANGING MY MIND

HISTORIANS WRITE FROM THE EVIDENCE, BUT ALSO FROM their understanding of how the world works and how they would like it to work. A historian who thinks large impersonal forces have shaped our destiny will write a different history from one who thinks that great leaders have turned the tide – or made a tide. A socialist will not write approvingly of the rise of modern capitalist society. A free marketeer will be hard put to treat socialists sympathetically.

The great majority of the historians of Australia over the last forty or fifty years have been left-leaning, progressive people. I was taught Australian history by them and their books. I was brought up on Russel Ward *The Australian Legend* (1958) and Robin Gollan *Radical and Working Class Politics* (1960); my first teacher at the University of Adelaide in the early 1960s was Ian Turner. These three, as it happens, were more than left-leaning: they had all been members of the Communist Party. They were all properly trained academic historians and none was a crude propagandist. They wrote under tighter control of their discipline than the next generation of radicals. I still value and draw on their books. But their sympathies were plain.

My sense of how the world works and my political allegiance were at first those of my teachers. They are now different. With this change, my history-writing has changed. I am not sure how these two changes relate to each other. I wonder if my study of history has changed my views or whether my views changed and then my history-writing.

*

By the time I acquired my BA I believed that the Labor Party was the only party decent people could support. Labor promised a new, just social order; Liberals were the tools of big business, selfish and stupid.

I proceeded immediately to study for a PhD. The topic I chose for my thesis required me to study the South Australian history of both the Labor and Liberal parties. They both had their origins in Adelaide; the Labor Party in the trade unions and the Liberals among the city's businessmen and large property holders. If either group was to be a governing party, it had to gain support in the country. It took them some time to realise that country people were not automatically going to support a city organisation and its program.

The Labor Party had to drop its plan to tax all land, big farms and small, and it had to give country branches a real say at conferences. With these concessions made, it did win office in its own right for the first time in 1910. But the hard men in the trade unions were disgusted at the moderation of the Labor government. They turned on the Labor politicians, one of whose offences was to have made these concessions to the country. During World War I the hard men expelled the leading Labor politicians (for supporting conscription) and they reduced country branches to a nullity at Labor conferences. In future delegates had as many votes as the number of members they represented. A trade union delegate might have 10,000 votes and a country branch delegate ten.

As I followed this struggle, I found my sympathies were very much with parliamentarians. I was a Labor supporter (I was never a party member) but I was perfectly happy for parliamentarians to accept the restraints that winning government required.

The Liberal Party in South Australia took final shape in 1910, the year Labor first ruled. Most of its money came from big business and large landholders, but they had no influence over the choice of candidates. In the countryside, which was the Liberals' stronghold, party members insisted on selecting their own candidates without interference from head office. The farmers who wanted more land for themselves and their sons had also insisted that the party program include the compulsory purchase by the government of large pastoral estates and their subdivision into farms. It was to resist just such a measure that the big businessmen and landowners had first formed a political organisation. Now they were bankrolling a party that supported it! They were not happy.

*

The discipline of studying the evidence had led me to put aside the view that Liberals were just the voice of big business. But I was unusual among Australian historians in spending time on the Liberal Party. When they write political history, they generally study causes with which they sympathise. Some years ago an American colleague of mine expressed his amazement at this narrowness: 'There are shelves of books in the library on the Labor Party, even a small shelf on Communists and the Communist Party, but you are lucky to find two or three volumes on the Liberal Party – but haven't they governed the country for most of its history?' The imbalance is not quite as bad as this. Part of the difference arises because Liberals themselves are not as interested in their history and write fewer memoirs and reminiscences. But I think academic historians can be criticised for their lack of interest in the Liberals or for simply adopting the Labor view of them. You might think that left-leaning historians would study them if only to understand the enemy. Fortunately we now have two very revealing books on the Liberals written by left-leaning Judith Brett: *Robert Menzies' Forgotten People* and *The Australian Liberals and the Moral Middle Class*.

So why was I more ready to spend time on the Liberals? Was it just that I was writing a general history and I needed to look at them as well as Labor? Or was it that my mother was a Liberal voter and did not appear to be the willing tool of big business? She voted Labor for the first time in 1966 (against the landslide for Harold Holt) because she did not want my younger brother to be conscripted for Vietnam. She was not a passionate or a vocal Liberal; she did not take much interest in politics. She was calm and non-judgmental; very unwilling to see wickedness. This is a useful trait for a historian who first of all has to understand.

If I was now less prejudiced about the Liberal Party, my political sympathies still lay with Labor and they strengthened when Gough Whitlam became leader. I was as elated by his 1972 victory and as angry at his 1975 dismissal as any party member.

My bedrock assumptions about the world changed while I was writing my book on convict society in New South Wales. It was published in 1983 when I was forty years old. I began my researches with the usual assumption that convict society was cruel and degraded with masters being corrupted by the power they held over the convicts. The question I posed for myself was how had this brutalised society been transformed into a free, democratic society. My conclusion was that I had asked the wrong question. This was not a brutalised society; it was much more a normal British colony which had convicts as part of its labour force and which had always preserved crucial legal rights and economic opportunities for convicts and ex-convicts. I was one of what is now called 'the normalising school' on convict society.

At the centre of the book were musings on the nature of power. As my ideas formed, I found I was contesting the liberal view that power corrupts and that if subordinates complain or rebel it is because they have been badly treated. I began the section in the book on masters and servants by questioning how much power the masters of convict servants had. They had the power to get their convicts flogged, but they got poorer service than the masters back in England with servants who were kept in line by the threat of being sacked without a reference. Even under threat of flogging, convict servants were inclined to be stroppy, to get drunk or run away. A minority were absolutely incorrigible. I explored the idea that some masters were driven to cruelty not by lust for power but through the frustrations of getting work out of convicts, of not having enough power. Cruelty was a standing temptation for those who began by thinking that gentle treatment would bring good service. The commonly accepted formula for success with convicts was a combination of kindness and firmness (that could include flogging). This was the practice of those known – by convicts and others – as 'good masters', an old notion of power being exercised justly that survived even in the convict colony.

I was more open to think in new ways about convict society because I had read the recent books on slavery in the United States which described a complex relationship between masters and slaves. In law slaves might be property to be bought and sold but slaves were not things, for things do not answer back, go slow or run away. I had also learnt the paradox that when you 'own' your labour force you are more responsible for its welfare than when you hire free workers for wages. More important, I think, was the fact that I was now a 'master' myself – of a very rebellious teenager. I was of course a decent and understanding parent but that did not lessen the ferociousness of the rebellion. I was under siege myself as I watched masters trying to control convicts. My fellow-spirit in convict Sydney was the very decent Christian master George Allen. He was reluctant to send his servants to court for punishment, but when John Crawley ignored his orders on the pretence that he was deaf, he felt he had no option. On the day Crawley returned after receiving twenty-five lashes, Allen noted in his diary: 'It is very strange that when Men are well treated they will not behave themselves.'

My family, without having read my convict book, but having some sense of its argument, mocked me for claiming that flogging did not hurt. Some of my colleagues made the same criticism in a different way. But in fact I pointed out that flogging did injure some convicts so badly that they were admitted to hospital. It was not true, as is sometimes alleged, that flogging was used as a punishment because it did not take the convict away from his work. What I did not do in my book was to denounce flogging and be constantly outraged by it. By our standards it is an outrage, but I have this historian's quirk of knowing that the people who flogged criminals would think our practice of locking criminals up in all male institutions for thirty years or more cruel and unnatural. So I hesitate to condemn the past, but I recognise that I run the danger of not seeing horror when it is truly there.

*

The writing of my convict book set my mind in a new direction. Like a good historian I can offer the evidence for this in the notable sayings I have recorded in a little notebook I always have with me:

History shows there is no such thing as absolute power.
    —F. Eggleston, *State Socialism in Victoria*, p. 315

Mild, just, but exact in discipline; he was father to his people who were attached to him from affection and obedient from confidence.
—Tribute to James Cook on contemporary monument, copy in Maritime Museum Greenwich

Surely of all the 'rights of man', this right of the ignorant man to be guided by the wiser, to be gently or forcibly held in the true course by him is the indisputablest.
—Thomas Carlyle, *Chartism*, chapter 6

Thomas Carlyle, the historian-philosopher of the nineteenth century, became my favourite guide. He lived through the industrial revolution and hated its tendency to reduce all human relations to a cash nexus. But he did not believe that the liberal and democratic programs of his day would meet humankind's deepest needs. I was myself living in a new age of revolution, the libertarianism of the 1970s and after. I could not believe its promise that the loosening of social ties and the questioning of all authority would produce a better world. It was on this issue that I parted company with left-leaning, progressive people. I was, and am still, a supporter of the old left causes of a fairer distribution of wealth and opportunity.

I do not have the temperament of the liberationist. When authority is attacked my instinct is to come to its defence. I am very sympathetic to the problems of governing. I think our society has become too suspicious of authority and forgetful that we have cultural restraints on power that have produced and may still produce good leaders, bosses and teachers. The modern formula for governing is to be open and accountable and to consult widely and be inclusive. But the pleasures of sitting in committees can be exaggerated. In a committee we are instantly aware that some people are more fluent, forthright and determined than others; that we are not equals. With a good boss we are all equals in that he or she is equally concerned for us and will judge us equitably. That is a very satisfying environment in which to work.

I was not favouring a more authoritarian government for the state. There we need the checks and balances. The danger, as I saw it, was that democratic principles and rights were being applied to all subordinate institutions, which rendered them less able to do their job. A school that has so little control over its pupils that it has to call the police is a failed institution.

From Carlyle, who was much influenced by German idealist philosophy, I received the encouragement to think differently about human motivation and the course of history. Here are some extracts from my notebook:

It is a calumny on men to say that they are roused to heroic action by ease, hope of pleasure, recompense – sugar plums of any kind, in this world or the next. In the meanest mortal there lies something nobler. The poor swearing soldier, hired to be shot, has his 'honour of the soldier', different from drill regulations and the shilling a day. It is not to taste sweet things, but to do noble and true things, and vindicate himself under God's heaven as a god-made Man that the poorest son of Adam dimly longs ... Difficulty, abnegation, martyrdom, death are the *allurements* that act on the heart of man.

—Carlyle, *On Heroes and Hero-Worship*, Lecture 2

It is not what a man outwardly has or wants that constitutes the happiness or misery of him ... The real smart is the soul's pain and stigma, the hurt inflicted in the moral self.

—Carlyle, *Chartism*, chapter 5

From my teachers in Australian history I learned a sort of debased Marxism which looked to economic interests to explain events. This was somewhat offset by the lectures Professor Hugh Stretton gave on European history. I was probably not well attuned to his message. I do remember gaining a sense that the world was more open than is sometimes portrayed and that men with fresh ideas can be influential. In an aside he declared that the trouble with the Labor Party was that it had stopped thinking, which was no doubt true of the Labor Party circa 1963, pre Whitlam. We students were in the dark about Stretton. He had written nothing, though he was rumoured to be working on a magnum opus of whose subject there were conflicting reports. It was only later that all became clear when I read *The Political Sciences* and *Ideas for Australian Cities*.

The Australian historians had done a regular job on the history of the making of the Australian Commonwealth. I can remember at university reading on the economic interests that underlay the federation movement. Many times thereafter I had to read that federation was a business deal with very little idealism about it. It gave me great satisfaction for the celebration of the hundredth anniversary in 2001 to write a book that inverted this claim, and put the ideal before the material.

My book began with the idealists, the people who worked for federation who called it, publicly and privately, a noble, holy or sacred cause. That was the first sign that the old interpretation had missed the animating spirit of the movement. My job then was to explain why the making of a nation could be viewed this way. I hope I was not too starry eyed about these people. They had an interest in the creating of a nation, not an economic interest but a status interest, the quintessential selfish interest, what Carlyle called the moral self. They wanted to avoid the stigma of being thought second-rate. While the colonies were separate those who lived in them were known as colonists, a second-class people. If the colonies combined, the colonists would become citizens of a nation and share the standing of other nations round the globe.

Businessmen wanted the colonies to combine. My knock-down case against their influence on federation was that they wanted a customs union, not a federation. A customs union would yield immediate economic benefits: this was the practical proposal. Federation would deliver a customs union but since it involved the setting up of a whole new system of government it would be immensely difficult and would take too long. Until the very last, businessmen opposed moves to federation.

Over many years the businessmen advanced plans for a customs union, but they always failed because of the different economic interests and policies of the different colonies. It was the 'impractical' men, the politicians, the patriots and the poets, who created the union, which then delivered a customs union.

I called my book *The Sentimental Nation*. I think of it as a tribute to Carlyle. It has of course to pass the test of the discipline: has the evidence been produced to support this interpretation? But the making of an interpretation of this sort is also evidence of what has happened to my mind and self since I left my first teachers.

2004

FROM CONVICT SOCIETY TO COLONIAL SOCIETY

HOW DID A PENAL COLONY CHANGE PEACEFULLY TO A DEMOCRACY?

THE PENAL COLONY OF NEW SOUTH WALES, ESTABLISHED IN 1788, became by 1860 a self-governing colony and a democracy, with all men having the right to vote. How did this amazing transformation happen? Some books do not pose this question at all; others give a variety of unconvincing answers, which mark the change rather than explain it.

The vagueness and thinness of the answers arise because the question has been wrongly posed. New South Wales did not begin as a penal colony; it is better to think of it beginning as a colony of convicts. Its history can be represented in this way:

Colony of convicts   →   Failed attempt at a penal colony 1820s–1830s   →   Colony of free people

Why wasn't early New South Wales a penal colony? The short answer is that British officials in 1786 could not conceive of such a beast: a society of warders and prisoners designed for punishment and control, as the French ran much later on Devil's Island. In Britain in the eighteenth century there was no institutional treatment of convicted criminals; they were flogged or hanged or sent to the American colonies.

There were gaols but only for short-term imprisonment. They were prisons without prison discipline. There was a men's ward and a women's ward, and no bar to the men and women intermixing. One convict couple who came on the First Fleet had met and conceived a child in gaol. If you were a prisoner of some means you could send out for food and other comforts, and maybe pay the gaoler in order to occupy a room in his house. Running an institution without reference to the birth, wealth and connections of the inmates was unimaginable.

We can understand the mindset of the ministers and officials who established New South Wales by looking at what they planned when the convicts were to be sent to the west coast of Africa (a plan that was abandoned because the climate was too hostile).

The convicts were to be dumped on an island in the Gambia River and left to their own devices. They were to elect a chief and a council to make laws and administer the settlement. It was to be a little republic of convicts. They were to cultivate the ground to support themselves; at this, some would undoubtedly do better than others, and they would become employers of the rest. The British government would keep a ship at the mouth of the river to see that they did not escape. Clearly, ministers were not concerned to punish these men according to their crimes; the punishment was to be exile. The men most likely to emerge on top in this little republic would be the most hardened and enterprising offenders.

With New South Wales, the government was much more involved: there was a governor and a contingent of marines. But quite quickly this new settlement began to look something like a republic of convicts. On day one the marines went on strike: they refused to supervise the work of the convicts. They refused to supervise the convicts even when they were clearing the ground for the marines' own tents. So Governor Phillip was forced to appoint convicts to oversee the work of other convicts. Their pay was the freedom not to work. The official rule was that convicts were to work from dawn to dusk, but the convict overseers soon adopted their own system to get work out of convicts. They fixed a daily task – so many trees felled; so much ground hoed – and when that was done the convicts were free to leave. If the convicts applied themselves, their task could be finished by midday.

This is how the convicts developed what they called their 'own time', which they defended ferociously. If the weather was bad in the morning and the government task could not be done, they refused to work for the government in the afternoon. In their 'own time' the convicts could laze about, steal, or take work and get paid for it.

It took years for governors to claim back at least some of the afternoon. The final rule was that the convicts had to stay at work either for the government or their private master until three o'clock. Governor Macquarie in 1814 declared that convicts had to work the full day for their private masters, but the masters had to pay for the work they did after three o'clock. This became known as their wage. For the convicts who worked for the government in Sydney, Macquarie built a barracks, which still stands in Macquarie Street. Once they had full board and lodging, the convicts did not need to earn money after three p.m. to pay for their private lodgings. But the convicts' 'own time' was not forgotten; at weekends they were free to leave the barracks and live it up or work in the town.

In the second year at Sydney Cove, food supplies were shrinking and starvation loomed. Desperate to stop robberies, Phillip created a police force and had no choice but to staff it with convicts. These convicted felons were given authority over free men, the sailors and the marines; in particular, they were to detain any marines or sailors who were wandering around the camp at night.

Under these orders, the convict police did detain marines, but after several months the head of the military (and lieutenant governor), Major Robert Ross, raised a furious objection when a marine was detained. Phillip had trouble eliciting his reasons; he was almost apoplectic with rage and could only repeat that the power given to the convict police was an insult to his corps. Which, by all ordinary standards, it was. Phillip yielded so far as to alter the rules for the police so that they could detain marines only if they were actually committing a robbery. Then he sent Major Ross to take charge at Norfolk Island. The convict police remained.

Convict overseers and police: this was just the beginning. For all professional services, the governors drew on the convicts: lawyers, architects, surveyors, doctors, teachers, artists (who were former forgers). It was hard to get free people to come to the colony to do these tasks. The second governor, John Hunter, told the British government to stop looking for eligible free people; whatever he wanted doing, there was a convict who could do it. Free settlers also employed these convict professionals; a convict tutor was a regular feature of a gentleman's home.

This so-called penal colony was run according to the principles of the ordinary English law. This was a late decision in the planning of the colony, taken, it seems, by Lord Sydney, the British home secretary, which is enough to warrant the immortality he has acquired through the city that bears his name. The first plan was for the colony to be governed under military law. The operation of the normal law meant that convicts could not receive any further punishment except by order of a court, and that before the court they appeared in the usual way, as innocents until proven guilty.

In fact, it became inadmissible to refer to a convict in court as a convict or ex-convict. In the magistrates' court, where convicts were taken by their masters for offences against the labour code – being lazy, running away, getting drunk – they were unlikely to get off, though it was a great access to their dignity that their masters could not punish them themselves. Convicts did not work under the lash. For serious offences in the higher courts, the rate of acquittal was quite high – between a quarter and a third of all cases. The juries in these trials were six military or naval officers, who were partial when cases touching on their honour and interests arose, but otherwise were conscientious and willing to let a convict or ex-convict go free if the evidence against them was insufficient.

Convicts acquired more legal rights in the colony than they had at home. Convicts in England could not give evidence, own property or bring actions in court. Since in New South Wales most people were convicts, they had to be allowed to give evidence if the court was to learn what it needed to know about a case. Because convicts could testify, they could give evidence against their masters. Convicts also had to be considered as owners of property, otherwise other convicts could not be charged with pinching it. The first case in the criminal court concerned a convict who had stolen another convict's bread ration.

If convicts were to protect their property, they had to be able to bring actions in court. The first case in the civil court was brought by a convict couple against the captain of their ship for losing their baggage. These were the convicts who had met in gaol, Henry Kable and Susannah Holmes. The government had at first planned to separate them, sending only Susannah and her baby to the colony. When the gaoler delivered

Susannah and the baby to the ship, the captain refused to take the baby. The gaoler left Susannah at the ship and took the baby to London, where he camped outside the offices of Lord Sydney until he agreed that the baby and its mother and father could go to the new colony together. The case became famous and a fund was opened to equip the family for their new life. This was the baggage that the captain of the ship lost as they sailed to Australia. The court ruled that the captain had to pay the couple compensation.

The early governors were given no instructions as to the punishment of the convicts. The first job of the governors was survival; the second was economic growth, so that the colony could pay for itself. So they used the convicts according to their skills and diligence. They readily granted pardons to those who did good service, as well as to those who brought recommendations from home. The 'ticket of leave', which became a reward for good behaviour, was at first given to convicts who could get their own living and so be taken off the ration rolls. That reduced expenditure, which was what the British government was most concerned with.

Convicts had in this free-wheeling outfit plenty of opportunity to make money. The convicts who did best worked for the officers who had gone into the business of trading. Like all officers, they offset the tedium of a foreign posting by enriching themselves. They could import rum, tea, sugar and tobacco, but they could not actually set up a shop to sell them without damaging their claim to be gentlemen. The convict servants assigned to them ran the shops, and quite soon set themselves up in business on their own account, becoming traders, shipbuilders and bankers. These ex-convict businesspeople – men and women – were assigned convicts to work for them on the same terms as the officers and the few free settlers.

On becoming free, convicts were granted thirty acres as a farm and convict servants to help them work it. Few of the convicts were experienced or determined farmers. Most drank too much, fell into debt and sold off their lands, which were then bought by the more enterprising settlers, whether free or ex-convict. Some ex-convicts became wealthy landowners, but the route to this was in the first place through trade; starting with thirty acres was not the way fortunes were made.

Only one barrier was erected against the successful ex-convicts: no matter how much money they made, the officers and free settlers would not accept them as social equals. They did not expect to meet them at balls and dinners at Government House, which set the standards of 'good society'. To modern Australians this seems snobbishness, but the other side of this social exclusion was economic opportunity: the officers and free settlers did not care what positions ex-convicts held or how much money they made because they would remain socially their inferiors.

Governor Macquarie thought the free settlers were always bitching, and that it was the ex-convicts who had made the place. He 'went native' and, fully accepting the logic of a convict republic, appointed three ex-convicts as magistrates; he invited them to Government House and expected the rest of the Government House crowd to accept them as equals. They deeply resented this, and this was one complaint that led to an official enquiry into the running of the colony. Macquarie was to be the last ruler of a colony of convicts.

But what about the floggings? This is what everyone knows about early New South Wales. There was a good deal of it. It was a regular punishment of the time used in the armed forces, the schools and the home. It is so obnoxious to us that it fosters misleading views of how the colony operated. When a flogging is depicted in film or on TV, a cruel, sneering free settler sends his convict off to the court for a trifling offence. The magistrate, who is a friend of the master, takes little time to convict him. The order of the court is that the man be flogged. There is a rattle of a drum; a small contingent of soldiers leads the culprit forth; an officer gives an order; the culprit is tied to the triangle; a soldier wields the whip.

This is entirely fanciful. The military had nothing to do with convict punishments. A convict or ex-convict policeman supervised the floggings, which were performed by a convict flogger. The convict could as well be sent for punishment by an ex-convict master. During the Macquarie madness, the magistrate might have been an ex-convict. That's the picture to hold on to: an ex-convict master sends his convict to court; he is tried by an ex-convict magistrate; his punishment is supervised by an ex-convict policeman and he is flogged by a convict. Is this a penal colony?

No, it's a unique social formation.

New South Wales was entirely different from the penal settlements, properly called, that were established by the French in the 1850s in colonies that already existed, Guinea and New Caledonia. The warders and the prisoners were in a special separate settlement. The warders did their job – they kept the convicts to hard labour – and the convicts and their skills were not called on to secure survival. The settlements were all-male affairs. They did not have a transforming effect on the colonies in which they were placed.

It was, finally, the presence of women in New South Wales that makes 'penal colony' so inappropriate a term. The rulers of Britain were happy to hang and flog prisoners but they thought locking men away from female company for a long period was unnatural and cruel. So 191 women convicts were sent on the First Fleet to accompany the 568 men. Governor Phillip planned to bring other women from the Pacific islands to service the men, but once he arrived he decided that it would be unkind to bring them to a colony close to starvation.

Men and women together: this was a source of much disorder – and also of babies. There were babies conceived on the First Fleet. These infants were free British subjects. So before it began, this 'penal colony' was producing free people who grew up to call it home and thought of it as a nation in the making. Not even in its first year was this society composed just of convicts and their guards. In any case, the guards, as we have seen, were non-players in the penal department.

*

New South Wales was founded just as the cause of prison reform was taking off in Britain. The reformers wanted prisons to be well run, clean and healthy; the prisoners were to be classified, with men and women separated; and they were to be kept at work and attention given to their reformation. Solitary confinement was to be provided as a mode of punishment and an encouragement to reflection and reformation. When the reformers triumphed in the 1840s, solitary confinement was to be the lot of all prisoners. This was the terrible end point of a movement that thought of itself as humane and whose supporters worked as well on the abolition of slavery.

As these principles of punishment were accepted, New South Wales became a blot on the system. Here there was no classification, an indiscriminate mixing of the convicts, and no matching of punishment to crime or attempt at reformation. How could there be reformation when the convicts themselves composed almost the whole of the population? How could transportation be a deterrent when convicts lived well and some made fortunes? The reformers wanted transportation to New South Wales to be abandoned and all prisoners confined to prisons of the new type.

Building prisons according to the new principles was very expensive; expelling convicts out of the country was cheaper and psychologically very satisfying. Governments would not readily give up transportation but they had to take notice of the new principles. To this end, the government sent a commissioner of enquiry, John Bigge, to New South Wales in 1819. His brief was to find a way to make New South Wales a fit place for punishment, both for deterrence and reformation. After eighteen months of enquiry he produced his recommendations, which the British government adopted and Governors Brisbane (1821–1825) and Darling (1825–1831) carried out. This was the second stage in the colony's history: the attempt to make it into a penal colony. How far was it successful?

In future, tickets of leave were to be given only to those who had been well behaved. Governor Macquarie had set rules so that convicts could not get a ticket until they had served a certain proportion of their sentence; seven-year men had to serve at least three years. But he had frequently broken his own rules, and the convicts, in their bolshie way, had come to assume they had a *right* to a ticket as soon as they had served the required time, no matter whether they had convictions for drunkenness or running away.

To ensure that each convict's record could be known, there were now to be central records kept of all offences committed. This took some time to organise and the records were never perfect. They were much better in Tasmania, where on one page in the 'Black Books' all the details of the convict's career were recorded. Most of the New South Wales records were destroyed; the Tasmanian records survive and are a wonderful resource for family historians.

So on this matter convicts were now handled in a bureaucratic way, with like cases treated alike – the same mindset from which came the notion of the well-ordered prison. The new system was a benefit to the convict who had no outstanding skill and no one to speak for him; if he kept his head down and did his work, he would get his ticket. Exceptions still had to be made: tickets were given out to those who caught bushrangers or gave useful information about the hard men and their plans, or agreed to go on an exploring expedition. And letters of recommendation from home could sometimes still get a result – an early ticket of leave. But the problem of what to do with gentlemen convicts was partly solved. A special settlement was created for them, but they were not to be put to ordinary labour; no one could contemplate that.

Convicts were no longer to receive a wage. But this did not mean that all convicts got their ration and nothing else. Skilled men would be given extra rations and the opportunity to do work in their own time and be paid for it, either by a master or a neighbouring settler. In 1833 the leader of one of the rare convict rebellions claimed in court that he and his fellow convicts had been repeatedly flogged and starved on the property of James Mudie in the Hunter Valley. Governor Bourke ordered an enquiry, which showed that these claims were untrue. It revealed that the leader of the rebellion, John Poole, was a carpenter in charge of a group of convicts who were building a windmill on the property. He got extra rations, including wine, and wore a white shirt. Mudie brought him a flute and a music book from Sydney. He got extra work making ploughs for other settlers. He got on well with Mudie but not with his son-in-law, who managed the property. When the son-in-law sent him to be flogged for insolence (his first flogging), Poole organised the revolt.

The food ration for convicts had been set down in London. It had been cut down in starvation time, restored and varied, but it survived as a standard that had to be met. It became the convict's right to receive seven pounds of flour and seven pounds of meat per week. In 1823 this was abandoned and convicts were to receive what was 'adequate'. About this there were many disputes. Convicts up on a charge of being lazy would claim they were being starved, and magistrates would have the difficult job of working out whether the food they received was 'adequate'. Convicts thought anything other than white bread was definitely not adequate; they were not going to eat brown bread or maize meal. In 1831 the official ration was restored.

Regular and uniform discipline was now to operate in the places of secondary punishment. These were the settlements at Port Macquarie and Moreton Bay, where convicts who had committed serious offences in the colony were sent. They had been as lax as early New South Wales itself. The military ran their own farms and employed convicts on them. Friends of the convicts could send them food, clothing and other goods – free of carriage on the government supply boats – so convicts could run shops while they were being punished. Married convicts were allowed to have their wives and children join them, and they were allowed time off to work in their support. From the ranks of double-convicted prisoners, constables and over-seers were recruited. Now private farming and business were banned; all convicts had to be kept at hard work, with the hoe, not the plough, except that skilled men could work at their trades in cases of urgency – but only as a temporary measure. Well-behaved men could still have their wives join them. The overseers remained the convicts themselves.

In 1825 Norfolk Island was reopened. It had been an important adjunct to the early colony because it was so fertile, but it had not been used as a place of further punishment. Now it was to be a dreaded place of secondary punishment, the horror to keep men in order in New South Wales proper. Governor Darling ordered that no women were to be allowed, either wives of convicts or of soldiers. He acknowledged that the absence of women would lead to an increase in homosexuality, but he thought that the presence of a few women would not make much difference to its prevalence. In any case, his aim was deterrence; he didn't mind how bad a place he created. Whether he was right about homosexuality or not, Darling correctly gauged the significance of barring women. He did not want the regularity of his prison disturbed by the comforting regularities of family life, or by the irregularities of the casual congress between men and women which had been part of life in every other settlement in New

South Wales. Norfolk Island came closest to being a penal settlement, and could be so described if the convicts themselves were not the warders. Hated by the men as traitors and fearing always for the security of their jobs, they were the more tyrannical and cruel.

At Norfolk Island and at Port Arthur, in Tasmania, another place of secondary punishment, there are ruins of prisons built on the new principles of solitary confinement. At Port Arthur a wing of the separate prison has been restored, which includes the chapel where prisoners were seated in winged stalls to prevent them from seeing one another – so that solitary confinement would continue even in church. These relics are taken to be symbols of the convict system in Australia and its studied cruelty. They were actually built very late, to the formula of the British penal reformers who opposed transportation to Australia and the customary treatment of the convicts there. What was normal in the convict system has left no distinctive relics because most convicts saw out their time working for private masters, living in attics or separate kitchens, in the men's huts at a sheep station or in a shepherd's hut in the bush, or sharing bed and board with a small farmer.

That was the difficulty of running New South Wales proper according to penal principles. Private employers would never be concerned with punishment and reformation. They wanted to get work done, and they would cut deals and turn a blind eye as required. Bigge's plan to forestall this criticism was that more free settlers should be encouraged to come to the colony. They would make better masters for convicts than the ex-convicts. If all convicts were sent to do hard work on their estates in the country, there would be consistency in punishment and more chance of reformation away from the fleshpots of Sydney. It was a neat solution but this part of Bigge's report could not easily be implemented.

Four years after Bigge's policy was adopted, the British colonial secretary told Governor Darling that there were still too many skilled convicts in Sydney. He wanted them sent to the country and put to hard labour. Darling explained that he could not obey this instruction: if he did, how would the various trades of Sydney – tailor, shoemaker, etc. – be carried on? The building workers were even more important; they worked for the government during the week and took private work at the weekend:

'Thus has the Town of Sydney been built.' These were very stubborn facts to be put against penal principles. Whitehall let the matter drop.

One further difficulty about arranging hard labour in the country was that, increasingly, the work was minding sheep (boring but not hard) or rounding up cattle (exciting, with the freedom of being mounted on horseback). As pastoralism spread beyond the boundaries, the men who owned the stock usually did not supervise the enterprise themselves. So convicts had overseers who were ex-convicts, ticket-of-leave men or even other convicts. This was not a recipe for good order and tight discipline. The perpetrators of the 1838 Myall Creek massacre, in which thirty Aborigines were slaughtered, were convict and ex-convict stockmen who had been roaming the district on horseback for days, looking for Aborigines to kill.

Better order could have been established over convicts, and better protection for the Aborigines provided, if the rush to new lands beyond the boundaries had been stopped. But the British government wanted the wool that the colony provided. A booming colonial economy trumped penal principles.

More free settlers with capital did arrive in the 1820s, and were allocated land and convicts to work it. The Hunter Valley, settled at this time, did develop as Bigge had wished. In other new areas some ex-convicts were among the pioneers, especially in cattle, which required less capital. Ex-convicts were strongest in trading, shops, pubs, farming and other small businesses. Overall, they employed about half of the convicts working for private masters. No one (not even Bigge) proposed that they should be deprived of their convict workers. To do so would have knocked out half the economy, something that would have damaged free settlers as well. Since ex-convicts were so well established so early, it would take a long time before the great majority of convicts had free settlers as masters.

A court ruling just before Bigge arrived in the colony had cast doubt on the legitimacy of the pardons the ex-convicts had received. If the pardons were doubtful, the next query might concern their capacity to hold property. Though Bigge doubted their quality as masters, he could see that the prosperity of the colony depended on the security of their property. He added his support to the petition already sent to Britain asking for the pardons to be validated by parliament. This was done in 1823. That gave the ex-convicts what the certificate of freedom (a local invention) had long claimed: that the holder was 'restored to all the rights and privileges of free subjects'.

Overall, the changes made to the convict system following Bigge's report fell a long way short of his plan for all the convicts to be working in the country under the supervision of respectable free settlers. That arrangement might warrant the title 'penal colony'; I call the efforts made after his report a failed attempt at a penal colony. Too much could not be undone or bent to penal purposes.

*

The danger to New South Wales evolving into a free and democratic society came from the free settlers. If they had had their way, they would have made themselves into a ruling class and excluded the ex-convicts from power. The British government, which kept firm control over the colony, was the force that prevented this.

Britain was the pioneer liberal state. In the seventeenth century, parliament had tamed the monarchy by beheading one King and exiling another. The King still ruled but only parliament could pass laws and approve taxes. The King appointed judges but only parliament could dismiss them, an arrangement that established the law's independence. That all Englishmen were entitled to the protection of the law, conducted without fear and favour, was a deeply entrenched belief. Only a few Englishmen voted, but all had the right to the security of their property and persons, and to be tried by a jury of their peers. This view was held strongly enough by Lord Sydney that he felt that the convicts in New South Wales should be subject to the rule of law and not to some arbitrary authority. They did miss out on having a jury of their peers.

The American Revolution of 1776 proclaimed liberal principles, and the French revolution of 1789 liberal and then democratic principles. Democracy made liberalism look dangerous, for the French people had used their new power to chop off the heads of aristocrats and support a reign of terror. While the French revolutionary regimes survived, the British government hounded democrats and refused to contemplate any further liberal reform. But after 1815, when Napoleon was defeated, liberalism strengthened in Britain, with its chief aim the widening of the ranks of those who could vote for parliament.

In 1830, after long years of Tory rule, the Whigs, the reforming party, came to power in Britain. In the first *Reform Bill* of 1832 they gave middle-class men the vote and rearranged electorates, taking members away from small and decaying towns and allotting them to the new industrial cities. To New South Wales they sent a liberal governor, Richard Bourke. The ministers concerned with this oddball colony took their responsibility very seriously. They were appalled at what their predecessors had done: establishing a society of convicts, which was bound to create a degraded and immoral society. The concern for morality was strengthening alongside support for liberalism. The assumption that a colony of convicts must be degraded overlooked all the ex-convicts who had acquired property and so become defenders of law and order. Still, there was enough crime and drunkenness in New South Wales to give moralists cause for concern.

Viscount Howick, the son of the Whig prime minister, Earl Grey, was the minister responsible for colonial policy. He introduced a scheme to encourage free working people to migrate to New South Wales. In the 1830s there were thus two streams of migration: convicts and free working people. The convicts were still nearly all men; the free workers were men and women in equal number, which would help to redress the sex imbalance, a prime cause of immorality and disorder.

Working people could not afford to pay for the long journey to Australia. Howick got the money for their fares by introducing the sale of the colony's crown land, rather than giving it away. This was the formula advanced by the colonial reformer Edward Gibbon Wakefield. The selling of land would stop settlement spreading too far, and with the proceeds spent on the emigration of free people the colonies would not have to depend on convicts for their labour force.

The free settlers of New South Wales had not requested such a scheme and were dismayed that the land, which had been available as a free grant from the crown, now had to be paid for. They were even more dismayed when the price of land was ramped up during the 1830s to match the price in South Australia, which had been founded on Wakefield principles without convicts in 1836. The landholders of New South Wales were perfectly happy to go on relying on convicts. But the Whig government had now provided a way for the colony to continue to prosper if transportation were ever to cease.

With the support of the Whig government, Governor Bourke set new principles of equality in the government's dealing with the churches. Bourke was an Irishman, a Protestant but a liberal Protestant who had seen firsthand the bitterness and conflict caused in Ireland by the British government enforcing support of a Protestant church. Though most of the Irish were Catholic, they had to pay church rates to support Protestant ministers whose services they did not attend. The Whig government was contemplating directing funds to the Catholic Church in Ireland, but it was tricky: there were Protestant dissenters in England who did not want to pay church rates to the established Church of England and would be eager to take changes in Ireland as a precedent. The Whigs had no wish to encourage debate about the funding of the Church of England in England.

New South Wales was easier; the government approved Bourke's plan to support the Anglican, Catholic and Presbyterian churches on the same basis: the government would pay the salaries of their clergymen and would match the monies they raised for church building. The Catholics had been not altogether excluded from government support in New South Wales but now, at a stroke, they were to gain full equality with the Protestants. It was an amazing measure for Protestant Britain to sanction for its convict colony, and vital for social peace when almost a third of the population was Catholic. The Anglican bishop and other Protestant leaders did not like the government supporting the 'error' of Roman Catholicism, but they were pleased to have the promise of more generous support for their own churches. No one denomination could have proposed that others should receive government support as well as itself. This was a measure which only a benevolent despot could propose.

The fight for religious equality was one of the great liberal and radical causes in Britain throughout the nineteenth century. This highly charged issue had been put to rest in New South Wales long before the colony began to govern itself.

Again with the support of the Whig government, Governor Bourke introduced juries of citizens to try criminal cases in the place of juries made up of military and naval officers. In the usual way, jurymen had to own or occupy property of a certain value in order to be eligible to serve. Despite the fierce objections of the free settlers, Bourke allowed ex-convicts who met the property test to serve. The free settlers had some reason for their objection: there was an oddity, to say no more, in inviting former criminals to determine guilt or innocence in criminal trials. In their eyes, that would threaten the integrity of the legal system and damage the reputation of the colony – and their own for living in it. But a larger question was at issue: as the colony acquired the normal legal and political institutions, were the ex-convicts, a large and prosperous class, to be marked for exclusion? Bourke had given his answer.

If ex-convicts could serve on juries, what could be said against allowing them to vote? The battle over juries took place in a larger dispute over the future government of the colony. The British government was contemplating allowing New South Wales the traditional right of a colony to have an elected assembly that could pass local laws.

The demand for an assembly had been pushed by William Wentworth, who had the ambition to confer all the rights of self-government on his native land. He was the son of a convict mother. His father, well connected in the Irish aristocracy, had been three times charged with highway robbery but never convicted. He went into voluntary exile in New South Wales and became very rich. His son was sent home to be educated at Cambridge University. On his return in 1824, he started the first independent newspaper in the colony, *The Australian*, which agitated for a popular assembly. Wentworth would allow the ex-convicts to vote, and he proposed a property qualification so low that nearly all ex-convict men would qualify. They easily outnumbered the free settlers, so the colony would fall into their hands. This pleased Wentworth no end because he had been snubbed and humiliated by the free settlers.

Governor Darling had tried to curb *The Australian* and other independent papers but had been frustrated by a liberal chief justice, so that the press was freer in the convict colony than in Britain. Darling could not believe it: he had been sent to make New South Wales a credible place of punishment, and the ex-prisoners had their own newspaper to clamour for their rights and denounce him!

The free settlers were alarmed at Wentworth's campaign for an assembly and feared that the Whigs might be persuaded by it. They insisted that if there were to be an assembly, property rights alone could not be the qualification for the vote. Ex-convicts would have to show some sign of rehabilitation.

The Whigs came close to setting up an assembly but they worried and delayed. They did not want to impose some contentious test on ex-convicts as qualification for the vote, but nor did they want the colony to fall completely into their hands. Ministers solved the problem another way: they decided to abandon transportation. Once the flow of convicts stopped, the free settlers were less concerned about voting rights for ex-convicts, who would now constitute a declining proportion of the population. Free settlers and the native-born would soon outnumber them.

This is how it was managed. Transportation stopped in 1840, and in 1842 ex-convicts were allowed to vote and stand for a Legislative Council, two-thirds of whose members were elected and one-third nominated by the governor. This body would pass local laws, but the governor and his officials, appointed by the Colonial Office, still constituted the government. Full self-government had not been granted but the impasse over ex-convict rights had been solved.

The free settlers had not proposed the ending of transportation; nor had Wentworth and his ex-convict supporters. Both groups were appalled at the decision because it seemed to threaten the colony's prosperity and was accompanied by wholesale denunciations of the colony. The Whigs had abolished slavery in the empire in 1834, and now the case against slavery was extended to New South Wales. Society was said to be as debased there as in the West Indian slave colonies. It was not only that the convicts were not properly punished or reformed, but also that the masters had been corrupted by the absolute power they wielded over their 'slaves'. New South Wales was in fact very different from the slave societies: its 'slaves' had rights under the law, and many had former 'slaves' as their masters. But the passion now aroused by slavery was enough for the British government to make a decision, which created huge problems for itself: what to do with the convicts? Prisons of the new type would have to be built for them. Meanwhile, transportation was to continue to Van Diemen's Land, which got many more convicts than it could cope with.

New South Wales was set on the path to becoming a self-governing colony of free people. The convicts already arrived would serve out their terms or gain tickets of leave; ex-convicts had the same legal and political rights as the free settlers; the native-born, chiefly the children of convicts, had always been full British subjects. The need for more labour would be met by the migration of free working people. The process of becoming a colony of free people proceeded smoothly because of the decisions of the British government or its endorsement of what Governor Bourke proposed. In summary, these were the key measures:

- A scheme for the migration of free working people was introduced (which made it possible to stop transportation).
- The Catholic Church (whose members were overwhelmingly ex-convicts or convicts) was granted government funding on the same terms as the Protestant churches.
- Ex-convicts were allowed to serve on juries.
- A local assembly was not granted while ex-convicts and free settlers were in dispute over its composition.
- Transportation was abandoned, which allowed free settlers to accept that ex-convicts could vote and stand for the assembly.

It is a great record of statecraft, but this is not usually highlighted in histories of Australia: who wants to acknowledge that Australia owes so much to the Poms?

Britain was becoming a more liberal society during Australia's early years but was itself still far from democratic. Amazingly, the British, having laid the foundations for a liberal state in New South Wales, helped to ensure that it was democratic.

The qualifications for voting for the partly elected Legislative Council established in 1842 were set by the British government. It knew that property values were higher in the colony than in England, so the English qualifications would not be appropriate. In England the lowest qualification for the vote was the rental of a house at £10 per year. This gave the middle class the vote in the towns but not the working class. For New South Wales the rate was to be double that: £20 per year. Rents were so high in Sydney that this allowed some skilled workingmen the vote. Overall, though, the rent and property qualifications set for the colony had the same result as in England: only about one man in five had the vote.

With such a narrow electorate the members elected to the Legislative Council were the colony's elite: large landowners, squatters, merchants and professional men. One of the members elected in 1843 was Dr William Bland, an ex-convict who had been sentenced to transportation for killing his opponent in a duel. William Wentworth, the son of a convict mother, was the leader of the elected members who harassed the governor's officials (who were nominated members of the council) and demanded that the colony be granted full powers of self-government. Wentworth was putting his rabble-rousing past behind him. The free settlers were now willing to accept him as their political leader, though still not as their social equal.

In 1848 a small group of Sydney democrats – skilled workers and small traders – formed a reform association. They did not dare to demand votes for all men; they asked that the franchise for the Legislative Council be widened. They sent a petition to this effect to the British Colonial Office. The petition would have had no impact, except that it acquired a very effective advocate in London. This was Robert Lowe, a clever lawyer who had made his fortune in the colony and had returned to make his mark in England. He had won one of the seats for Sydney in the 1848 council election with the support of the democrats. He was no democrat himself, but in London he supported a wider franchise for the colony with an argument that could not be used in the colony. He said that under the existing rules, many ex-convicts qualified for the vote but the newly arrived free workingman did not. The usual rules did not apply (was not everything topsy-turvy in the convict colony?): you would get a more respectable electorate by *lowering* the qualifications.

It happened that a bill dealing with the government of the Australian colonies was passing through parliament as Lowe set up his scare about convict influence in the electorate of New South Wales. The bill provided that the system of a partly elected Legislative Council would be extended to South Australia, Tasmania and the new colony of Victoria, now to be separated from New South Wales. The voting qualifications in these colonies were to be the same as in New South Wales.

By the time this measure reached the House of Lords, Lowe's argument had prompted a moral panic about convict influence, and their lordships – for the first and last time in their history – made an electoral measure *more* radical: they halved the household qualification in the towns and gave the vote to small tenant farmers in the country. No one had asked for this in South Australia, Tasmania and Victoria; the group petitioning for it in Sydney was totally marginal. The House of Lords had given the democratic cause in Australia a great boost. Sydney's elite could not believe it. At the next election, in 1851, Wentworth told the newly enfranchised Sydney electors to their faces that they should not have been given the vote. He only just scraped back in as the third member for the city.

Just as these new qualifications came into operation, the gold rushes began. Property values soared and, as they did, more and more people qualified for the vote. With no change to the law, every householder in Sydney (and in Melbourne) qualified. Every hovel carried a rent of at least £10 per year. Household suffrage was only one step away from manhood suffrage.

In 1852 the British government finally announced that the Australian colonies (except Western Australia) could become self-governing. Each Legislative Council was invited to draw up a constitution for a parliament of two houses. Wentworth was in charge of this process in New South Wales, where the argument over constitution-making was most intense. In this colony, now over sixty years old, a well-established old order was determined to protect itself. Wentworth announced that he planned a

'British not a Yankee' constitution. To offset the influence of the working-man householders of Sydney, who already had the vote, he added to the electorate the respectable young men who were lodgers. It was a desperate ploy: he was staving off democracy by giving more people the vote!

Since Sydney and the other towns were the heartland of liberals and democrats, Wentworth allotted most electorates to the country. For the upper house he planned a colonial aristocracy to mimic the House of Lords. When that was laughed out of court, he substituted a nominated house to be chosen by the governor. He protected these two bulwarks against democracy – the imbalance of electorates and the nominated upper house – by providing that they could be altered only by a two-thirds vote in the parliament, a most un-British measure, borrowed from the United States' constitution.

The Australian constitution was sent to London to be enacted by the British parliament. The officials who checked it noticed that Wentworth had not provided for any general power of amendment. He had been so concerned to ensure that its key provisions could not be readily amended that he had not included any process for the amendment of its other provisions. The officials inserted a general power of amendment for *all* provisions by a simple majority. This meant that the two-thirds clauses could be repealed by a simple majority.

Wentworth was in London at the time, and protested at this gutting of his work. But he had a formidable antagonist in the secretary of state for colonies, Lord John Russell, who had been a Whig prime minister in the 1840s and the hero of the struggle to pass the *Reform Bill* in 1832. He wanted the colony to be free to reconsider any part of its constitution, so the new provision which undid Wentworth's two-thirds device stood.

The first ministry under self-government was conservative, but it promised to repeal the two-thirds clauses. How could this be resisted when the minister in London had so clearly endorsed it? With that barrier gone, a liberal government in 1858 was able to redress the great imbalance in the allocation of electorates. This was more crucial for the establishment of democracy than the adoption of manhood suffrage, which was also carried. That measure added far fewer men to the electoral roll than the changes made by the House of Lords, by property inflation and by

Wentworth himself. It *disqualified* some men, because electors now had to have resided in the electorate for six months to get on the roll and in the colony for three years. The nominated upper house survived because it turned out to be more amenable to popular control than one elected on a narrow property franchise, which was what the other colonies had established. If the upper house of New South Wales was too obstructive, the government could recommend to the governor that new appointments be made.

It is sometimes said that Australian women did not have to struggle as hard to get the vote as their sisters in Britain and America. Australian women got the vote in the new Commonwealth in 1902 and in all the states by 1909. It was nevertheless a struggle from the time of the formation of the first women's suffrage league in 1884: a long series of meetings, deputations and petitions. Australian women had to stick at it much longer than the men; Australian men got the vote quickly and with almost no struggle at all.

2016

TRANSFORMATION ON THE LAND

IN 1850 NEARLY ALL THE GOOD LAND IN AUSTRALIA'S FERTILE crescent – the strip of land 200 miles wide along the eastern and south-eastern coast of the continent – was occupied by pastoralists who grew wool for the British market and supplied meat to the local market. The pastoral holdings were huge, the labour employed small, and throughout the huge pastoral domain there was only a thin scattering of townships. A pastoralist carted his wool to the coastal ports, and from there frequently he obtained his stores – flour, tea, sugar, tobacco. During the next eighty years this landscape was transformed. Wheat had joined wool as a major product of the region. In many areas the large pastoral holdings had disappeared completely and been replaced by wheat farms and other small holdings; in others, portion of a few large holdings survived; in some places most of the land was still held in large holdings, and the smallholders were few. At the beginning of this period the small man grew wheat and the large man ran sheep. By the early twentieth century this distinction had almost disappeared. On their much reduced holdings pastoralists frequently planted some land to wheat, and the farmers, who were increasing the size of their holdings, spread their risks and rested their land by running some sheep. In this period the coastal cities had continued to grow – they now handled wheat as well as wool – but third-order service towns of one or two thousand people, occasionally more, were now spread throughout the wheat and sheep belt and between them smaller villages and hamlets.

The concerted campaign against the pastoralists' monopoly of the land began in the early 1850s in Victoria and New South Wales, the two best-endowed and the two most populous colonies, and achieved its first legislative success in the early 1860s with the passage of the Selection Acts. These provided that anyone could select a farm on the pastoralists' holdings – in Victoria, certain areas were set aside and surveyed for selection, and in New South Wales the selector could select anywhere, even before the land was surveyed. A relatively high price for the land was maintained – at least £1 per acre – but the selector was able to pay this off over a number of years. He was obliged to reside on his selection, cultivate it and improve it. These first attempts to break up the pastoral holdings and settle an industrious yeomanry on the land were in the short term at least dismal failures. The pastoralists were able to secure their holdings, or key sections of them, by employing mediums – known as dummies – who selected land on their behalf, and then transferred it to them; and because cash sales at auctions continued at which the pastoralists met no competition from small men.

The early historians of this period ascribed the failure to develop small holdings and agriculture to the power of the pastoralists to outbid other buyers, and their willingness to subvert the intention of the selection legislation.

Subsequently, economic historians who considered the technology, markets and transport available to smallholders in the 1860s, declared the conditions were not favourable for agriculture, and that no legislation could have guaranteed success to smallholders. Only patchy success was possible in areas where farmers could supply local markets. In the 1870s and 1880s, however, the railways reached further inland, and so gave farmers access to wider markets and improved technology was available from the long-established farming areas in South Australia. Then the wheat belt could develop across northern Victoria and through western New South Wales. The early failure, and the later success, could thus be explained with little reference to the land laws at all. This conclusion was held to the more firmly, I suspect, because it freed the historian from the tedium of actually examining the land laws, which are very complex, and in Victoria at least were frequently amended.

Appropriate markets, technology and transport were necessary conditions for the establishment of the wheat belt, but they won't explain why most of the farmers in the wheat belt were owners rather than tenants. Why didn't the pastoral runs turn into landed estates, to be rented out to farmers when wheat-growing became possible? That is what happened in Argentina when pastoralism gave way to wheat-growing. To explain the triumph of the family farm in Australia we are driven back to politics and to the land laws.

Some writers who have noticed the similarity of the pastoral economies of Australia and Argentina in the middle years of the nineteenth century have made the mistake of attributing the same power and position to the pastoral land holders in the two countries. It is very important to understand that in Australia in 1850 the pastoralists did not own their land, they only leased it; and that their political power in the matters they cared about most was severely limited. Let me explain this further.

When the pastoralists first moved out beyond the older settled districts around Sydney they were occupying Crown lands illegally – hence the origin of the term 'squatter' by which they were known. The British government's policy in the 1830s was to restrict the spread of settlement to maintain order and civilisation and reduce the costs of administration. Within the settled districts they sold land for relatively high prices (it reached £1 an acre in 1842) and used some of the proceeds to pay for the immigration of free labourers. Wool-growing wouldn't pay on land acquired at such prices, and so the pastoralists took their sheep out on to the unoccupied land, and within fifteen years they had taken up most of the best land in south-eastern Australia. Having failed to stop this movement, the government was nevertheless determined to control it, and it obliged squatters to take out annual licences, and insisted they had acquired no permanent right to the land. The squatters of course wanted security. They demanded that they be able to buy their land at much-reduced prices – 2/6d. or less an acre (one-eighth of the ruling price), or that their occupancy of the land which had transferred a barren waste into a valuable possession should be sufficient to give them a freehold title without further payment. In Argentina the right to take a certain number of cattle on the pampas became a right to own the land on which the cattle grazed. But the British government refused to yield to such demands. It insisted that the Crown lands should be held in trust for the whole empire, and in particular for the immigrants who would subsequently go to Australia. Land should not be given away to the lucky first-comers. It recognised that pastoral land was not then worth £1 an acre, but its value would rise as settlement spread, and access to markets improved. It refused to believe the squatters' claim that the land would only ever be suitable for sheep.

However, in 1846 and 1847 the British government did make substantial concessions to the squatters. This followed a spirited campaign mounted by them in Sydney and London after they had been angered by the local government's proposals to raise more revenue from them in return for some security, and after they had been made desperate by the crippling depression which hit the industry in the 1840s. In 1847 the British government gave the squatters leases instead of annual licences, to run for eight to fourteen years depending on the locality of their holdings. During the lease they could purchase the land, but at the standard rate of £1 per acre. They had no right to a renewal of their lease, but they were to be compensated for improvements at its expiry. Contemporary opponents of the squatters, and many historians, have claimed that this was a great victory for the squatters and they declared that the leases on these terms gave the squatters a virtual freehold to their property. This was far from the truth. How the squatters would fare in the future would depend in part on who held political power and hence the right to interpret the terms of the leases, and how their leaseholds would be treated when they expired.

The three major colonies – New South Wales, Victoria and South Australia – did not obtain the full right to self-government until the mid-1850s. Before then landowners and squatters dominated the local legislature, but those bodies had limited power. Executive authority rested with the British appointed governor and his officials. The limitation which the pastoralists felt most keenly was their inability to control land legislation. That matter, as we have seen, was in the hands of the British government. It was the eagerness of the pastoralists to gain control of the land which had fuelled their demands for self-government in the 1840s. After the squatters had obtained their leases in 1847 they became less concerned to gain self-government, but if any became complacent they were rudely awakened by the social and economic transformation brought about by the discovery of gold in 1851 and 1852. The population, particularly in Victoria, rose spectacularly; the thousands of gold diggers who rushed from find to find in the interior, were turning over the soil in the heart of the pastoral domain.

Business in the coastal capitals boomed, merchants and importers were no longer chiefly reliant on the fortunes of the pastoral industry. For the next two decades exports of gold were as valuable as exports of wool. Opposition to the pastoralists' monopoly of the land became intense. Those who had made money in the towns or on the diggings wanted to invest in land, and those immigrants who hadn't made their fortunes – and these were the majority – wanted the chance to settle on the land. The middle class led the attack against the squatters, and they had an enthusiastic following among the workers and gold-miners.

In Victoria, the pressure against the squatters was overwhelming, and many squatters soon saw how little security they had. To appease the land hunger the governor, with the support of his superiors in London, used a loophole in the lease – the power to reserve land for 'public purposes' such as townships or roads or 'for otherwise facilitating the improvement and settlement of the colony' – to withdraw thousands of acres from the squatters' holdings around the new goldfields, and to offer them for sale. The squatters were furious, but when their representatives in London failed to persuade the British government to disallow the governor's measure, there was nothing more for them to do. Competition for the land was keen, and it fetched high prices. Lots of it went to speculators. More land would have to be opened up and special facilities given to the poor man before the land cry would disappear.

Self-government was established in 1856–57. The new constitutions provided for two houses of parliament on the Westminster model – an Assembly and a Council – with the government being formed in the Assembly. Landowners and pastoralists dominated the new Councils – in New South Wales the Council was a nominated body, and in Victoria it was elected on a narrow property franchise – but the Assemblies were, from the beginning, in the hands of their enemies, the Liberals and Democrats from the towns and the goldfields. The Assemblies were initially elected on a very wide franchise, and very quickly this was extended to adult male suffrage; the secret ballot was introduced and electorates redrawn to reduce the weighting in favour of rural areas. Land reform was the issue which sustained the Liberal/Democratic advance, and after a short struggle the first measures for land reform were carried in the early 1860s. In political life at least the pastoralists had been over-whelmed. They remained a significant political force, particularly in the Council, where they could thwart or distort popular measures, but they never controlled governments or set the agenda of politics.

Notwithstanding this, for a time they won the battle for the land. Large areas of their leaseholds were being transferred into freehold. The loopholes and vagueness in the selection legislation which the squatters exploited were partly there because of their influence in the Legislative Councils.

Their economic resources were of course much greater than potential smallholders, and their local influence in rural areas meant that land officials were sometimes working in their interest. But governments and the popular Assemblies did not give up the battle. At the outset land reform had been a crusade which had rallied thousands in the towns and goldfields with the hope that the pastoralists would be turned off their land and every man would gain his farm. The issue never reached the same intensity again – most of the diggers and immigrants found jobs in the towns rather than on the land – but land reform was kept alive by the constant and continuing interest of those smallholders who were on the land – tenants in the original farming districts near the coast still wanted to escape landlords and own their own properties, those selectors who had managed to find a farm wanted to move to larger holdings, or better land, or to induce governments to allow them more generous terms for the purchase of their holdings. Farmers of all sorts wanted to get more land for their sons. Farmers and Selectors Associations were developed. The squatters' lack of political power finally told against them.

Briefly the measures which were adopted to give the small man a better chance to acquire land were these:

1. The abolition or limitation of open sales at auction. The Selection Acts had been designed because small men couldn't hope to compete against the pastoralists at auction sales, but Liberal and Democratic governments continued them because it was an easy way of raising money.

2. Dummying – that is, the employment by squatters of men who selected on their behalf – was made more difficult by the insistence that a selector couldn't obtain a title to the land unless he had resided on it and improved it over a considerable number of years. The early Victorian legislation allowed a selector to obtain title immediately if he had the funds. That meant a dummy only had to be employed by the squatter for a few days. He'd select the land, pay for it, and transfer it to the squatter. It was a much riskier and expensive business for the squatter if his dummy had to be employed for years before the title could be obtained.

3. The terms of repayment for the selector were made more generous and eventually a system of leasing at low rental was introduced. This meant that the selector could afford to take more land and he could spend more of his capital on improvements and machinery.

4. More effective and flexible administrative procedures were developed. Land Boards were set up to examine all applications for land. This helped to screen out dummies and to reduce the squatter's influence in the local administration of the law. Ministers of Lands gained more power. They could cancel selections if they considered they were not bona fide. This proved much more effective than taking offenders through the courts.

Those writers who downgrade the importance of the land laws in Australia usually overlook these improvements in the law. In Victoria the improvements were most marked in the 1860s, in New South Wales in the 1880s and 1890s. After these measures had been adopted there was in these colonies a great expansion in the area planted to wheat. These were also the years when conditions became more favourable for wheat-growing, but I believe that the more favourable laws were in themselves a stimulus. With more confidence we can assert that the amended land laws and the political weakness of the pastoralists ensured that the new wheat belt would be worked by men who owned their farms and not by tenants of those who originally held the land.

In the 1890s Australian politics was transformed. The Labor Party and a new radical liberalism emerged which supported a more interventionist government and were prepared to carry the program of land reform a stage further. Labor men and radical Liberals were interested in land reform partly because the huge estates established in the early years of settlement and during the first years of the Selection Acts were the clearest examples of monopoly in Australia, and also because both groups had significant support from small farmers and labourers in the country. They proposed that progressive taxes should be levied on large estates, and that the government should repurchase them, compulsorily if necessary, for sub-division to smallholders. They favoured the establishment of state banks to lend money on favourable terms to smallholders, and state assistance for the marketing of primary produce. The conservative groupings which formed in reaction to the emergence of the Labor Party and the radical Liberals, originally opposed measures of this sort – but to survive electorally they had eventually to support or acquiesce in their adoption. The re-purchase of large estates was carried on extensively in the early twentieth century, and after World War I for soldier settlement, and this meant that there were very few areas left where large estates predominated. Some of the large holders, under pressure from the Land Tax, and wishing to realise on the increased value of the land, sold out voluntarily to smallholders. Once small holding predominated, there was much less prestige or power to be had from the ownership of a large estate. In Australia, landed estates were the most vulnerable form of property. Even the anti-Labor parties would not, or could not, defend them. Those parties increasingly represented the interest of business, manufacturing and mining enterprises.

One of the leading issues in politics for the eighty years after 1850 was the settlement of smallholders on the land. In this sense politics determined the nature of rural society, rather than the other way about. This process of small-scale settlement of owner-occupiers was made possible by the political defeat of the squatters in the 1850s and 1860s. It is important to realise that, though pastoral activities were, for the most of the nineteenth century, the basis of the economy, the pastoralists themselves were never a ruling class. Before self-government they occupied a pre-eminent place in the local political institutions, but these bodies had limited powers and executive authority was vested in a British-appointed governor and his officials; after self-government Liberals and Democrats ruled. This explains why a landed oligarchy could not establish itself and become a constant threat to a democratic polity as happened in Argentina.

1979

DISTANCE –
WAS IT A TYRANT?

IN 1966 PROFESSOR GEOFFREY BLAINEY PUBLISHED *THE Tyranny of Distance*. The book is subtitled 'How distance shaped Australia's history' and its preface claims that 'Distance is as characteristic of Australia as mountains are of Switzerland'. Blainey is concerned both with the distance of Australia from Britain and distance within Australia. His first theme explores what he terms the 'contradiction' that Australia 'depended intimately and comprehensively on a country which was further away than almost any other in the world'. This is the more satisfying section of the book. It includes an account of the British decision to settle Australia which gives particular emphasis to its potential as a supplier of naval stores. This portion of the book attracted most attention from reviewers and has since been the subject of scholarly dispute. This critique, however, is solely concerned with the second of Blainey's themes: distance *in* Australia.

The chapters relating to this theme are chapter 6, 'Land Barrier', which deals chiefly with the establishment of the pastoral industry, and chapters 9, 10, 11 and 13 in Part Two, 'The Taming of Distance', which deals with the introduction, development and influence of railways, steamships, cars and aeroplanes. With the detailed argument of these chapters there can be very little quarrel. They are vintage Blainey: informative, lively, provocative and wide-ranging. My objections arise when Blainey expects these chapters to sustain an argument which he outlines only very sketchily in his introductory sections: that distances were very great in Australia and that the problem of overcoming distance was particularly obstinate, so much so that its malign effects can be described as tyranny.

*

In the preface to the book Blainey notes that the Australian coast encloses as much land as the United States excluding Alaska. One recalls the school atlas maps which made the same point by fitting all the countries of Europe inside Australia. Yet it is misleading to suggest that the historian of Australian social and economic life is concerned with continental Australia. Portus and Hancock, who in the 1920s and 1930s preceded Blainey in pointing to the special problems of distance and isolation in Australia, were notable offenders in this regard. To estimate the density of population in Australia Portus divided the population by the total area of the continent, two-thirds or more of which was uninhabited. Hancock highlighted the problem of distance in Australia by noting that there was no doctor between Hawker on the northern fringe of the settled areas in South Australia and Darwin, 1300 miles away. Of course there were virtually no people there either. That situation was not typical of the settled areas of rural Australia.

In the body of the book Blainey is much more careful in his analysis. He is at pains to explain why most of Australia's people and its economic activities are concentrated in its south-eastern perimeter, the Boomerang Coast, an area less than one-tenth the size of the continent. In several places Blainey emphasises that in the nineteenth century there was no national economy, but a number of separate economies. This is the crucial factor in his explanation of the development of the three railway gauges. Railways were designed to take the produce of each region to a coastal port; they were not needed to move goods from one region to another. What trade there was between the regions could be carried more cheaply by sea. When the various rail networks were connected, the break of gauge was not felt to be a great drawback, because passengers and mail could move easily from one train to another. Many passengers and goods continued to go by sea. So continental Australia disappears from view. Settlement is confined to the Boomerang Coast and within that area there are a number of separate economies with their own access to the sea. But is not this a different picture from a country having an area as large as the United States? Blainey says distance is a 'manageable problem' in the Boomerang Coast. Is it just, then, to describe it elsewhere as a tyrant?

Even within the settled areas in the south-east of the continent it may be urged that distances were comparatively great and difficult to overcome. In chapter 6, 'Land Barrier', he explains what effect distance had on the nature of settlement in the Boomerang Coast. In this area there were no navigable rivers stretching inland through the mountain ranges, and the terrain made the construction of canals impossible. Hence most of inland Australia could not be served by the cheapest means of transport, water carriage. The cost of land transport was so high that severe limitations were placed upon what could be produced there. The land later proved capable of growing wheat, but for most of the nineteenth century it could not be utilised for this, because wheat is a 'heavy' product, expensive to transport. Grazing solved the problem of distance behind the ranges because wool is a 'light' product – a ton of wool was worth between ten and twenty times a ton of wheat – and so it could be carted long distances to the coast, shipped overseas, and still return a profit.

One can accept this analysis and still question the nature of the tyranny which distance exercised. Is it simply that it forced the production of one commodity rather than another? Blainey's chapter is in fact a celebration of the ease and speed with which the inland plains were settled and integrated into a market economy. It would be difficult to persuade someone acquainted with the slower development of other colonies of settlement that distance here was a difficult problem, let alone a tyrant. In new societies where the problem of distance has really been intractable settlers have been forced to adopt a subsistence economy.

Consider the situation of the settlers beyond the Appalachian Mountains in the United States in the early nineteenth century. They could send some goods down the Mississippi river system, but until the development of the steam river boats they could not receive goods upstream. They were connected to the coastal settlements by roads, but cartage was too expensive for them to send wheat to those markets. With little opportunity for them to sell their produce, they could buy few manufactured or imported goods. In 1815 the two million people west of the mountains were largely self-sufficient and only peripherally connected to the market economy. Their isolation only ended when British capital built canals which connected them to the east and steam boats reached them from the south.

Blainey notes the advantage the United States enjoyed over Australia in being able to use water carriage to serve these inland areas. But settlers in these areas had been on the land some time before they could enjoy the benefit of water carriage which eventually made them part of the market economy. Because inland Australia was settled in the nineteenth century when there was a growing demand for wool in Britain, no squatter beyond the Divide ever moved outside the market economy. Wool was carted to the coast and shipped to Britain; stores were carted from the coast, and some of these – tea, sugar, tobacco, and clothing – had themselves been shipped halfway round the world. The immediate integration of the inland plains into a market economy must be considered *prima facie* evidence that the problem of distance was not particularly intractable.

In the old world working people seldom moved far from their own village. Witness the scene in Hardy's *The Mayor of Casterbridge* when a young couple are about to part because the man has to take work elsewhere:

'I'm sorry to leave ye, Nelly,' said the young man with emotion. 'But, you see, I can't starve father, and he's out o' work at Lady-day. 'Tis only thirty-five mile.' The girl's lips quivered. 'Thirty-five mile!' she murmured. 'Ah! 'tis enough! I shall never see 'ee again!'

At no stage in its history could such a scene be set in Australia. As Russel Ward has made plain, the labour force up the country was from the earliest times remarkable for its mobility. Bush men moved readily from one job to another and after working some time, they would go on a spending spree – quite frequently to the coastal capitals as these were the only substantial towns. Melbourne, perhaps even more so than Sydney, was the labour centre of its hinterland. Squatters and their overseers rode down to hire men or arranged to have them sent. Such mobility in the workforce was made possible because of the shortage of labour. Fear of unemployment did not tie men to one place or employer. Decent wages also enabled men to save enough to support themselves between jobs, and the hospitality of the bush greatly reduced the expenses of travelling. As Blainey has pointed out elsewhere, when his theme was climate and not distance, men could walk between jobs all the year round because the Australian winter was not severe. So in the pastoral age in Australia, working men moved more freely and over much greater distances than in the old world.

Blainey's claims about distance in Australia are implicitly comparative: Australia has greater distances than most other countries and has suffered more from the 'tyrannies' of distance. But with what is the comparison to be made? If we compare Australia in the 1830s and 1840s with Britain at the same period, it is certainly true that goods moved more readily and cheaply on the British canals and railways than they did by bullock wagon in Australia. But if the comparison is made between the general economic and social development of Australia and that of other countries, then the response must be very different. In Britain, as in the rest of Europe and North America, the unified economy which the canals and railways made possible replaced a series of localised economies and communities. It is to societies constituted in this way that the term 'tyranny of distance' could perhaps be more appropriately applied. Nearly all the needs of the great mass of the population had to be met by what could be produced in the immediate locality. Movement of people was rare. Australia, even before the construction of the railways, had no experience of this localism either in its economy or society. If the 'tyranny of distance' is interpreted in this way, its application to Australia is peculiarly inappropriate. Europe and North America still bear more marks of the 'tyranny of distance' – in the variety of speech and dialect, the institutions of local government, and the distribution of towns and villages – than Australia does.

*

Part Two of the book, 'The Taming of Distance', deals with the introduction of railways, steamships, cars and aeroplanes in the years after 1850. Lest one should think the story of these triumphs is at odds with the book's title, Blainey adds a cryptic final sentence to the brief note which precedes Part Two: 'The long era in which distance was a tyrant seemed suddenly, but mistakenly, to be fading away.' The implications of 'mistakenly' (as it concerns distance within Australia) are not pursued at all in the chapters that follow. In the 1850s when the first of these innovations reached Australia, the settlement at Sydney Cove was seventy years old. That might be a 'long era' in Australian history, but for most of Australia the gap between first white settlement and the arrival of these innovations was much shorter. Thirty years after the squatters took possession of Victoria a railway ran across the colony from Melbourne to the River Murray, and every significant town was connected to the electric telegraph network. That these innovations were available so early in the country's history is a further reason for doubting that distance was a particularly intractable problem in Australia. The benefit which the colonies derived from the technological developments in the old world was, in fact, greater than Blainey allowed. By treating the 'taming of distance' for only the period after 1850 he makes no concentrated study of the innovations which were used before 1850 in roads, bridges and coastal shipping. In the period after 1850 he has given scant attention to the development of the telegraph within Australia.

Australia was first settled by white men at the opening of a great age of road and bridge building in Britain. Large sums were invested in these works and new construction techniques were developed. Metcalfe, the first modern road engineer, began work in the 1760s, Telford and Macadam, whose name was given to his road-building method, early in the nineteenth century. Blainey gives some account of early road building in Australia, but he does not refer to the advantage enjoyed by the Australian settlement in being able to use these new road-building techniques. The roads built through the settled districts of New South Wales in the 1810s and 1820s were constructed on Macadam's principle. Contemporary observers declared they were as good as the highways of Britain. From the 1820s a regular service of stage coaches connect Sydney with Parramatta, Liverpool and Windsor. Stage coaches may now seem a primitive form of transport, but when Australia was settled, they were a comparatively recent innovation in Britain. Though they had first appeared in the seventeenth century, they remained unimportant until the last half of the eighteenth century when the heyday of coaching began. Before that, most of the travelling had been done on horseback. Peter Cunningham, who reported favourably on the roads and coaches of New South Wales in his *Two Years in New South Wales*, published in 1827, noted that many parts of Europe still did not enjoy such advanced means of transport as New South Wales.

As settlement spread beyond the Cumberland Plain, the same standard of road building could not be maintained. The Surveyor General, Sir Thomas Mitchell, realigned many miles of main roads and devoted his resources to improving the most difficult sections of the routes. His most notable achievement was the Mount Victoria pass in the Blue Mountains on the road to Bathurst. The young Charles Darwin was most impressed with this work. He wrote that in both design and execution it was worthy of any road in England. For his bridge building Mitchell was fortunate to have the services of David Lennox, who had worked with Telford on the Menai suspension bridge and a single-span stone bridge across the Severn near Gloucester. Lennox was Superintendent of Bridges in New South Wales from 1833 to 1844, when he was given the same job for the Port Phillip District. His work is a clear example of how the pioneering colony benefited from skills developed in the first industrialised nation.

From the 1840s fewer convicts were available for road building and the care of main roads passed to a multitude of local authorities which allowed them to fall into disrepair. The next concerted road-making program was undertaken in the new colony of Victoria. The Central Road Board was appointed in 1853 and by 1857 it had macadamised virtually the full length of the two chief roads in the colony: from Melbourne to Bendigo and from Geelong to Ballarat. This rapid improvement in the roads led to a sharp drop in the costs of carriage. Echuca, on the River Murray, forty miles north of Bendigo, had developed a substantial trade with the goldfields since it was less expensive to ship goods up the river from South Australia than to cart them the 100 miles from Melbourne. Once the road had been improved, however, the river trade fell away and Bendigo was linked firmly to Melbourne.

The improvement of the road also led to a quicker passenger service between Melbourne and Bendigo, especially after Cobb and Co. entered the business in January 1854 with their lighter and sturdier coaches and more frequent stages. Cobb and Co.'s coaches left Melbourne at 6 a.m. and reached Castlemaine, eighty miles away, by evening. On the next morning they completed the journey to Bendigo. By January 1856 the road had improved to such an extent that they took only one day for the trip. The Melbourne newspapers were then available in Bendigo on the day of publication. In the winter of 1854 the service had to be suspended, but thereafter the coaches ran right through the year. Cobb and Co.'s Bendigo coaches maintained an average speed of between nine and ten miles an hour. In the eighteenth century in Britain no coach travelled at this speed. In 1750 the average speed was approximately five miles per hour. Regular speeds of nine or ten miles an hour were not achieved until the 1820s. The Bendigo coaches travelled at this rate five years after the city's foundation.

The first steamship in Australian waters came into service in 1831. Blainey dismisses the contribution of steamships before 1850 as insignificant. He rightly says that in 1850 most of the coastal trade was still carried by sailing vessels, but the role of the coastal steamers as carriers of passengers and mail cannot be ignored. The first steamship service on the Australian coast was between Sydney and the towns and settlements along the Hunter River, 100 miles to the north. The Hunter River Valley was separated from Sydney by very difficult country. All the trade between Sydney and the river was carried by sea. Before the 1830s travellers who wanted to avoid a voyage in the small sailing vessels, which by turns could be dangerous or tedious, had the alternative of a three-day journey on horseback. The introduction of the steamships brought a great improvement. By the late 1830s there was a daily steamship service between Sydney and Newcastle and the time for the journey was a mere eight hours. As well as carrying the mail for the Hunter River and the country beyond, the steamers were used by the government to transport soldiers, convicts and stores.

Along the coast north of Newcastle the introduction of steamships coincided with the first settlement of the land. A group of graziers and their agents hired the steamer *King William IV* to inspect the land along the Clarence River. Steamships took away convicts from Moreton Bay and brought some of the first free settlers. Governor Gipps visited the settlement by steamship in 1842 and fixed on Brisbane as its port. A regular steamship service was established between Sydney and Brisbane the following year. At the same time, a service was begun between Sydney and Melbourne, but the seas along the southern coast were more boisterous

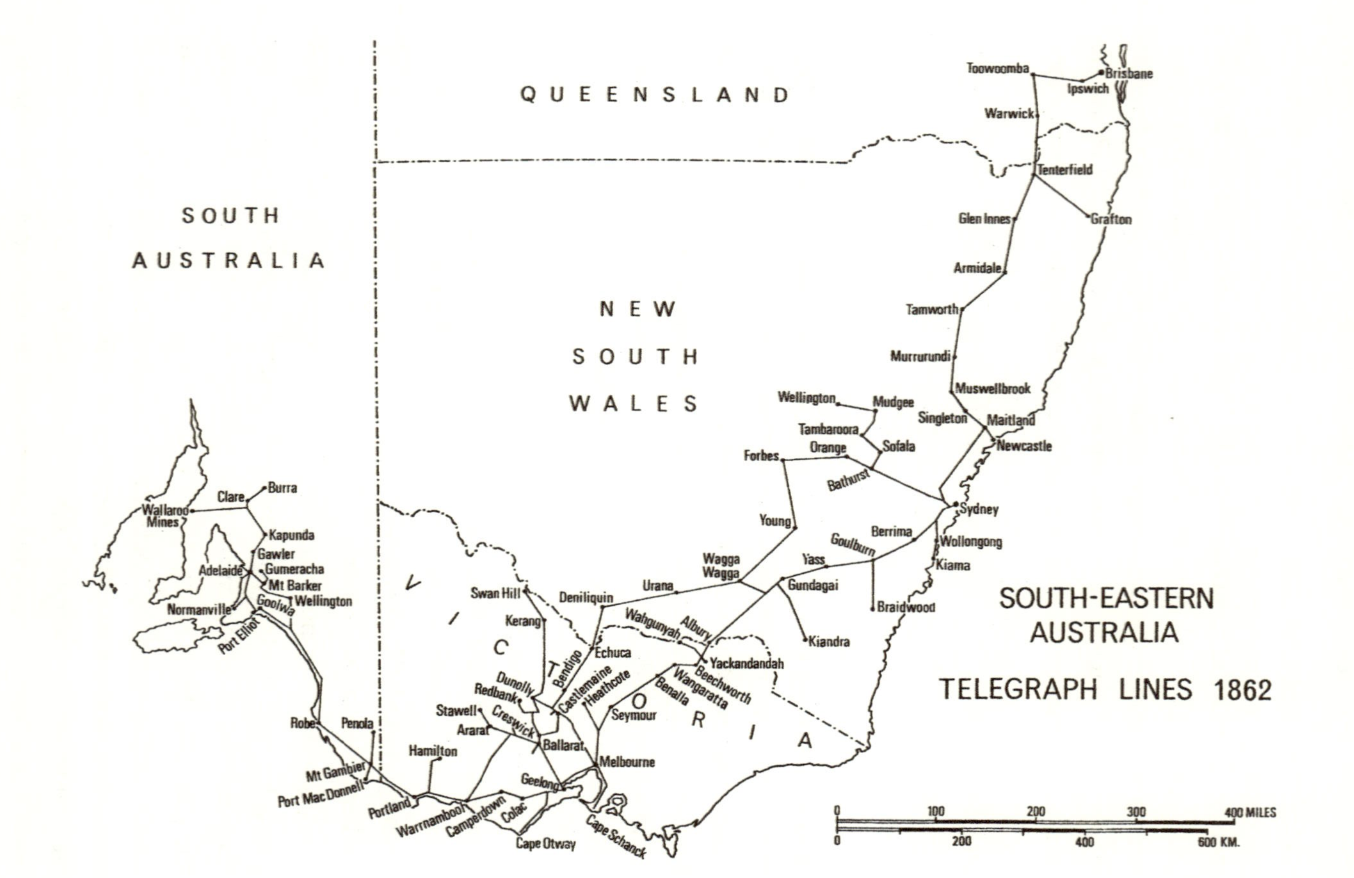

SOUTH-EASTERN AUSTRALIA
TELEGRAPH LINES 1862
QUEENSLAND
NEW SOUTH WALES
SOUTH AUSTRALIA
VICTORIA
Brisbane
Ipswich
Toowoomba
Warwick
Tenterfield
Grafton
Glen Innes
Armidale
Tamworth
Murrurundi
Muswellbrook
Singleton
Maitland
Newcastle
Sydney
Wollongong
Kiama
Braidwood
Berrima
Goulburn
Mudgee
Sofala
Tambaroora
Orange
Bathurst
Wellington
Yass
Gundagai
Kiandra
Forbes
Young
Wagga Wagga
Urana
Wahguniyah
Albury
Yackandandah
Beechworth
Wangaratta
Benalla
Seymour
Melbourne
Cape Schanck
Deniliquin
Echuca
Castlemaine
Heathcote
Bendigo
Ballarat
Geelong
Cape Otway
Swan Hill
Kerang
Dunolly
Redbank
Creswick
Stawell
Ararat
Maryborough
Camperdown
Hamilton
Warrnambool
Portland
Penola
Robe
Mt Gambier
Port Mac Donnell
Clare
Burra
Kapunda
Gawler
Gumeracha
Mt Barker
Wellington
Goolwa
Port Elliot
Normanville
Adelaide
Wallaroo Mines
400 MILES
600 KM.
300
400
200
200
100
100
0
0

and the steamer had to seek shelter on every other voyage. The mail between Sydney and Melbourne continued to be taken overland. Within the calm water of Port Phillip Bay a steamer began to ply between Melbourne and Geelong, the second town in the District, in 1841. Within a few months the mail service was transferred to the steamer which was quicker and more reliable than the mail cart. From 1843 there was a daily steamer service each way between the two centres.

The omission of any discussion of the telegraph within Australia is a serious distortion in Blainey's account of the techniques available to conquer distance. The first telegraph line, between Melbourne and Williamstown, was opened in 1854. The telegraph was relatively cheap and could be put up quickly. Within eight years, as the accompanying map shows, it connected the capital cities and every substantial town in south-eastern Australia. There was nothing 'mistaken' about this rapid triumph.

The telegraph was used chiefly for commercial messages. By this means country storekeepers could send urgent orders to the capital cities and wheat buyers receive daily instructions from their principals. Private personal messages were sent by the rich and by the rest of the population in cases of emergency. Its public uses were quite extensive. Information about the weather and the movement of ships was collected and distributed by telegraph both within and between colonies. After the opening of the intercolonial telegraph the newspapers printed each day a few items of news from the other colonial capitals and gradually they added telegraphic dispatches from country centres as well. The telegraph enabled country newspapers to present important news from the capital and up-to-date information on prices and markets. In 1859 the line between Adelaide and Melbourne enabled newspapers for the first time to give on-the-spot reporting from the scene of a disaster. On the 6th of August the steamship *Admella* bound from Adelaide to Melbourne was wrecked on the coast near the Victorian–South Australian border. Some of the passengers and crew survived on the aft portion of the ship which remained above the water line. It was five days before the survivors could be taken off, and day by day the newspapers carried accounts of the rescue attempts and estimates of how many were still on the wreck and who they were. The *South Australian Register* described the impact of this new form of journalism:

Never before, perhaps, were the horrors of a shipwreck so intensely realised by those who were not actual sharers in them. Every sweep of the waves over the wreck, every effort of the brave men who went to the rescue, every shriek of despair from the forlorn sufferers – in fact, almost every emotion, whether of hope or dread, on the part of those engaged in the desperate struggle for life – were flashed along the electric wires to Adelaide, and sympathised in by thousands of anxious beating hearts. The calamity was one which afflicted all.

For the conveying of information, the telegraph had annihilated distance.

The colonial governments were the largest single users of the telegraph. In Victoria, where government messages did not have to be paid for, they constituted in the 1860s about one-quarter of all messages sent. In New South Wales, where departments had to pay for their messages, they constituted a smaller, though increasing share of the total. The telegraph enabled the colonial governments, which in the absence of strong local bodies performed a multitude of functions, to rule their territories more effectively.

*

Two years after *The Tyranny of Distance*, Blainey published *Across a Red World*, which records his impressions of a rail journey through China and Russia. Here he encountered vastness on a new scale. Not only are the territories of these nations immense, they have people distributed right across them. In an interesting chapter entitled 'The Red Mass' Blainey considers the effects of the huge size of Russia and China on their political history and in particular on the triumph of communism. He assumes that the large area of both countries made them more difficult to govern. So far China and Russia are the only countries for which Blainey has considered the relationship between distance and the forms and functioning of government. If he were now to consider the effective functioning of the highly centralised colonial governments in Australia, could he avoid the conclusion that distance – or more precisely in this case the conveying of information – was not a great problem in the Australian colonies?

The rule of powerful central authorities in the Australian colonies was most severely tested in New South Wales during the 1830s and 1840s when there was a rapid expansion of the pastoral frontier. Part of the new pastoral areas formed a separate economy based on Melbourne, and this was administered by a superintendent under the governor's authority, but the government in Sydney remained directly responsible for all of what is now New South Wales and Queensland. The government's officers in the pastoral areas were the commissioners of Crown lands and their bands of mounted police. The commissioners supervised the licensing of the squatters and all other occupiers of Crown lands – mechanics, doctors, shipwrights, storekeepers and cedar getters. Their constant task was the settling of disputes between the squatters over the boundaries and possession of their runs. They also collected statistics, made assessments for the stock tax, controlled the ticket-of-leave men, held inquests and dealt with the property of deceased persons. They have been described as petty dictators, but their rule was subject to scrutiny from Sydney. Squatters, aggrieved at their decisions, complained to the colonial secretary and commissioners were frequently called on to explain their actions. In a cause célèbre at Deniliquin, 500 miles south-west of Sydney, the big squatter Ben Boyd had a commissioner's ruling overturned. The commissioner had granted a licence to a former employee of Boyd to set up a store on Boyd's run which would have competed with the station store.

In the administration of their office and staff the commissioners were very closely tied to Sydney. All except very minor expenditure had to be approved by the colonial treasurer in advance and explained to the auditor-general at the end of the year. A commissioner could not put new shingles on his hut without asking Sydney first. He had to send a form each month to the auditor-general to receive pay for himself and his men. He had to give a regular account of all the stores and equipment in his possession to the colonial storekeeper. The cooking pots of the commissioners and their men were numbered in Sydney. Red tape seems to have had an effortless conquest over the bush.

The licensing system was also administered from Sydney. The commissioners did not issue licences. They made recommendations about the applicants, but the licence itself was issued by the colonial treasurer after he had received payment in Sydney. The squatter's Sydney agent made the payment and collected the licence for him. The register of licence holders was kept by the treasurer and he had to be informed of all alterations in the ownership of runs. This centralisation of administration mirrored that of the economy. It could be assumed that the squatter would have an agent in Sydney to transact business with the treasurer, because it was from there most of the wool was exported. Sydney's position as both trading and administrative centre was not threatened even though settlement had spread hundreds of miles into the interior.

*

It may be difficult to resolve arguments as to whether distances in Australia were great or not, though it is helpful to define what the relevant distances are. (Of course, there may be arguments about this, but such disputes will be an advance on the simple practice of using the dimensions of the whole continent.) It is a commonplace that distances are relative. The freedom with which goods move in a society is not related primarily to distance, but to the nature of goods that can be produced, the markets for them, and the means and costs of transport. The mobility of population depends on social structures, attitudes and expectations, as well as on personal means and the means of transport. Whatever the distances, the other circumstances of Australian settlement have been such that, from the beginning, goods, people and information have been highly mobile. Blainey's chapters speak of this movement, and it may seem churlish to object to the introductory sections and the title. However, it is my impression that the title of the book has an influence apart from the book itself. It diverts attention from the mobility which has made the Australian experience distinctive.

1975

COLONIAL SOCIETY

OUR TASK AS AUSTRALIAN HISTORIANS IS TO UNDERSTAND a dependent culture. Two forces continue to distract us. As nationalists we want to establish what is distinctive about our society so we seek out those aspects which are as un-English as possible. The bushman, the digger, the pioneer have done noble service. That British institutions, habits or ideas may have been distinctively modified in substance or import in Australia may seem a tame theme by comparison. We are also distracted because in our desire to have a mature historiography we look to Europe to guide us in theme and method. So we practise family history, psycho-biography, the new social history. But the Europeans cannot help us with our central problem. They are not historians of dependent cultures. Our independence as historians will be achieved when we have developed the methods to cope with the dependence of our culture.

We have already a stock of ideas to deal with the relationship of the colonial and metropolitan culture. There is the British 'background'; there is colonial improvisation, usually limited to the material culture – stringy-bark and greenhide; there is British society in Australia deprived of its top and bottom elements (the aristocracy and gentry and the poor mostly did not come); there is the copying of British models, sometimes ahead of their implementation in Britain because of there being fewer obstacles to change in a new society, sometimes behind because of 'cultural lag'. There is, at another level, W. K. Hancock's *Australia*, Douglas Pike's *Paradise of Dissent*, Michael Roe's *Quest for Authority in Eastern Australia*, which all take seriously the dependent nature of our culture.

My aim in this paper is to explore the Australian careers of some British institutions in the hope that I can extend the stock of our ideas for the interpretation of a dependent culture. The first part of the paper refers to an institution which was not transported to Australia – the English poor law. The dependent relationship is of course as evident in what a colonial society rejects as in what it adopts from the mother culture. I am particularly interested in the consequences of the absence of the poor law for the treatment of the unemployed. The second part of this paper examines three institutions which were transferred to Australia – the mechanics institutes, the friendly societies, and the labour party – and flourished wondrously here.

In exploring the nature of a dependent culture we are fortunately not alone – we can borrow from the historians of other dependent cultures. The work of the grand theorist of dependence, the American Louis Hartz, is now well known here, though *The Founding of New Societies* has generally been regarded as not very helpful. Hartz's central idea is that Europe's colonies of settlement are fragments of Europe whose nature and course are determined by the ideology which prevailed at the time they left the mother culture. So Latin America is a feudal fragment, the United States is a liberal, bourgeois fragment, and Australia is variously a radical, proletarian, or collectivist fragment. In the new world the fragment ideology is nationalised so that its European references are lost and it comes to be regarded as a distinctive indigenous ethos. The liberal ideology becomes Americanisation; the radical and collectivist ideology becomes mateship. Europe remains a dynamic society with ideologies in contention and new ideologies forming, but the fragment societies become conservative, their development limited and controlled by their founding ideology. In the twentieth century, however, the isolated and inwardly-looking fragments have to face those European developments which they have hitherto escaped. A new generation knows more of the wider world and realises that the fragment is not a whole universe, that it has been impoverished by its isolation.

What follows will reveal me as a poor man's Hartz. *The Founding of New Societies* has been criticised as theory on altogether too grand a scale which passes sometimes into metaphor. When the facts are not wrong, there are no facts at all. The processes discussed below are, I hope, sufficiently plain and concrete. To the extent that they can be interpreted in Hartzian terms they take on added significance and if they redirect attention to Hartz's work they will have done very good service indeed.

*

The time at which the Australian colonies were founded was certainly crucial to their determination not to reproduce the English poor law. The American colonies, some of them critical of much in England, adopted poor laws as a matter of course. However, during the period of the founding of the Australian colonies – from the late eighteenth century to the 1830s – the poor law ceased to be an accepted part of English life. It was subjected to concerted criticism and after its amendment in 1834 became a matter of savage contention.

The poor law provided a complete service for those in need or distress. It was administered on a parish basis by the magistrates and financed by a rate on the occupiers of land. Under the old poor law parishes ran poor houses or work houses, but the chief relief afforded was out-of-doors in the form of doles, pensions, fuel and assistance with rent. The able-bodied poor in work received a supplement to their wages or an allowance for their children if their family was large; out of work they received a money payment or were put to work with the ratepayers and occasionally given jobs on some local public work. From the late eighteenth century onwards the cost of poor relief rose dramatically, for which during war and rapid industrial growth there were many reasons, but at the time the chief was thought to be the practice of supplementing wages. This had long been a part of the poor law but from 1795 the practice became widespread and permanent in the southern counties. Farmers had every incentive to keep their wages low knowing that their workers could be kept alive by payments contributed to by all the landholders in the parish.

The reforming Whig government, which took office in 1830, came to the rescue of the ratepayers. Under the new poor law which it passed in 1834 no able-bodied person was to receive relief unless he entered a workhouse where work was to be arduous and the standard of provisions lower than what the worst paid labourer could secure outside. For him, there were to be no more supplements to his wage, family allowances, or money payments. The new system was introduced without trouble in the southern counties at a time of prosperity. When it was introduced in the north, unemployment was rife and there was determined and sometimes violent opposition to the new workhouses from the working classes. They felt that the traditional right of an Englishman to a living in his own country was being taken from them. The terms on which relief was to be offered were totally repugnant. They called the workhouses with their studied harshness, bastilles, engines of tyranny. In fact the principle of the new poor law could never be fully implemented. In some areas outdoor relief to the able-bodied had to be allowed, but in return the unemployed had to come daily to the workhouse and break stones or pick oakum.

Nineteenth-century Australians formed their notion of the poor law from these experiences. The nightmare increase in the poor rates so that industry and enterprise were crippled to pay them was a powerful folk memory. Australian landowners did not want to pay a tax on land and in particular a poor rate whose incidence was so unpredictable and so likely to increase. Those who might need assistance were equally unwilling to be subjected to the meanness and cruelty of the new-style workhouses which were the institutions most likely to be recreated if poor relief was made a charge on landowners. Generally, Australians regarded the poor law as symbolising what they wanted to escape in the old world: potential ratepayers and potential inmates were united in the belief that there should be opportunity for all and no need for a poor law. Working men should have work, and those who had property should not be hindered in their pursuit of more.

The determination not to have a poor law or anything like it was very clear, but Australians had no firm ideas as to what was to replace it. Though they refused to have a poor law they had to cope with the situations which the poor law was designed to meet. Even in a new country where labour was generally scarce unemployment was sometimes acute; there were still the aged and invalid poor, the unemployables and deserted wives. The colonial governments themselves took on some of the responsibilities met by the poor law guardians, but nowhere did they provide a complete service and particularly in the larger colonies of New South Wales and Victoria the reliance on another English method of relieving distress – charity – became greater than in the mother country itself.

Charity in England was an optional extra; the poor law guardians provided for all those in distress and incapable of looking after themselves.

Charity took care of those who were thought worthy of more generous and less humiliating treatment. It operated on the principle of the deserving and undeserving poor, the deserving being those whose misfortune was not caused by any failing in their moral character. The undeserving missed out on charity but they were left not to starve but to whatever the penny-pinching poor law guardians were prepared to provide. In Australia when charitable bodies were running institutions or providing outdoor relief, they frequently had to deal with the undeserving as well as the deserving, which put a strain not only on their resources but also their philosophy for they were reluctant to give up the English distinctions. Shurlee Swain, who has made a thorough study of the charity network in Melbourne in the late nineteenth century, reports that the people dispensing outdoor relief were well aware that the greatest distress occurred amongst the less deserving and that reluctantly they had to give aid in these cases, though less than to the deserving. Nothing else stood between these people and starvation. Since charity was a vital institution its own inadequate funds had to be supported by government money. It might look as if Australia by this arrangement had acquired a poor law. The charitable bodies maintained institutions for the aged poor, orphans and 'fallen' women; they distributed outdoor relief to people whose distress arose from a variety of causes; and the taxpayer met a large part of the bill. No-one at the time considered these arrangements were remotely like a poor law, though the inmates of the various asylums and refuges might have had difficulty distinguishing these places from workhouses. The arrangements were indirect in more ways than one. Until the late nineteenth century no colonial government imposed a direct tax on land, income or wealth. The governments survived by selling off their capital assets – land – and by regressive taxes on imports. The government-supported charities did not involve a tax on land; it was that which was the distinguishing mark of the poor law.

The independence of the charities from government control meant that they could not be directed to take everyone. In New South Wales the hospitals run by charities were reluctant to accept the invalid aged. In Victoria the benevolent asylums did not have accommodation for all the aged poor who needed it. Police and magistrates presented with an invalid or destitute old person who was refused admission to a hospital or an asylum had to improvise. The nearest thing the state had to a network of caring institutions were its jails. To these the sick and aged poor were occasionally committed. In England the workhouses were condemned as prisons; in Australia the anxiety to avoid the cruelty of the workhouses meant prisons were actually being used in their place. As the population aged in the late nineteenth century the problems of finding accommodation for all who needed it became more acute. The agitation for the introduction of the old age pension in Victoria in the 1890s was greatly strengthened by revelations about the practice of committing the old to jail. The reluctance to have the English method of dealing with the aged poor pushed the society into accepting, before England did, the alternative of pensions, for which there were already distinguished English advocates.

The absence of a poor law led to innovation as well as improvisation. In England when a wife was deserted by her husband, she was given support by the poor law guardians who had the power through the courts to get the husband to pay maintenance. In Australia the need to get husbands to support their wives was met in a novel way. From 1840 in New South Wales a deserted wife herself was allowed to sue her husband in the courts for maintenance, a right not granted in England until 1886. So long as the husband could be found – and this was often a difficulty – the wife by this means had a cheap and ready way of getting some assistance for herself and her children without the aid of government or charity. It was, as Margaret James writes in her work on divorce and marital breakdown, 'a significant addition to the rights of women'.

In the absence of a poor law the unemployed in Australia were able to demand with a good deal of success that governments provide work for them. In times of unemployment the charitable bodies gave aid, chiefly food, but the men always insisted that they wanted work not charity. When this demand was first made the men were recent immigrants who had been brought out on assisted passages. They claimed they had been lured to the colony with promises of abundant work at good wages and that the government must provide work to keep faith with them. The founders of South Australia had indeed gone so far as to promise government work to the immigrant working men if private employers did not take them all. Since governments wanted to continue recruiting labour they were to a certain extent at the mercy of the unemployed, for their future recruiting efforts would be undermined if immigrants sent home damaging stories. Once the principle of giving work had been conceded – in Sydney in 1843, in Melbourne in 1842 by the corporation and in 1855 by the government, in Adelaide in 1837 – it became easier to make the demand at the next recession. In the second half of the century as governments became builders and constructors on a large scale, they had greater opportunities to adjust their works program to provide relief for the unemployed. Developing the resources of the country was truly the consensus program of nineteenth-century politics, supported as enthusiastically by working men who wanted employment kept up as by merchants, farmers and land speculators.

The methods by which the unemployed made their demands for work soon fell into a regular pattern. They met in the open, marched around the city, and assembled regularly at parliament house or the government offices to seek an interview with the premier or minister of public works. Invariably the ministers agreed to receive a deputation. Reporters were present to record the interview. The men spoke first detailing the numbers who were out of work, the rebuffs they had encountered, the distress which was being felt, and frequently they suggested specific projects which the government should undertake. The minister in reply said that in every large city there was always a number of men out of work and he hoped that the present distress, which he felt sure was not as great as had been represented, would soon pass. There was plenty of work, he was informed, available in the country and he offered free railway passes to any who wanted to seek it. Railway contractors in the country could also offer jobs and in a few weeks new contracts for a variety of works would be let. The men then had to explain as they did a hundred times that jobs in the country were of no use to married men. The minister's claims about the availability of work might be contradicted by the deputation which could point to men who had already tried and failed to find work at the places he had mentioned. But for the moment the minister would offer nothing more than railway passes, though he might promise to send telegrams to the country to check on what work was available. The deputation reported back to another meeting of the unemployed and further meetings and marches were planned. The unemployed frequently met daily and agitations could last for several weeks. Considerable ingenuity was needed to devise ways to occupy the men and increase the pressure on government. The unemployed marched to government house, to the chambers of the leader of the opposition, to the bishops' residences and sought interviews with their distinguished occupants to put their case, with the press always in attendance. Deputations were sent to sympathetic members of the House and particular attention was given to the city members in whose constituencies some of the unemployed had votes. On one occasion the unemployed marched up Collins Street in Melbourne with shovels to show that they were ready for work. If the agitation did continue the minister would receive more deputations and agree to accept a list of names of those who claimed to be unemployed. The list, when completed, was passed over to the police for the authenticity of the names and claims to be checked. The police invariably could not find a good number of those who claimed to be unemployed, which allowed the minister to prove that distress was not as extensive as had been claimed, but he agreed to create a special work project for the genuine unemployed (these were known as relief works) or to bring forward or expand some regular public works project. As soon as this had been conceded there were further meetings and deputations about pay and conditions, the men insisting that the work be performed by day labour and not contract. Ministers always hoped that the unemployed would disappear and an alternative tactic to stalling was to give in at once and offer some not very attractive work, for which the number of applicants could usually be depended upon to be much fewer than the number claimed to be unemployed. This might settle the matter for a time.

The politics of the unemployed were simple – they wanted governments to give them work. They were sometimes led by men who sought to teach them the true origin of their discontents and to use them to achieve those reforms which would eliminate unemployment for the future. Land reformers, protectionists, free traders, socialists and in the twentieth century, communists, offered their services to the unemployed. Other leaders were more idiosyncratic stump orators, well-known characters at the traditional Sunday meeting places. Leaders were usually already known to the reporters but occasionally a man would emerge from the ranks and would be recorded among the speakers or deputation members as 'a young man called West' or 'a strong young man named Richard Elliott, who stated that he was a baker'. The unemployed were regularly warned that their cause was imperilled by 'agitators'. There were instances of them disowning their leaders – asking them to stay away from their meetings and assuring a minister that the genuine unemployed were perfectly satisfied with his proposals – and of them passing votes of confidence in their leaders after ministers indicated they would do better without them. The skills of the leaders who were already involved in public life, even if only at the fringes, were clearly important for the launching of an unemployed agitation. However, the unemployed were poor materials for the wider influence which these leaders sought. Whatever the message preached, meetings always ended with a deputation to the minister. If the deputation succeeded, the leaders lost their constituency as the men went off to their new jobs. Ministers no doubt were more ready to offer work knowing that the leaders had bigger barrows to push. The only cause apart from work to which the unemployed themselves were enthusiastically committed was the cessation of further immigration.

Work was regularly provided for the unemployed, but reluctantly and with due care. Real and widespread distress had to be proved. In the 1890s when unemployment was most acute and funds at their lowest, governments could do little and the chief relief to unemployment in the east was migration to the west. Officialdom never acceded to the *rights* which the unemployed claimed: 'the first and great primary right of all others – the right to live by their labour and support their wives and families in moderate comfort and decent respectability'; or (from a hostile source) 'the monstrous doctrine ... that because a man had served seven years to a trade he had a right to have work found for him, and he could not be expected to take any other employment than that to which he had been accustomed'. Harassed ministers would sometimes declare against all the evidence of their predecessors' actions that it was no business of the government to find work for the unemployed and lecture deputations on the need for savings and greater initiative, or a willingness to accept lower wages. A good leader of the unemployed could cope with that:

> He did not say that it was the duty of the Government to find work for people out of employment, but he did say that when there was a large body of men who could not get work, it was the duty of the government to step in and give that relief which they could not get elsewhere.

And ministers were finally responsible or why else did they agree to admit the deputations?

I have gone into the unemployed agitations and the responses to them in some detail because frequently in our history we forget the scale of the societies with which we are dealing. To say that central governments gave jobs to the unemployed on public works in Australia whereas in England local poor law guardians ran workhouses would miss so much. What could be more 'local' than the face-to-face encounters between ministers and the unemployed, the discussion and argument about particular job sites and wage rates, the invitations to deputations to call back tomorrow when the results of telegrams sent to contractors in the country would be known? Australian ministers dealing with the unemployed were not unlike the English magistrates who ran the old poor law, who had to deal with crowds complaining about the price of bread, who supplemented wages, and occasionally provided public works for the unemployed. The similarity is not fortuitous. In the special circumstances of Australia's founding, working men were able to maintain those rights to a decent living in their own land which the English poor lost in 1834.

With the advent to parliament in the late nineteenth century of Labor and radical Liberal members, governments came under more pressure to provide work and be model employers. Labor men and radical Liberals had their critiques of capitalism to justify such a positive role for government and what had been done for the unemployed under the lap, as it were, when self-help was the prevailing ideology, was now forthrightly proclaimed as sound policy. These members insisted that in all government work and in any special relief schemes for the unemployed a living wage must be paid. The formula of 'living wage', applied first to government work, was transformed into the ruling principle of the nation when the federal Liberal government led by Deakin with Labor support made the payment of a 'fair and reasonable' wage a condition of manufacturers enjoying tariff protection. Justice Higgins in his Harvester Judgment in the Arbitration Court in 1907 laid down what that wage should be and the figure he adopted for the basic wage, seven shillings a day, was the amount which had been fixed on by radical Liberals and Labor representatives as the 'living wage' for government work. The Higgins decision became the basis for all the courts' awards.

A 'living wage' established on a needs basis and enforced by legal tribunal was a great contribution to social welfare. If men were in work they could be assumed to be adequately provided for. Men out of work could be employed by the government at the basic wage and it was settled policy in the early twentieth century for the state governments to expand their works in winter, which was the slack period for private employment. These measures were not however sufficient to take up all the unemployed, and in the 1920s unemployment rose sharply. Australia now had a new model for coping with unemployment. Britain had adopted unemployment insurance and health insurance in 1911 and there was a growing interest in comprehensive social security insurance in Australia. Leader writers, intellectuals and political leaders espoused it. Insurance had a particular appeal to conservatives worried about the sapping of self-reliance if people received benefits to which they had made no contribution. The federal government authorised detailed examinations of social insurance and made two attempts to introduce insurance schemes, in the 1920s and the 1930s. Its particular interest, Rob Watts argues, was in reversing the 'mistake' of funding the Commonwealth old age pension out of consolidated revenue. A comprehensive social insurance scheme would establish contributions for pensions as well as other benefits and reduce the drain on the Treasury. In its 1928 proposals the government decided not to include a scheme of unemployment insurance. For this omission it had the sanction of its *Royal Commission on National Insurance*. Under the British system of unemployment insurance, employers, employees and government contributed equal shares to the insurance fund. The Commission had examined employer and union representatives around the country and found that most were opposed to a contributory scheme and generally to any scheme of unemployment insurance. The Commission summarised the views it had encountered:

> The giving of food or sustenance is not advocated as it is stated that there is no other solution worth considering than that of providing work for the unemployed in order that they may retain their self-respect and independence. There should be no payment without work in return, as the genuine unemployed wants work and not charity. Further, that it is undesirable to hand out charity to men willing to work when so much national work of a reproductive nature is required to be done in Australia. It is contended that every person in the community should have the right to work, and that if a man is willing and able to work, and work is not forthcoming, then the government should provide full sustenance for him and his family while he is unemployed. Full sustenance is said to be the basic wage ... It is suggested that this financial responsibility would force the government to provide work for the unemployed.

'There is no other solution worth considering than that of providing work': this was Australia's defiance of Britain and all those European countries which had adopted unemployment insurance. The Commission recommended that state governments should develop and refine their existing practice of expanding public works to give the unemployed work.

There was a remarkable tendency towards convergence in the views of those employer and union representatives whom the Commission examined. There were differences in emphasis and different reasons for holding the same opinion but in substance their approach to dealing with unemployment was similar. The unions stressed the right to work, but employers supported the policy of providing public works which was how the 'right' was to be exercised. It was employers rather than unionists who pointed to how much scope there was for public works and were more nationalistic in claiming that unemployment insurance was inappropriate for a young country where there was so much still to be done. Both groups feared the consequences of supplying a money dole. The employers were afraid that it would lead to a weakening of work discipline, though they conceded, as the unionists insisted, that most men wanted work rather than handouts. The unionists were afraid that if a dole were provided there would be less incentive for governments to provide work. Hence the demand that if there was a dole it should be equivalent to the basic wage so that governments would want to get work in return, which employers insisted should always be done when benefits were granted. Employers and unionists were completely at one in the desire not to pay contributions to an unemployed insurance fund, the employers arguing that it was a further tax on industry which would lead to less employment opportunities, the unions because workers on the basic wage were barely surviving as it was.

The attitude of the Labor Party and the unions made the introduction of any contributory insurance scheme difficult if not impossible. The Labor Party line was that if there were to be money payments to the unemployed they should be paid for out of consolidated revenue and the extra funds needed should come from taxing the rich. Despite this, a few union witnesses before the Commission were prepared to consider contributory schemes. They were pounced on by the Labor appointees among the Commissioners and asked whether they would not prefer all the funds to come from consolidated revenue, to which it seemed churlish not to agree. Where he could, Senator Grant (ALP, New South Wales) encouraged witnesses to say that unemployment would never be completely solved until the Labor platform was fully implemented and society was entirely remade. The unemployment insurance schemes in Germany and Britain had been implemented before the workers' party was a major force in the state and in part in an attempt to prevent it from becoming so. A contributory scheme which required a wide measure of support to succeed would be difficult to launch against opposition from the party which was the alternative government. If it were launched, the unions had a weapon to thwart it. They made it quite clear to the Commission that if compulsory contributions were levied they would seek an increase in the basic wage to cover their costs. Employers would then pay both their share and that of the workers.

To read the evidence and report of the Royal Commission on unemployment insurance is to become aware how inappropriate, for this matter at least, is the standard question being asked about our welfare history: why after such promising beginnings at the turn of the century did Australia lag behind the rest of the developed world? Australia did not 'lag behind': it was holding out for something much better than the rest of the world had settled for. It wanted regular work for all at a living wage – an ideal generally supported and the aim, though far from realised, of its official policy – and its workers insisted that if there were to be a dole they should not have to pay for it.

The Depression of the 1930s, as everywhere else, took the problem of coping with the unemployed into a new dimension. It removed one relic of Australia's founding years – the benevolent asylums and societies, still the major source of outdoor relief in some states, could not cope with the massive numbers and were superseded. The state governments themselves all provided food to the unemployed. But to have thousands of men and their families existing on these handouts was repugnant to the unemployed themselves and to the community at large. All states except South Australia introduced special taxes on those still in work to pay for the food doles and to provide relief work for the unemployed. The relief work was rationed: a man was allotted so many days work a week according to the number of his dependants. The wages were below award level, but were designed so that men earned considerably more than the value of their food entitlement. By 1934 in New South Wales, 75 per cent of those in receipt of relief were working for it. Western Australia did best – by 1935, 95 per cent of those on relief were at work. That other relic of the founding years – the practice of finding work for the unemployed – still survived.

The distinctiveness of this response to the Depression has not been generally realised. In Britain in the 1920s when unemployment was already high there was some relief work rationed according to need, but it catered for only a tiny proportion of the unemployed and was abandoned in 1931. In the United States massive sums were spent by the federal government to provide relief work in the 1930s. At first the work was arranged by local bodies on the rationing system, but from 1935 the federal government itself controlled the program and the rationing system was dropped. It was condemned as inefficient since work could not be properly organised with men constantly coming and going and as failing to provide what the men could regard as a proper job. Under the federal scheme all work was on a full-time basis. This was clearly better for those who obtained it, but many missed out. At best one-half of the unemployed were on relief work; the usual figure was between one-quarter and a third. In Australia there was a stronger determination to get everyone in work whatever the imperfections of the work offered.

The federal government made a concerted attempt to introduce a national insurance scheme in 1938. Two British experts were brought out to design it. The expert on unemployment insurance drew up a scheme based on the British system of contributions from employer, employee and government. He criticised the system of relief works and judging the matter with the values of an accountant explained that jobs were more expensive for governments to provide than doles, something which Australians well knew since they had paid special taxes rather than see men left without work. He attempted to shame Australians with their backwardness:

> Relief works had been adopted in many countries from time to time
> as a temporary method of relieving unemployment, but the method
> that is being most universally adopted as a permanent means of
> relieving unemployment is that of unemployment insurance.

He was at pains to point out that unemployment insurance only provided relief to the unemployed; it did not cure unemployment. The method he condemned as temporary and ad hoc, which Australians had been following for a hundred years, was much more a cure since it gave the unemployed not 'relief' but a job. The federal government accepted his scheme, but wanted the states to pay two-thirds of the government contribution. The premiers refused and the scheme lapsed.

During the war the Labor government introduced the unemployment benefit along with other new social welfare measures. They were to be paid for out of consolidated revenue, but the scope of the income tax was widened so that for the first time workers had to pay it. They were to contribute to their welfare benefits. The government well knew that the unemployment benefit was not a cure for unemployment and it committed itself to a Keynesian policy of managing the economy so that serious unemployment would not occur. It is only in recent times that it has become possible to assess the full consequences of these policies. What happens when the management of the economy falters? The workers were right to fear that once there was a dole there would be less incentive for governments to provide work. Ministers now govern without having to encounter deputations from the unemployed demanding work. After its colonial defiance, Australia has rejoined the old world.

*

Mechanics institutes began in Britain in the 1820s. Their aim was to instruct mechanics – that is, skilled men – in the rules and principles of their own trades and in science generally. There were to be lectures, classes, and the provision of scientific reading matter. The institutes spread rapidly, but very quickly their social composition and purposes changed. They ceased to be exclusively institutes for working men and were usually composed of the highest sections of the working class and the lower sections of the middle class. Their lectures, if they continued to be given, were on literary and historical topics or matters of current interest. Dramatic and musical recitals were held. The running of a library became a central function of the institutes but the books were general rather than scientific literature and increasingly works of fiction.

Institutes were established in Australia from the 1830s. In Victoria and Western Australia they were called mechanics institutes; in New South Wales and Queensland the alternative British name of school of arts was used (by 'arts' had been meant mechanical arts); in South Australia they were called simply institutes. A similar change occurred in their purpose and a much more marked change in their social composition. The migrants who came to Australia from the 1830s to the 1850s were overwhelmingly from those groups for which the British institutes catered – the upper sections of the working class and the lower middle class. In Britain they comprised a part of the population; in Australia very near the whole. In Australia, particularly in the suburbs and country towns, the institutes became community centres used by people from a wide range of occupations. They were not established by one group for the use of another as the first Australian institutes had been on the British model; the men who established them wanted to use their services themselves. They provided a place for meetings, lectures, debates by the 'model parliament' societies, entertainment, and dances; they ran a library; they frequently had a billiard room. Throughout the nineteenth century the number of institutes continued to increase and there were mechanics institutes and schools of arts where there might be no more than a handful of mechanics. But providing for them in particular had long ceased to be thought of as their function, though the original names were not abandoned. By 1900 there were about 1000 institutes, a greater number than ever existed in Britain. The vital function they played in Australian society was recognised by governments which gave financial aid for the building and the running of a library.

In the 1930s the institutes still ran Australia's public libraries apart from the one central library maintained by state governments in each of the capitals. In 1934 Ralph Munn, director of the Carnegie Library of Pittsburg, was invited to Australia to survey its libraries and suggest improvements. He was appalled at the institute libraries. Most were run by amateurs; only in a few large institutes was there full-time paid staff; in the medium size there might be a librarian cum billiard marker cum janitor. The books were overwhelmingly light, ephemeral novels. What non-fiction there was was usually hopelessly outdated. 'It is pathetic,' he wrote, 'to observe the pride and complacency with which local committees exhibit wretched little institutes which have long since become cemeteries of old and forgotten books.' Munn was an advocate of rate-supported free municipal libraries run by professionals. These would be better libraries and reach more people than the institutes which still required a subscription from their library users. He was puzzled why Australia, which had 'led the world towards government ownership of public service and socialised activity', should lag so far behind the rest of the English-speaking world in the provision of free libraries.

In Britain municipal councils were empowered by the 1850 Public Libraries Act to set up free libraries. As councils opened libraries, the mechanics institutes libraries were either absorbed or superseded. The number of mechanics institutes reached their peak in the 1860s and then declined. In Australia there was no need to follow the example of the Public Libraries Act for the institutes provided a comprehensive service. As Munn reported, on the evidence of the books they still held, the libraries were much better in the nineteenth century than they were by the 1930s, and as he had to concede they were able to function in places too small to support a professionally run rate-supported service. Despite their rapid growth, the mechanics institutes in Britain never covered the whole country, and there would have been many people reluctant to use a library housed in a building called a mechanics institute.

From the 1930s dates the campaign to establish free municipal libraries in Australia. The leading campaigners were the Australian Council for Educational Research, funded by the Carnegie Foundation, and the professional librarians. The report by the American library expert on Australian backwardness was one of their most powerful weapons. The new municipal libraries are undoubtedly better than what they replaced, but I imagine their chief business is still in ephemeral fiction. Not all is gain, however. The professional librarians have a quaint belief that children should read only wholesome fiction. So they banned from their shelves Enid Blyton and Biggles and whatever the modern equivalents are. I borrowed scarcely anything else from our library, though I always had to look hard to find them for there was neither catalogue, nor book numbering, nor alphabetical order at the Clarence Park Institute.

*

Friendly societies underwent a transformation similar to that of the mechanics institutes when they were transferred to Australia. Friendly societies were mutual benefit associations which flourished in England from the late eighteenth century. The societies which came to Australia were the affiliated orders such as Manchester Unity and Foresters which had a central organisation co-ordinating the activities and pooling the resources of numerous local lodges. These provided the most comprehensive benefit packages – in return for a weekly contribution members were eligible to receive free health care, sick pay, and a decent funeral. The cost of these services meant that the poorer sections of the working class were excluded from membership. The membership, as with the mechanics institutes, came generally from the higher section of the working class and the lower section of the middle class.

In Australia the friendly societies had a much wider membership. My information on their membership and much else besides comes from Nancy Renfree's excellent study of the societies in Victoria. Men who had done well and no longer had the financial need for the benefits remained subscribers and continued to associate at the weekly lodge meetings with those who had not been so fortunate. Employer and employee within the lodge called each other brother. Skilled working men were the largest occupational group in the lodges, but membership extended as it did not in England to include significant numbers of labourers. Information on the occupation of lodge members was gathered in official returns. The religion of members was not officially recorded but in her detailed study of Castlemaine, Renfree established that Protestants and Catholics were members of the same lodge. In the suburbs and larger country towns a very high proportion of the adult males were members of lodges – in the early 1870s in Collingwood 53 per cent, Williamstown 62 per cent, Maldon 45 per cent, Creswick 51 per cent and Castlemaine 63 per cent. It was entirely fitting that the leading nationalist institution in the late nineteenth century should have been a friendly society – the Australian Natives Association, which has been wrongly characterised as 'middle-class'; its membership ranged from professional men to labourers.

The doctors came to regard the friendly societies with hostility. The societies contracted with the doctors to provide a service to their members for which they were paid so much per member per year. The societies reserved the right to carpet the doctors for poor performance and to reduce their payment as punishment. The strength of the societies meant that doctors had fewer patients paying the full fee for a consultation and they were forced into relationships which they increasingly saw as incompatible with their social and professional standing. They were particularly incensed that men who could well afford to pay their fees came to them as lodge patients. At the intercolonial Medical Congress in 1887 it was noted:

> In Australia the most prominent feature is the extent of the club practice … To the newcomer the extent to which the lodge system is carried is astonishing. He is amazed to find well-to-do and opulent men – Members of Parliament, lawyers, Government officials – not only ordinary members of a lodge, but expecting, and demanding, treatment as lodge patients. This should not be, and could only have arisen from a misconception of the origins of Friendly Societies.

The origins of the societies were working class, and while they remained chiefly that in England doctors were prepared to make special arrangements for servicing their members; as community organisations in the new world they were threatening.

Once the doctors' professional organisation became more powerful they were better able to reduce the friendly societies to their proper role. The Australian division of the BMA insisted that contracts with friendly societies were unacceptable unless the societies excluded from their benefit schemes those whose incomes exceeded a certain amount. The societies did their best to stave off these demands, but they could do little finally against the doctors' power simply to boycott them. In 1909 the New South Wales societies implemented an income limit on membership. After a long dispute in Victoria during which over 400 lodge doctors refused to renew their contracts the societies conceded in 1918.

But for the doctors greater dangers loomed in the new century. They had to fight off the plans of the state to introduce national health insurance schemes which, if they were to follow the British model of 1911, would give them the same relationship with the state as they had with the friendly society lodges. They would have a panel of patients and be paid so much per head. In fighting the government's insurance schemes in 1938 the doctors were joined by the friendly societies which feared a further downgrading of their own role. The opposition of these two bodies helped kill that proposal, but the doctors knew they could not forever forestall plans to make health care more accessible. From the 1930s they encouraged and themselves founded new insurance organisations which gave contributors a cash payment to offset the costs of doctors' services. This kept doctors from being subject to the insurance body and allowed them to charge fees to all-comers. Doctors insisted that this should be the model for any national scheme of health insurance. The Menzies government introduced a scheme of this type in 1953 by making federal health benefits available to those who insured with organisations which made cash payments. In 1950 the BMA had announced that all contracts with the friendly society lodges would cease. The friendly societies survived by becoming insuring bodies of the new sort. They now have more members than they ever did, but not members who meet together in brotherhood and sit in judgment on doctors.

The association of men of very different economic circumstances in the lodges was paralleled by the attendance of children from across the community at the new state schools. In the first decade of their operation in Victoria there was a great shift of children into state-supported education, the newcomers being made up of both poorer children (since fees were no longer charged and attendance was compulsory) and the well-to-do (since the teaching was superior to that of many small private schools). After the introduction of the 1872 Education Act the state school in South Yarra was swamped by 'young ladies'. At St Kilda, 'the children of doctors, the children of clergymen, the children of professional men and the children of everyday labourers ... sit side by side'. The elite generally continued to regard such schools as unsuitable for their children, but what a tiny elite it was! After ten years operation the state schools had 82 per cent of all school enrolments. If those attending Catholic schools are set aside as a religious rather than a status minority, the proportion was 92 per cent. The new schools were modelled on the Board Schools set up in England in 1870. These were provided by town councils to educate working-class children not reached by the National Society and the British and Foreign Society whose schools continued to receive government support. Varying from locality to locality there were status differences as between these schools which all catered for the working class and lower middle class. A London artisan would keep his children away from the Board school so that they might mix in better company at a National school. And beyond were the gulfs which separated all these schools from the grammar schools and public schools. In Australia, by contrast, setting the Catholics aside, what would have been known as Board Schools in England took virtually all children at the primary level.

The transformation of the mechanics institutes and friendly societies can be understood chiefly in the social composition of the migrating population – the institutions of a section of the population became those of the whole as migrants distributed themselves across the occupational structure in the new land. But this does not wholly explain why these institutions lost their sectional character. In Britain they were identified in the social order according to those who belonged to them. In the new world the colonists, anxious for the best sanction of all for their activities, gave them a new dimension by identifying them as British and using them to establish those civilising activities which made the colonies seem more like home. The social bearing of these institutions became even more indeterminate because in the new society there was not in the same configuration the social groups in which they originated and by which they were originally defined. They were ready for new purposes and a new membership. It is thus that we can understand why men who had no experience of these institutions in the mother country or had positively shunned them were ready to join them; why they continued to hold a membership diverging in economic circumstances; and why few saw the incongruity of maintaining such names as mechanics institutes.

*

It is this second process which we should bear in mind when attempting to understand the colonial career of the last of the British working-class institutions to come to Australia – the labour party. Whatever the local circumstances precipitating its foundation, it was undoubtedly a borrowed institution, something which those historians who seek to explain its origins and success by reference to class configuration in Australia sometimes overlook. The trade unions, the Trades and Labour Councils and their parliamentary committees were replicas of British models. Many of the movement's members and most of its leaders had come to Australia in the migration of working men in the 1870s and 1880s. The great development of new unions in Britain and the increased interest in parliamentary representation in the late 1880s were spurs to similar developments here. In 1886 the British Trade Union Congress established a Labour Electoral Association which was soon describing itself as the National Labour Party. Its aim was to increase working-class political influence though not necessarily by running its own candidates. Their first attempt to elect an independent Labour man occurred in 1888 when Keir Hardie ran for Mid-Lanark in a by-election which attracted national interest. Support for independent political action was strongest in the industrial north. The Scottish Labour Party was formed in 1888; the Bradford Labour Union in 1891; and at Bradford in 1893 the Independent Labour Party, which was constituted chiefly from associations in the north and Scotland, was established. When the Australian labour parties were launched in the early nineties they immediately achieved much more than had been secured in Britain, but their leaders had the encouragement and sanction of British practice. The legitimacy of what they were attempting in the labour interest was generally accepted and so they brought to this agricultural and pastoral country with its commercial cities a class institution of an advanced industrial economy.

The rapid expansion in electoral support for the Labor Party, especially in the early years of the twentieth century, was phenomenal. In Britain the Labour Party was and was seen to be a party of the working class, a group quite rigidly separated geographically, in status and style of life from the rest of the population. In Australia the party could not have this identity. The workers who formed it were members of mechanics institutes and friendly societies; they sent their children to the state schools – institutions which in England had a distinct lower-class character but in Australia were patronised by wide sections of the population. In these circumstances so long as Labor had suitable policies there was less to inhibit those outside the ranks of the unions and manual workers from supporting the party. Adelaide and its suburbs, the small farmers, the Tasmanian apple-growers were all won over to Labor. Labour in Britain was the party of the working class; in Australia the party of those who worked and on this basis could be persuasively presented as both a 'class' and a 'national' party.

But the Labor Party in this society without a large industrial working class became a different party from the British one. In 1918 when the British party adopted its socialist objective it had only fifty-seven seats in the House of Commons. It gradually consolidated its support in the working class and sought support outside with a socialist program, which it went some way to implementing when it first obtained office in its own right in 1945. When the Australian party adopted its socialist objective in 1921, it had already ruled in the Commonwealth and in five of the states, and what Labor governments did and did not do had been settled.

*

Hartz has difficulty in deciding on the essential nature of Australian colonial society: was it collectivist, proletarian, or radical? The impulse behind the determination not to have a poor law can scarcely be identified as collectivist or proletarian. 'Radical' may be closer, but in a specific sense which Hartz does not envisage – opposition to burdensome taxation which was an important part of the radical program in the early nineteenth century. Those in Australia who wanted to increase opportunity by removing the threat of taxation were nevertheless in their refusal to set up a poor law committing themselves, however indirectly, to the view that Australia would not have Britain's social problems. When unemployment did occur, the unemployed were thus well placed to get their demands met. The *Argus* said of Governor Hotham's provision of roadworks for the unemployed in 1855 that it would 'greatly relieve the public mind, and we shall no longer be oppressed by the supposition that poverty and misery find lurking places here almost as numerous as those of the old world'. It is in the provision of work for the unemployed that we can trace the origins of the Australian living wage which was a distinctive characteristic of this fragment. In his attempt to characterise the ideologies of the fragments Hartz sometimes attaches them to certain key European figures. When among other stabs he fixes on Cobbett for the Australian ideology he may have chosen well. Cobbett was neither proletarian nor collectivist, but he was radical. He wanted to reduce the taxation of the old order which oppressed small property holders and producers and yet he insisted that labourers must live in decent comfort.

Hartz wrote of a proletarian or collectivist ideology being nationalised in Australia. I have outlined instead how British working-class institutions were nationalised in this country. The mechanics institutes and the friendly societies were of course far from being collectivist in spirit. Their aim was to help their members to self-improvement in a moral and cultural sense and to better their economic circumstances. Hartz's account of Australia is seriously flawed because he followed the old Whig view of Australia's history which posits a weak middle class, and a large, confident working class and he derived from this the view that Australian democracy was 'dedicated much less to the capitalist dream than to mateship'. Australians did want a career open to talent and the desire for economic independence was strong. But the membership of the mechanics institutes and the friendly societies suggests some limitations on this which may not have their equivalent in that liberal capitalist society par excellence – the United States. Those who had done well were willing to associate with respectable working men whose worth and respectability were not impugned because they had failed to make fortunes. The mutual seeking of self-improvement is not collectivism, but nor is it unalloyed individualism. The respectable working man was part of a culture which spread a long way beyond his ranks. It is in these terms that I would explain the widespread acceptance of the Labor Party.

Hartz, by contrast, ascribes the easy victory of the Labor Party to a pre-existing collective ethos. One of the difficulties with his thesis is to know when the fragment 'breaks away'. He implies that this had happened before the formation of the Labor Party, but if this were so he has the difficulty of explaining why an inward-looking fragment should be borrowing a British institution. One of the reasons for the absence of a strong labour or socialist party in the United States is that by the time these movements emerged in Europe the United States was a self-confident society, absolutely sure of its superiority to Europe and ready to condemn labour organisations and socialism as alien and un-American.

The social structure of Australia in the late nineteenth century was much closer to that of the United States than of Britain, and indeed Australia may have been a more open society, but the continuing eagerness to follow British models brought to it with a large measure of acceptance what was regarded as alien in America.

It is difficult for even a friendly critic of Hartz to date the 'departure' of the Australian fragment and impossible to see the multifarious activities which are following or departing from British models as moving in unison. When Australia borrowed the new unions and the Labor Party, other matters were already settled in ways which were no longer British – mechanics institutes as the chief providers of libraries, for instance. In some places Hartz dates the departure of the fragment when the society is composed chiefly of the native-born who do not know Europe and for whom the fragment is naturally the whole world. That would put Australia's departure about 1900. But its separate life would then be very short-lived for, as this paper has detailed, in the twentieth century the intelligentsia and the professionals were in Hartzian terms taking Australia back to the old world. They successfully attacked the institutions of the migrant population of the nineteenth century – mechanics institutes libraries, public works for the unemployed, lodges for health insurance. The attackers were the people most open to outside influence and whose professional standing was most threatened by the 'amateurism' of the migrant institutions.

I do not want to suggest that *The Founding of New Societies* or some refinement of it should be our sole guide. There are other ways that dependence must be explored. But Hartz is worth a second look and the issue he dealt with we must continue to confront.

1984

EGALITARIANISM

'EGALITARIANISM – SEE UNDER MYTHS': SO RUNS THE index entry in a standard sociological text on Australian society, and it illustrates a stock way of handling this vexed question. One can understand the despair behind this approach – why won't the populace who believes this is an egalitarian society read the books on social stratification and class formation? To this there may be an obvious answer. While historians are also interested in the development of myth, for them egalitarianism has a more substantial existence. The desire for equality in social, political and economic realms has been a major force in our history, with results that are quite palpable.

One of the difficulties of the term is the variety both of the equalities which have been sought and the standards by which they have been measured. This applies even to historians or sociologists studying egalitarianism in Australia, who have not always made their own positions clear enough or taken care to separate them from those of the people they are studying. Some egalitarians, for example, seek equality of opportunity: they regard unequal outcomes in wealth and social prestige as acceptable so long as all have an equal chance of obtaining them. To egalitarians of another sort such outcomes are unacceptable: they wish to see equal material outcomes, or at least no gross differences in material rewards between various occupations. There have been egalitarians of these two sorts both in our history and among the observers of our society. Those who deride the view that Australia is an egalitarian society point to the undoubted existence of class structures and status hierarchies. On the other hand, Australians who claim their society is egalitarian may believe that opportunity is open to all or be pleased that people of different status address each other as equals and that everyone has the vote. This introduces two other kinds of equality: that of manners, and that of political rights. The failure to distinguish between various forms of egalitarianism has not only produced confusion; it has precluded discussion of the relationship between them, now and in the past. I don't intend to offer here anything like a full account of egalitarianism in our history. The paper gives some impressions derived from my study of nineteenth-century New South Wales society, and it bears mainly on equality of opportunity, of political rights, and of manners. Much of the paper is concerned with some of the inequalities that developed when equality of opportunity was the ideal.

*

Egalitarianism, in the sense of opportunity for all regardless of birth, has rightly been considered as something which the great bulk of the free migrants of the mid-nineteenth century wanted to see enshrined in the new country. Any attempt to recreate here a closed system of privilege was fiercely resisted. Nominated members of Legislative Councils were anathema to a generation brought up on the battles against Old Corruption. Wentworth's attempt in 1853 to found a colonial aristocracy for his constitution was laughed out of court. The terms on which squatters held their land were seen as an attempt to restrict land ownership to a few hands, and (worse) to re-establish a feudal order of lords and serfs. The squatters were relentlessly pursued and politically crushed. The land, the prime resource of colonial society, was thrown open to all.

There is a widespread view, to which serious historians have given support, that the migrants were also egalitarian in another sense: having escaped an old-world society, they are said to have been opposed to the creation here of a society of deference, ranks and titles. On this view, the history of the egalitarianism of manners would begin at this point. On the face of it, there are grounds for doubting this. The old society which denied migrants their opportunities would also have ingrained in them its own signs of success. In so far as the motive for migration is the desire for social advancement, a society of migrants will not forget the old marks of social pre-eminence.

Political democracy was not part of the old world, and its establishment in New South Wales in the 1850s might be thought to signal an acceptance of the intrinsic worth of every man which would also have affected manners. Clearly, democracy does imply the social worth of every man, or it may be justified in such terms, but this was not the bearing it had in New South Wales at its foundation. The introduction of political democracy was not accompanied by the establishment of a democratic ideology. There were many reasons for this, not the least of them being that the word 'democracy' itself was still suspect. It had not altogether lost its associations with direct popular rule and republicanism. The Liberals could not afford to be seen as un-British in their constitutional plans, for the British constitution was still widely revered. When Wentworth had declared that he wanted a British and not a Yankee constitution, the Liberals accepted this, and argued that their plan for two elected houses was a better embodiment of the principles of the British constitution than his own, given the colony's different social composition. In this they were fortunate to have the authority of leading British statesmen, who declared that there was no longer any necessity for colonial constitutions to be closely modelled on the British. The time was past when a departure from a nominated upper house in a colonial constitution was taken as threatening to the House of Lords at home.

There were also in the 1850s respectable British precedents for widening the franchise. Chartism, which had been a handicap to the cause of colonial democracy, was finally defeated in 1848. Middle-class reform groups then reappeared with more limited programs, and the cause had been taken up in the House of Commons by no less a figure than Lord John Russell, the hero of the first Reform Bill, who had now renounced his earlier view that that measure was final.

These movements in British opinion were relied on heavily by the Liberals and were crucial to their success. Such a strategy precluded the emergence of a democratic ideology that would have implied too thorough a denunciation of British society, from which the colonial constitution still had to be able to derive its authority and to which colonial society still gave its loyalty. There is a striking contrast between the fierceness with which the privileges of nominated Legislative Councillors and pastoral lessees were attacked and the gingerly approach to manhood suffrage. Indeed, the very form in which the franchise was extended indicates the limited commitment to democracy: the old property qual-ifications for the vote were retained and the manhood qualification was merely added to them.

The introduction of political democracy can best be seen as a measure adopted by those who were close to success in order to strengthen their hands for the final battle against the squatters. The supporters of man-hood suffrage were warned that they would eventually become victims of the forces they were prepared to unleash. These warnings were ignored; some say because there was less reason in Australia to fear the multitude. Perhaps so; but the impatience and recklessness of the aspiring migrant must also be considered. He had no care or respect for society until he had attained what he considered his proper place. This was the migrant's dilemma: would he in his destructive phase be so successful that there would be no basis finally upon which to claim the distinction he craved?

What would be the basis for distinction in a colonial society was a central concern of a very perceptive lecture given in Melbourne by Archibald Michie in 1859. Michie was a Liberal, a supporter of man-hood suffrage and a defender of the Eureka rebels. He gave his lecture the rather cumbersome but pertinent title, 'Colonists: Socially and in their Relations with the Mother Country'. It begins by welcoming those aspects of colonial society which distinguish it from England: here everyone – gentle and simple, educated or ignorant – works for his liv-ing. There is no disdain for manual labour, and no pathetic attempts by the genteel poor to keep up appearances. 'The revolution set in when gentlemen began to dress sheep for the scab. The revolution surely is complete when a French marquis is driving a dray in Collingwood and the son of an English peer is in the police, and ex-fellows of colleges are in the deep sinkings of Ballarat.' But these changes in fortunes and in old certainties have not established – and, Michie insists, never can establish – entire social equality. Like-minded people will want to asso-ciate with each other; and what is seen and criticised as exclusiveness is frequently no more than that. Furthermore, men will continue to want to be distinguished from their fellows by titles and other marks of hon-our. In democratic America men grasp at any title they can lay claim to and are constantly be-captaining each other. This is a natural human vanity – and a beneficial one; for would it not be 'disastrous for society – nay, could society even exist? – if we were in the mass utterly indifferent to the good or ill opinions of our fellow citizens'. For Michie, the colonists were merely Britons overseas, and they should be eligible for all the titles available to the inhabitants of the United Kingdom – a surprising view for a colonial Liberal to voice while the battle against privilege still raged. Michie went so far as to put in a good word for Wentworth's peerage scheme. A peerage should perhaps only be conferred in rare cases, but the principle for which Wentworth contended was correct: a colonist held a degraded rank as a British citizen if he were deprived of the opportunity of gaining British honours.

The *Sydney Morning Herald* was delighted by Michie's lecture. Fighting a losing battle against the New South Wales Liberals, it was pleased to take up and strengthen Michie's views. The affected contempt for titles of honour, it claimed, was hypocrisy: 'Social distinction is everywhere desired, and nowhere more than in democratic countries, where the passion for rising in the world is stimulated by the possibility of it.' Was the *Herald*'s view of its enemies correct? Were the distinctions of the old society still sought in the new democracy?

*

The social distinction most readily available to the aspiring colonist was that of becoming a gentleman. Gentlemen had a distinctive dress – frock-coat, top hat, kid gloves – and received public recognition from other gentlemen. Policemen were instructed to salute them. In letters addressed to them and in any formal listing of names they were given the title 'Esquire'. Working people addressed them as 'Sir'.

The history of the gentleman in Australia has suffered much from the aristocratic bent of its historians. Paul de Serville in his study of Port Phillip gentlemen is much concerned with gentle birth and good family. Geoffrey Bolton associates the colonial gentleman with the ownership of broad acres. By traditional English standards, these are the correct criteria to adopt; but in the colonies, gentlemen did not have to meet them. In the 1850s in New South Wales the men claiming to be gentlemen and recognised as such were squatters, landowners, merchants, bankers, professional men, chief clerks and those of independent means. This rather lax conception is reflected in Burke's *Colonial Gentry* published in the 1890s – a work that both Bolton and de Serville find puzzling. De Serville takes it to task for belying its title:

> The genealogies are exiguous, often covering no more than three generations although attempts are made at times to graft new branches onto old trees. The heraldic aspects are even less impressive. An English critic pointed out that at least a third of the entrants are technically not gentlemen, lacking coats of arms … Nor could the 563 odd entrants be said to compose a gentry in the accepted sense of the term, since many were not landed, much less members of historical or ancient families of the untitled nobilities.

Bolton is a little more prepared to see standards relaxed but was it not, he asks, 'generous to include W. O. Hodgkinson, Micawber-like journalist and mining speculator who happened to be Minister for Mines in Queensland in 1891 and had neither wealth, permanent position, nor ancestry beyond a father who was a Mr Hodgkinson of Birmingham?' No, it was not generous. He was certainly a gentleman – as was Mr Micawber of course, once he was in Australia and had become a sheepfarmer.

The widening of the ranks of the gentleman in the colony was made possible because in England there was a long-standing ambiguity about the term, pressure for widening of the ranks, and uncertainty about where the line of exclusion fell. Gentlemen were of good family and held land, but they also had to possess the gentlemanly virtues – they were scrupulously honest and considerate. A man who lacked these virtues could be described as 'no real gentleman' even though he had land and an ancient lineage. But if this were so, could the practice of the gentlemanly virtues entitle one to the status of gentleman even without land and lineage? It was at this point that those without the traditional claims could exert pressure. Not that gentlemen had ever formed a closed order; old families had married new wealth, and after one or two generations, new wealth was old enough. Undoubtedly, it was now much easier, in the nineteenth century, to become a gentleman, or to seem to become one; but the uncertainty about the term was still only at the edges of a group that could be recognised clearly enough by the old criteria.

In Australia the balance changed. The core of true gentlemen was small and not self-sustaining; the claimants at the edges numerous. There were enough true gentlemen to retain the rank's traditional prestige, but too few, owning too few resources, for the traditional criteria to maintain a commanding influence. Everyone in the colonies – including those with the best claims to be gentlemen – was closely involved in money-making. This was traditionally forbidden the English gentleman, who could invest his fortune to advantage but was essentially a man of leisure, not preoccupied with money matters. If trade in sheep or cattle, or speculation in squatting runs, was allowable, on what grounds could merchants be excluded from the gentlemanly ranks? Both the Australian Club in Sydney and the Melbourne Club – the institutions of the gentlemanly elite – had merchants among their founding members. No doubt these were men who came closest to the gentlemanly ideal in character and education, but their acceptance into the Clubs meant that the traditional prejudice against trade could not be used to deny gentlemanly status to other merchants. All merchants became gentlemen, even if they were not all accepted into the Clubs. The rule against trade took on a new form in Australia: it was used to draw the line below merchants and so to exclude shopkeepers. Wholesale trade was allowable to a gentleman; retail trade was not.

The groups which became gentlemen in Australia were making (or were soon to make) claims to that status in England, but there, these claims could be resisted or made to look doubtful. In Australia, they could not, with the paradoxical result that there was ultimately less uncertainty about who was a gentleman in Australia than in England. In Australia, the criteria of good family (which was particularly limiting) and land ownership disappeared; 'gentleman' became the status of anyone holding a certain position in the occupational hierarchy or possessing independent means. Membership of a traditional English rank thus became available to the successful migrant of whatever background.

But one uncertainty remained. The new-made colonial gentlemen knew they were doubtful gentlemen by traditional English standards, which were overlooked in the colonies but not forgotten. The colonial gentlemen set about to meet them as best they could. By old-world standards many of these attempts were pathetic. Paul de Serville laughed at family trees that went back only three generations; what would he think of vague references to 'good yeoman stock'? Or of the ex-convict pastoralist claiming that his ancestors must have been people of some consequence because of the quality of their tombstones in the village churchyard? The gentlemen in Australian cities – merchants, bankers, company directors, professional men – frequently sought a country 'estate': ten acres, sometimes more, sometimes less, beyond the city proper where they built their mansions and villas. They worked in the city but lived in what might just be called country. The grand town house did not flourish in Australian cities, because town wealth immediately claimed gentlemanly status and tended to move out of town. In Adelaide, a country life for city gentlemen was most happily accomplished: the Adelaide Hunt Club met at the gentlemen's mansions and followed the trail over their estates and the neighbouring farms, all within sight of the city itself.

The widening of the ranks of gentlemen in the colonies was a fairly rapid but traumatic process. Gentlemen who had, or thought they had, good traditional claims to gentlemanly status regarded themselves as superior to the would-be gentlemen; but would-be gentlemen with the summit of their ambition in sight were not disposed to accept a subordinate place. They subjected any claims to superior status to remorseless analysis: How had so-and-so made his money? What was the real reason for his coming to the colony? Who were his wife's people? Such was the staple of day-to-day gossip, and often of public feuding. Men with new wealth, doubtfully acquired, could sometimes claim superior origins to those with old. Being an old family carried some status in New South Wales, but the old families were particularly vulnerable because some of the founders were of doubtful origin and all had made their money in ungentlemanly ways. Challengers could not meet the traditional criteria, but they used them to denigrate occupiers. Just because the new men could not be excluded, the contentions for place and precedence were fearsome. In small societies, where so many were parvenus and the traditional standards were being set aside, there could be no agreed basis for the ranking of gentleman. The result was the bitter personal feuding and the litigiousness we find in early Sydney and Melbourne – and in other colonial societies where status became problematic.

In England, a gentleman needed no title to have an unequivocal claim to his status. In the colony, as the traditional tests were being set aside, titles, official recognition and official position became more significant. If you could occupy an official position traditionally held by an English gentleman, then your claim to be a gentleman was more secure or precedence could be claimed over other gentlemen. In England, some men who had no other claims became gentlemen by this route – most notably, military officers. But though all officers were accepted as gentlemen, they were always eyed narrowly: there were regiments and regiments, and officers could well be rootless men, adventurers and jilters. As one officer was well pleased to find, no such suspicion attached to officers in New South Wales. A captain or a lieutenant – the title itself – was something solid and certain when other old-world claims were doubtful and contentious. In this uncertainty begins the amazing career of the Australian doctor whose title meant little in England but worked wonders here.

To be received at Government House became an important acknowledgment of gentlemanly status. Government House was not a court at the apex of society. Having begun as a place where all the colony's officers and gentlemen gathered, all who became gentlemen expected to be received there. At levees, they all could go. A levee at St James's was a gathering of the kingdom's elite, who in the 1850s and '60s still wore court dress to the Palace; at Government House in Sydney, it was a gathering of the colony's gentlemen, who wore gentlemen's evening dress. Governors differed in policy about whom they invited to dinners and balls, but because invitations to Government House held such significance, the tendency was to liberality. Certainly, invitations were not left unquestioningly to the governor's discretion. Lady Denison, whose husband was successively governor of Van Diemen's Land and New South Wales in the 1850s, records the difficulties they had with invitations. After invitations had gone out for a ball, every day brought a number of protest letters to the A.D.C. asking whether his Excellency had heard anything prejudicial to the writer's character or whether it was considered their situation disqualified them from the honour of an invitation. Some, more indignant, wrote direct to the governor. So vital to status was official recognition that the clerks in the Ordnance Office threatened to write home to the Board of Ordnance to complain at the indignity of being overlooked.

The House of Commons was a gathering of gentlemen, and those few members who might not have been true gentlemen enjoyed the title. Before responsible government in New South Wales, the Legislative Council was similarly composed overwhelmingly of those whose gentlemanly status was already secure. After responsible government and with the introduction of manhood suffrage, men of lower status entered the parliament: small traders and dealers, shopkeepers, publicans and country newspaper proprietors. These men and all their colleagues took the title of gentlemen. The securing of this status was one of the attractions of becoming an MP. A good many members who voted for manhood suffrage were still getting used to the feel of a top hat.

*

In England the Justice of the Peace was the epitome of the country gentleman, serving his monarch and dispensing justice to his inferiors. In New South Wales the Justices, as in England, constituted the Courts of Petty Sessions and took a large part in local administration. But the position became valued for its social prestige. In England the title of J.P. could add some lustre to a gentleman's name; in New South Wales it was the best endorsement of gentlemanly status and local pre-eminence. A place in the Commission of the Peace was therefore much coveted, and colonial success stories did not end merely with riches, but with the hero on the magisterial bench. This, for example, was the clearest way that Dickens could signal Mr Micawber's success; indeed, the position was especially valued by colonists just because its message was so clear not just to local eyes but to relatives and friends at home. Every aspiring emigrant was conscious of the audience he had left behind.

With responsible government the right of appointing Justices of the Peace passed from the governor to the ministry of the day, and the seal of gentlemanly status became one of the spoils of popular politics. Places in the Commission of Peace were used to secure support in the House and to reward constituents – just as with roads and bridges, but with the advantage to government that they cost nothing. The first NSW premier, Donaldson, a Conservative, asked all members to submit suggestions for additions to the magistracy. This resulted in 177 new appointments. The Liberals who quickly supplanted the Conservatives were more prodigal. In his five years of office to 1863, Cowper, the Liberal premier, made some 800 new appointments. At one time he reported he had 200 applications on his desk. There was no attempt at a careful scrutiny of these candidates. When there were complaints that new magistrates could not write or make themselves understood, Cowper blandly replied that all appointments were recommended by someone. He was a master of the patronage business. He always spoke as if magistrates were appointed in order to better supply the bench of the local courts. Certainly, there were regular complaints that court business had to be postponed because magistrates did not appear. But since a position in the magistracy was sought chiefly for its social prestige, and not because men wanted to spend one day every week on the bench, appointing more magistrates did not necessarily improve attendance at the courts. The 'need' for more magistrates was thus never ending.

In the country, the new Liberal appointments to the bench included storekeepers and other town business-people. These men were local leaders of the Liberal cause, but even by colonial standards had doubtful claims to be gentlemen. The existing country magistrates, chiefly landed men, were now being forced to accept them as equals. Cowper boasted that in making his appointments he broke with the usual practice of asking local magistrates whether new appointments were acceptable to them. In many cases they clearly were not, and Cowper provoked the old order into a counter-revolution. Magistrates declared that they would not sit with the new men and at Goulburn and Mudgee magistrates resigned en masse. They focused their objections on one particular appointment, declaring that the new man was unfit by social position and antecedents for the bench and was transparently being rewarded for political services. The townspeople of Goulburn and Mudgee enthusiastically supported the new appointments, and were angry that the local gentry should attempt to keep in their hands an honour which the Liberal government in Sydney was opening to them. In the colony at large, the grounds of objection taken by the resigning magistrates – social position and antecedents – were widely condemned. But the old magistrates won these battles, though not the war. It was true, as the Goulburn magistrates alleged, that the new appointment there, the editor of the local paper, had been dismissed in his youth from the Public Service for offering to bribe his supervisor. The government could not ignore this objection, and it was for this reason, and not because he had once run a pub on the Yass road, that his commission was withdrawn. At Mudgee the new appointment, a storekeeper, had once briefly served as a police constable under the supervision of the magisterial bench of which he had now been made a member. This was the particular circumstance used by the old magistrates to support their general case against appointments of this sort. The government ignored their protest, and the newcomer would have remained on the bench had he not over-played his hand. In answering the objections made to him, he proclaimed his own gentility – his father was an Irish gentleman of 'independent but not very large means', and many near relatives were peers of the realm – and attacked the antecedents of the local magistrates at their weakest point. Mr R. W. Blackman was now a landholder, but his parents had kept a public house at Mudgee. The storekeeper magistrate declared they had been suspected of sly-grogging and that the mother of the J.P., still living, was a drunk. When threatened with legal action for libel, he publicly apologised and lost his place on the bench.

'Social position', which the protesting country magistrates made a test for the bench, was rejected by the Liberals. Cowper said the tests were character and intelligence. A Select Committee that had examined the question in 1858 had opted for character and education but a requirement for formal education the premier thought too restrictive. Among what survived of the Conservatives in the Legislative Assembly, there was sympathy for the resigning magistrates, but given the constraints of popular politics they could not talk of 'social position' with impunity. James Martin, the Conservative leader in the House, and the *Sydney Morning Herald* accepted the tests of character and education, and criticised many of Cowper's appointments for failing to meet them. Under the protection of parliamentary privilege, Martin could detail his objections to new appointments. He declared that Chapman, a Sydney paper-hanger, was unfitted for the bench, but although the social slur in this reference to occupation was clear enough, Martin insisted that his objection concerned the paper-hanger's fitness and not his social position: the education a paper-hanger might receive suited him for mechanical pursuits, but not for dispensing justice. But such a test was no more acceptable than social position. Chapman's virtues were self-evident. As one of his many parliamentary defenders said, he was upright, honest and had raised himself by his own industry. And what could be said against a country-town worthy, also queried by Martin, who was as well-known as the town itself 'for he has grown with its growth and strengthened with its strength'? Education, as Cowper said, was too narrow a test. Instead, stress was laid on the virtues of shrewdness, knowledge of the world and sound common sense. A too close attention to the character and abilities actually needed to perform duties on the bench could not be allowed. Something other than a career open to talent was being contended for: a title had to be open to self-made wealth.

'Character and intelligence' rather than social position served their turn in opening the ranks of the magistracy, but they had their dangers. Strictly applied, they meant that anyone – no matter what his wealth, class or status – could be a magistrate. The ambiguity in the position of the magistrate – was he a man of a certain social rank or a man with certain abilities and qualities of character? – was similar to that surrounding a gentleman. If the virtues a gentleman should possess were made the sole defining characteristics of gentlemanly status, then gentlemen would cease to occupy a pre-eminent place in the social and economic hierarchy. Cowper's government had to face this implication of their policy when it was revealed that they had made a working man, a lowly employee at a sheep station, into a magistrate. The government was seriously embarrassed by this. No record could be found of who had made the recommendation. The government's final defence was that the appointment had been a mistake. Some Liberal supporters suggested that their enemies had smuggled the name in to discredit the government.

A few bold Liberals made a show of defending a working-class appointment to preserve the integrity of the 'character and intelligence' principle. But working men were by general consent not eligible for the honour. A limit had finally been reached.

James Martin became premier in 1863, and his government undertook a revision of the magisterial lists. Its declared aims were to exclude those unfit by education, means or character; all members but one of a family in the same neighbourhood; people in active business (this would exclude shopkeepers) unless no-one else was available; and those who rarely or never attended the bench. There were by now 1250 Justices of the Peace, and Martin reduced these to 628. It was generally conceded that a culling of the lists was necessary if only to exclude the dead and the departed, but a purge of these dimensions shook the social foundations. After the first howls of rage came demonstrations that the government had not been true to its own principles, and claims that it had been as much influenced by political allegiance as its predecessors. The gross inconsistencies, which even a cursory examination of the list reveals, suggest that this must have been so. The furore over the exclusions was such that Martin had to reinstate twenty-six of the excluded. His tampering with the Commission was partly responsible for his defeat in Parliament as soon as the House reassembled and at the election which followed. Cowper returned to power and ninety-eight more of the purged were reinstated within twelve months.

*

How far could the democratising of social distinction proceed? The distinctions became more defensible as access to them was widened, but would the new men so lower the tone that respect would vanish? My impression is that in the 1860s and 1870s the positions of gentleman, certainly, and of magistrate, more doubtfully, retained their prestige. With parliamentarians the case was different. There was a rapid collapse in respect for them. This was not solely a response to the widening of the social positions from which parliamentarians came, extreme though that was. A criminal record excluded a man from the magistracy but not from a seat in the House. What sealed the parliamentarians' fate was that in their deliberations they outraged the gentlemanly ideal. The House was frequently in uproar; insults and imputations were freely hurled; there was none of the restraint and good manners which should characterise the gentleman. The accounts of colonial history which describe this as the age of the bourgeoisie are a poor guide to the government and politics of the period. First, because the parliamentary benches were not filled by the solid bourgeois. As Chris Connolly concludes it is truer to say of the new Assemblies, as one Conservative did at the time, that they were made up in large part by 'publicans – expiree convicts – journeyman mechanics – Wesleyan lay preachers'. The great merchants who had helped the Liberal movement early soon deserted to the Conservative side. Connolly described the Assembly as 'middling class'. Secondly, the Assembly in its deliberations did not display the sobriety which one associates with the bourgeoisie. They failed as gentlemen, which was what they claimed to be; they could not even meet the tests of decency and respectability. But to the dismay of the respectable, the larrikin members were regularly returned by their constituencies. If the 'Age of the Bourgeoisie' is a poor guide to the politics of this period, the 'hegemony of the mercantile bourgeoisie' is worse. The wide popular franchise gave parliament a distinctly unrespectable odour.

Just as the respect for parliament and public life was falling, new honours became open to leading public men. An honour from the queen was immune from the dangers which might lower the value of colonial distinctions. It came from the fount of honour herself, and it associated its local recipients with the venerable orders of the mother country. The award of imperial honours remained a prerogative of the Colonial Office. It received recommendations from governors but even these were not always acted on. Governors were lobbied by ministers, individual aspirants and their friends. In the 1860s the Australian colonies were the most clamorous for honours of all the self-governing colonies, and received the most. Since I haven't examined the situation in other colonies, I cannot be sure of the reasons for this, but I suspect that imperial honours were sought more avidly in the Australian colonies because political power had passed from the hands of the social elite. Before responsible government, a place in the Legislative Council marked a man as one of the elite. With manhood suffrage and the coming of the 'middling class' to the Assembly, a place in the House, even a leading place in the House, no longer had this cachet, especially as there was a clear tendency for old wealth to shun and despise the parliament – to which in any case it had difficulty in gaining access. But what did old wealth matter, if the new political leaders could answer its taunts with royal honours?

During the 1860s the Colonial Office deliberated on how it could accommodate the growing demand for honours, chiefly from Australia. There were too few vacancies in the Order of the Bath. If the existing orders were expanded to take in the Australians, would they lose status in English eyes? If a special order were established for the colonies would Australians be prepared to accept it? Finally in 1868 the Order of St Michael and St George, which had been inherited by Britain with the Ionian Islands and which had been used to reward services in the Mediterranean, was expanded into a general colonial order. It had the advantage of a grand name and a lineage. It was to reward services for the colonies as well as in them. The first appointments to the new order included the distinguished Colonial Secretaries Lord Derby, Lord John Russell and Earl Grey. With these baits, the order was successfully launched and gratefully received in Australia.

The New South Wales Liberals took a prominent part in pressing for honours. The cabinet, meeting as the Executive Council, passed resolutions recommending particular people for honours, to the dismay of the Colonial Office which was not prepared to allow colonies to be self-governing on this issue. A continuing concern of the Liberal government was to secure an honour for its premier, Cowper. His Conservative predecessors had been honoured, even though their hold on office had been so brief; and the Liberals saw no incongruity in seeking a similar mark of royal favour for the man who had introduced manhood suffrage and swamped the Upper House.

I trust that I have said enough to show that liberal democrats, the victors of the battles against old world privilege, wished still to retain social distinctions which were marked by titles, special modes of address and of dress. Against this must be set the many features of late colonial society which shadow forth a different world, closer to our own, with less deference and more egalitarian manners. There was the independence of working men, arising from high wages and labour shortage; the disrespect of the Irish for English pretension; the 'egalitarianism tempered by the checks of respectability' that characterised the wide membership of friendly societies and mutual improvement groups; the wide support for common schooling in the new state schools. There is some evidence – I wish I had more – that the only acceptable terms for social mixing were those of equality, with the result, as de Tocqueville noted in America, that cross-class socialising declined. Yet for all these signs, commentators insisted on the Britishness of the colonial social order, especially in New South Wales, even while noting some aspects of life that we now take as constituent parts of our egalitarianism. Trollope referred to the maintenance of the British mode of thinking on 'social position', a view not disturbed by close observation of those archetypal egalitarians, the nomad pastoral workers whose attitude to their superiors he described as 'civil'. Froude, who visited Australia in 1886, detected no reluctance to respect men of high rank, and declared, 'There is room in Australia for all orders and degrees of men', though admittedly he did not move very far from the Government Houses and the people he met there. Twopeny observed more widely. He records the independence of servants, and the prickliness of tradesman if they thought they were going to be patronised, and yet he writes confidently of the gentlemanly order and of polite society, and takes a favourable view of the future of the Australian aristocracy after four generations. Australia's fascination for overseas observers was its newness and its democracy, and yet their message is that neither characteristic had had a transforming effect on social relations. Trollope specifically drew the comparison with the United States where:

> all institutions of the country tend to the creation of a level, to that which men call equality, – which cannot be obtained, because men's natural gifts are dissimilar, but to which a nearer approach is made in America than has ever been effected in Europe. In Australia, no doubt and especially in Victoria, there is a leaning in the same direction; but it is still so slightly in advance of that which prevails

among ourselves as to justify an observer in saying that the colonies
are rather a repetition of England than an imitation of America.

*

Colonial society wore a double aspect. It was a new society and by its
own standards an egalitarian one, in that opportunity was open to all
regardless of old-world tests of rank and birth. But so long as success
dressed itself in traditional garb, colonial society could also look, or be
made to look, like the old world reincarnated. This was its vulnerability. From the 1880s, a new radicalism and socialism reached the colony
from the mother culture. A democratic society committed to equality of
opportunity and the absence of old-world distinctions – like the United
States – might have been largely impervious to these forces. New South
Wales with only a half-hearted commitment to democracy, and nurturing
old-world distinctions, was not. Herein lies one answer to the question
which Geoffrey Bolton has asked: why did Australia, with a social structure like the United States, acquire British class institutions? It was from
this time also that the egalitarianisms with which we are familiar were
firmly established. I will briefly refer to three of the new egalitarian forces:
the Labor Party, the *Bulletin*, and the literature of Lawson and Paterson.

Those who want to highlight the tameness of the early Labor Party
draw attention to the number of items in its first programs concerned
with democratic reform: the abolition of plural voting, which the reten-
tion of the old property qualifications had allowed; the relaxation of
resident qualifications to give votes to nomadic workers; the reform of
the Upper House; the introduction of the referendum. Those who want
to explain Labor's success should note the great advantage it acquired
by being the first party in a democracy to be thoroughly committed to
democratic principles. It had everything to gain by democracy becoming
more complete; and its moral claim to represent the people was greatly
enhanced by advocating principles that could not readily be denied. The
party could use the principle of political equality to assert the worth of
the working man and to claim attention for his needs. But the working
men the party sent in to parliament were always suspected of being likely

to betray the cause; and for this reason, if no other, they did not put on the garb of gentlemen. Unlike some earlier members of low status, they were noted for their sobriety and attention to their duties. Previously men had used parliament to advance their own status; the effect of Labor in parliament was to dignify the working class.

The final catch-all point of Labor's first platform read: 'Any measure that will secure the wage-earner a fair and equitable return for his or her labour'. 'Fair and equitable': here begins the egalitarianism which Hancock traced in the pages of his *Australia*. The success of the Labor Party with that formulation derived in part from its ability to make it a democratic cause. The egalitarianism of equality of opportunity had, as we have seen, made little claim on political democracy; democracy was first fully exploited by an egalitarianism of distributive justice.

The *Bulletin* of J. F. Archibald exercised an immense influence, and yet it did not persuade Australians to renounce imperial titles or break the ties with Britain, two causes for which it campaigned relentlessly. What it conveyed more persuasively was a style: cheeky, irreverent, opposed to all humbug and pretence, delighting to find the hypocrite in the advocate of any cause it did not support. These attitudes are rightly taken to be widespread in Australia, and they form one of the cornerstones of the egalitarianism of manners. So integral are they to the Australian ethos that it is tempting to think that they must have been well entrenched long before the first *Bulletin* rolled off the press in 1880. Archibald himself did not think so. The natural tendency of Australians as British colonists was to toadyism and flunkeyism. He deplored the fact that while Australia was rightly expected to adopt ways and means best suited to itself for its 'commerce and money-grubbing', it slavishly followed England in 'politics, social relationships, and religion'.

Our understanding of Archibald has been greatly enhanced by Sylvia Lawson's biography, *The Archibald Paradox*, which presents him as a cosmopolitan nationalist. Archibald wanted Australia to sever its connection with the rottenness of aristocratic England, yet it was the English republican and radical movement which inspired and encouraged his republicanism. In the mid-'80s Archibald visited England, and sent back articles to the *Bulletin* on the caste, monopoly, and privilege that disfigured the society which Australians called 'home'. In London, he had his vision of what the future held: the Liberals as a reform party were finished; it was the party of idleness, privilege and great wealth, of that 'gilded bauble' the crown and the Whig nobles with broad acres stolen from the people. A social revolution was imminent. The Labor Leagues were rallying and had plans to send working men into the Commons. Soon there would be over 200 of them and they would wear cheap tweed suits or, better still, affront that perfumed Assembly with a grimy Crimean shirt. These men would speak for the toiling masses, the millions who lived in one room. Australians should follow this lead. The two representatives of labour in the New South Wales Assembly were a disgrace: they had put on top hats and frock-coats, which are as 'offensive ... marks of what the world calls social superiority as are stars and garters and Windsor uniforms'.

Archibald knew something of both sides of the coming revolution in the metropolis, and he used the standards of both in the *Bulletin* to show how pathetically provincial New South Wales was. He told the 'aspiring vulgarians' who scrambled after honours and Government House invitations what the old world thought of them. A travelling Lord, after being feted by these people in Australia, returns to his London club and says, 'A very good kind of people, you know; awfully vulgar and coarse, but anxious to please.' But what made Australia's hankering after old-world titles and distinctions even more pathetic was that the old world itself had seen through them. The social revolution would sweep them away. Australians, to universal laughter, would be running after the 'gewgaws of titles' while the rest of the world was discarding them. Archibald, the man from the provinces, who knew himself the disdain for the colonial, and feared the world's laughter for his country, saw the way to make the province into a metropolis. Australia could seize its chance and become the leading democracy of the new order. Without entrenched interests and ancient wrongs, it could quickly sweep away monopoly, caste and privilege. Then the rest of the world, still struggling with these evils, would turn to Australia for inspiration and instruction. To prepare Australia for this role, everything sacred had to be profaned. What we take to be typically Australian attitudes in Archibald's *Bulletin* were the responses of a cosmopolitan intellectual to a provincial culture.

The *Bulletin* made its impact through cartoons as much as text. One of its standard cartoon figures became the fat man, the bloated capitalist, dressed in top hat and frock-coat. During the coal-mines' strike of 1888, Capital as a portly gentleman first appeared in a tug-of-war with a working man. The working man says: 'Hello! Who's the joker in the white gaiters and shiny beaver? I've never seen him down in a mine.' The gentleman's garb signifies fastidiousness and remoteness from the realities of toil. Many wearing this dress in Australia were self-made men who had indeed known hard toil, but that is not how they dressed themselves to appear. They wore the clothes of an English gentleman for whom it was a point of honour not to work and never to have worked. But although this dress gave a false message about background, as indeed many of its wearers wished, it was a very good guide to Labor's enemies. The cartoonists of the *Bulletin*, and later in the Labor press, did not have to dress Capital up for ridicule; they found it already dressed fit to kill. There could be no doubt as to who would win in the image stakes between the soft hat and the bell-topper, and between sleeves rolled up and frock-coat. Gentleman's dress was now held up as a badge of shame. This was the cartoonists' contribution to an egalitarianism of manners.

The irony is that English gentlemen in the 1880s were abandoning the frock-coat and the top hat for ordinary street wear. Australian gentlemen were reluctant to follow this shift in fashion. Governors and their staffs, fresh from home, tried in vain to woo them from it by wearing tweeds and bowler hats, a style much less domineering than the old and more suitable to the climate. Men's fashion, writes one of its historians, tends to harden into a uniform, unlike women's which is always changing. Australian gentlemen might have clung to their uniform because it had assumed a greater significance in defining the gentlemanly order since the old-world tests did not apply. It was this uniform that many had struggled for the right to wear. However, from the 1890s tweeds and lounge-suits did become more common. Is it too fanciful to suggest that the cartoonists had succeeded where the Governors had failed? But the cartoonists were not happy with the change. Up until World War I they still dressed Capital in top hat and frock-coat even though the real capitalist was becoming inconspicuous.

The nationalist writers of the '80s and '90s, nurtured by the *Bulletin*, must be understood as operating in the same radical milieu as Archibald. This is a point insisted on by Graeme Davison and Richard White in recent times. Both have argued that Russel Ward's treatment of the writers in *The Australian Legend* is inadequate because he is too prone to regard the literature as a conduit, carrying the values and attitudes of the nomad bush workers to a wider audience, and because he underplays the creative power of the writers themselves. Graeme Davison insists that instead of studying the bush men as they were, a perplexing matter in itself, 'we do better to begin, as we would any other exercise in the history of ideas, with the collective experience and ideas of the poets and story-writers themselves'. I accept all that Davison and White say in this regard. The creative writers were chiefly urban men, influenced by the social and political reform movements of their day; they reacted to an urban environment with an idealised version of country life, giving an Australian celebration of the common man which was then a vogue in European society generally. But none of this excuses us from looking at the literature itself, and considering what constraints and opportunities faced the writers whose scene was pastoral Australia. The writers who were 'inventing Australia' did not work on *tabula rasa*.

Taboos were broken in pastoral life which were upheld everywhere else in Australia. Gentlemen worked with their hands; they worked alongside their men; and in pioneering days at least wore the same clothes as their men. An age-old inequality disappeared as employees took to horses and met their masters eye to eye. Pastoral properties were not managed from homestead offices. Whoever was in control had to ride as well as the stockmen and boundary riders he employed, to move around the property, to assist on occasion in the real work as well as supervise it. A pioneer squatter might eventually leave the work to a manager, and keep more to his homestead or retire to the city; some proprietors were absentees who had never left the city; but always there were gentlemen squatters directly involved in the dirty work of the pastoral industry. The term 'bushman' was first applied to those who possessed the bush skills, whether they were owners or workers.

The literature of Paterson and Lawson is described by Russel Ward as portraying the bush workers as egalitarian collectivists combining to outdo the wealthy squatters. Had the bush workers really been depicted in this way, the literature could not, in a capitalist society, have gained the acceptance and influence Ward claims for it. Certainly, when unions are mentioned – they are by no means a common theme – they are treated favourably, and good bush men support them. But squatters are not portrayed unsympathetically. They are respected as pioneers, and judged on an individual basis. The mateship between workers is generally personal and limited in scope; a man is loyal to his mate or mates, which is not quite the same as loyalty to the working class. The social dichotomies are not chiefly between employers and employees, but between bush and city, and between Australians and the English. The dominant impression of the bush workers is of their unassertive self-confidence. They are completely at home in their environment, suffering no enduring indignities on account of their status as employees. They become romantic figures in a way no peasant or yeoman farmer could, because of the roving nature of their work.

In most industries so to dignify and celebrate the life and skills of the worker would imply some devaluation of the owner and employer – as parasites, exploiters or simply effete. The cult of the peasant and manual worker in Europe had this subversive edge. But in the pastoral industry, as the literature takes no pains to hide and as everyone knew, the employing class possessed bush skills as well and had furthermore the aura of hard-working pioneers. Thus the unique character of the pastoral industry, where employers and employees at the extremes of the status hierarchy toiled in the same enterprise, allowed for a most potent yet unthreatening message to be conveyed about the worth of working-class figures. The literature is democratic in its implications, and not socialist; the status order is subverted, but not the economic. The more noble and romantic the bushman became, the more he confounded the socialist account of the plight of the working man under capitalism. The literature could thus be accepted into the schools and the homes of the middle class. Its acceptance has grown with time, and becoming as it were the Holy Writ of the Australian nation, it must be rated as one of the most powerful forces sustaining the view that Jack is as good as his master, a view that sustains in turn the egalitarianism of manners. Jacks have often enough thought themselves as good as their masters, even if only silently; what has been rare is for their masters to agree with them. We have to find in Australia the reasons why, to use Craig McGregor's words, the wealthy 'feel under some pressure to be accepted by ordinary working Australians rather than the other way round'.

The egalitarianism of manners is generally acknowledged to be one egalitarianism that does really exist in modern Australia. To give an adequate account of its history would require a much closer attention to the details of social life than I have been able to give. My impression is that it made its greatest advances, not in the 1850s, but in the 1880s and 1890s. Certainly, it was then that it first had firm ideological support, in the general sense that the worth of working people was being proclaimed and the pretensions of others were being derided, and issued in specific injunctions. Lawson's verse is well known:

> They tramp in mateship side by side –
> The Protestant and Roman,
> They call no biped lord or sir,
> And touch their hat to no man.

These lines would have had no point if these marks of deference had disappeared thirty or more years earlier.

The egalitarianism of manners is regarded as a trifling thing by those who want to see complete equality of opportunity or equality in the distribution of material goods. I don't think it should be undervalued. Despite the growth of the social sciences, most people still spend little time filling out questionnaires on status systems. They do spend a lot of time meeting other people. If those encounters do not induce the heartache and corroding anger that can be the other side of deference, then egalitarians of all sorts should rejoice.

1986

THE PIONEER LEGEND

S CHOOLS HAVE BEEN THE MOST INFLUENTIAL PURVEYORS OF the pioneer legend and in literature for children it occurs in its purest form. The first item in the Fifth Grade *Victorian School Reader*, in use for two generations or more earlier this century, was the poem 'Pioneers' by Frank Hudson:

We are the old world people,
Ours were the hearts to dare;
But our youth is spent, and our backs are bent,
    And the snow is on our hair ...

We wrought with a will unceasing.
We moulded, and fashioned, and planned,
And we fought with the black, and we blazed the track,
    That ye might inherit the land ...

Take now the fruit of our labour,
    Nourish and guard it with care,
For our youth is spent, and our backs are bent,
    And the snow is on our hair.

This legend is very different from the radical, collectivist legend of the bush worker discussed by Russel Ward in *The Australian Legend*. It celebrates courage, enterprise, hard work and perseverance; it usually applies to the people who first settled the land, whether as pastoralists or farmers, and not to those they employed, though these were never specifically excluded. It is a nationalist legend which deals in a heroic way with the central experience of European settlement in Australia: the taming of the new environment to man's use. The qualities with which it invests the pioneers – courage, enterprise and so on – perhaps do not strain too much at the truth, though it assumes wrongly that owners always did their own pioneering. Its legendary aspect lies more clearly in the claim that these people were not working merely for themselves or their families, but for us – 'That ye might inherit the land'. The pioneer story can also be described as legendary because of what it leaves out: there is usually no mention of the social, legal or economic determinants of land settlement. The pioneers are depicted in a world limited by the boundaries of their properties, subduing the land and battling the elements. Their enemies are drought, flood, fire, sometimes Aborigines; never low prices, middle men, lack of capital, or other pioneers.

The pioneer legend can scarcely help being conservative in its political implications. It encourages reverence for the past; it celebrates individual rather than collective or state enterprise; and it provides a classless view of society since all social and economic differences are obliterated by the generous application of the 'pioneer' label. In claiming that the pioneers were working for us, it puts on later generations a special obligation not to tamper with the world which the pioneers made. One of the first of the epic pioneer poems was written in 1898 by Robert Caldwell, a conservative politician in South Australia. It concluded with an attack on land reformers and socialists for wanting to deprive the pioneers of their rightful heritage. During the 1890 Maritime Strike the *Argus* declared 'this country should remain what the pioneers intended it to be – a land free for every man who is willing to work, no matter whether he belongs to a union or not'. The travelling lecturer of the Victorian Employers Federation used the same theme to keep the country safe from socialism and it has remained a minor strand in conservative rhetoric since.

Though the pioneer legend is very different from the other legend, in its origins it is quite closely linked to it: it began at the same time – in the 1880s and 1890s – and was celebrated by the same people. It owes much to Paterson and Lawson.

*

The term 'pioneer' came into common use in Victoria and South Australia sooner than in New South Wales. It was applied to those immigrants who had come to the colonies in their early years and so was not limited to those who had settled and worked the land. The pioneers were much honoured at the jubilee of South Australia in 1886 and during the Melbourne Centennial Exhibition of 1888. New South Wales could not look back with similar confidence to its origins or so readily identify its 'pioneers'. In Victoria the members of the Australian Natives Association, looking towards the future of the coming Australian race, showed only a formal respect for the pioneers – many of whom resented the arrogance of the native-born – and were seeking genuinely national symbols and causes. The honouring of early colonists as pioneers reflected the growth of colonial and local patriotisms; they clearly could not serve as heroes for the new nation.

'Pioneers' acquired its present primary meaning – that is, those who first settled and worked the land – in the 1890s. The older meaning survived, and still survives, but it now took second place. The shifting of meaning is nicely illustrated in the special Old Colonist number of the Melbourne *Tatler* in 1898. Under the heading 'The Pioneers of Victoria' appeared biographies of many early colonists, including bishops, officials, merchants, professional men, as well as settlers on the land. These were pioneers according to the earlier meaning of the word. But the cover illustration depicted a settler pushing his way through the bush and carried two lines from a woeful poem, 'The Pioneers', which appeared in full inside: 'Can you not follow them forth/Through the black treacherous bush'. This was the new meaning of the term, but it was not well-deserved by many of the worthies featured inside who had moved straight from the ship to Melbourne and had never pioneered in the bush. The pioneers as settlers on the land were a much more anonymous group than pioneers as early colonists, who always had an establishment, who's-who air about them. They were not identified with a particular colony and were much more closely connected with the land itself. The pioneers as immigrants had been first identified and honoured by the old colonists themselves. Pioneers as settlers and national heroes were the creation of poets and writers. It is to their work we now turn.

Ken Inglis in *The Australian Colonists* has outlined the largely unsuccessful search for national heroes in the years prior to 1870. We can see the difficulties facing a nationalist writer of this period in the work of Henry Kendall, the native-born poet who, like his friend Harpur, knew that poets can make a nation, and saw that as one of his tasks, but who never found the words or the audience to succeed. At the last, however, he touched on the pioneer theme which was left to others to develop. Kendall's views of what a proper hero should be were heavily influenced by the classical tradition of Greece and Rome. Heroes had to be statesmen or soldiers, preferably those who died for their country. For statesmen Kendall offered Governor Phillip, Wentworth, Blang, Lang and other politicians of the 1840s and '50s. This civic theme was extended by the celebration of those who built the Australian cities; this rather than the settlement of the land was the great triumph of colonisation, and one that could be described in classical terms. Melbourne is 'Like a dream of Athens, or of Rome'; Sydney is 'this Troy'. Australia had no great warriors, but the explorers in their bravery and in their deaths were acceptable substitutes. Kendall frequently celebrates Cook, Leichardt, Burke and Wills. In a later poem 'Blue Mountain Pioneers' (1880) he moves away from the more heroic big-name explorers and celebrates the work of Blaxland, Lawson and Wentworth in crossing the Blue Mountains in 1813. This was a short expedition and it didn't end in death, but it could be linked much more closely than other expeditions to the settlement of the land.

> Behind them were the conquered hills – they faced
> The vast green West, with glad, strange beauty graced;
> And every tone of every cave and tree
> Was a voice of splendid prophecy.

What that conquest foretold was the settlement of the western lands, but Kendall was tied so closely to the notion of the heroic as public and civic, that he never celebrated the coming of the settlers themselves. For him 'pioneers' was reserved for the explorers.

This poem was published posthumously in collected editions of Kendall's work in 1886 and 1890. There Paterson must have read it for it forms the basis of the historical section in his poem 'Song of the Future' which is the classic statement of the pioneer legend, frequently reproduced in anthologies and school magazines. This poem is much more ambitious than his usual ballad or bush-yarn work. It calls for a new response to landscape and nature in Australia, and to the history of European man in the continent. Paterson begins by criticising Adam Lindsay Gordon, Marcus Clarke and others who had written in gloomy terms about the Australian scene, and he rejects the stock claims that Australian birds were songless and its flowers scentless. On Australian history he acknowledges that there has been no 'hot blood spilt' – a commonly held prerequisite for worthwhile history – but Australians do have something to celebrate: 'honest toil and valiant life'. This introduces the historical section of the poem. The treatment of the crossing of the Blue Mountains is more extensive than Kendall's and it is told as a great saga of the people, rather than as a celebration of individual heroes. The names of the explorers, significantly, are not mentioned and the poem is more concerned with the achievements of those who came after them.

> The mountains saw them marching by:
> They faced the all-consuming drought,
> They would not rest in settled land:
> But, taking each his life in land,
> Their faces ever westward bent
> Beyond the farthest settlement,
> Responding to the challenge cry
> Of 'better country farther out'.

Paterson measures the extent of this achievement by dealing with a sceptic who declares 'it was not much' since the resistance to expansion was slight and – the stock objection – not much blood was split.

> It was not much! but we who knew
> The strange capricious land they trod –
> At times a stricken, parching sod,
> At times with raging floods beset –

Through which they found their lonely way,
Are quite content that you should say
It was not much, while we can feel
That nothing in the ages old,
In song or story written yet
On Grecian urn or Roman arch,
Though it should ring with clash of steel
Could braver histories unfold
Than this bush story, yet untold –
The story of their westward march.

This poem, more than any other single piece, did bring about that new perception of Australia's past which Paterson sought. He still had to defend his heroes against those of Greece and Rome, but soon the heroism of the pioneers was accepted without question and the reference to the classical tradition ceased.

Lawson was more consistently preoccupied with Australia's past than Paterson. In a contribution to the *Republican* in 1888 he called for much more Australian history to be taught in schools. As a nationalist, he wanted to give his country a past to be proud of. In the early stories and poems Lawson follows the orthodox line of dating Australia's greatness from the gold rushes, and so he accords heroic status to the diggers. These were the men 'who gave our country birth'. He rates their achievements higher than those of the explorers, the ranking heroes of the time: 'Talk about the heroic struggles of early explorers in a hostile country; but for dogged determination and courage in the face of poverty, illness, and distance, commend me to the old-time digger – the truest soldier Hope ever had!' For the settlers on the land and particularly the selectors, Lawson in his early years had scant respect. He criticises the selectors for their slovenliness, dirt and ignorance, and depicts settling on the land not as an heroic endeavour, but as a madness. But this attitude changed with time. His early emphasis on the wretchedness of the selector's life had had a political purpose, since he wanted to discredit those who saw small holdings as the cure for Australia's social ills. He never abandons the view that the life of small settlers could be wretched and narrow, but he becomes more willing to celebrate their powers of endurance and the co-operation between them, and, in the Joe Wilson series, the satisfactions and pleasures which their small successes gave them, though here Mrs Spicer, watering them geraniums, is still present as counterpoint being worn literally to death. In his verse, where he always wrote at a higher level of generality and usually with disastrous results, he came to see the settling of the land as the central theme of the nation's history, which could comprehend much more than the coming of the diggers. 'How the land was won' (1899) is a complete statement of this theme, and is the counterpart to Paterson's 'Song of the Future'. The settlers are described firstly as immigrants leaving the old world, and the poem tells of the variety of hardships and deprivations which they experienced in Australia. These two verses give the flavour of the whole, perhaps too favourable a view, since six verses of hardship become a little tedious, though the quality of the verse is better than Lawson's average:

> With God, or a dog, to watch, they slept
>   By the camp-fires' ghastly glow,
> Where the scrubs were dark as the blacks that crept
>   With 'nulla' and spear held low;
> Death was hidden amongst the trees,
>   And bare on the glaring sand
> They fought and perished by twos and threes –
>   And that's how they won the land!
>
> They toiled and they fought through the shame of it –
>   Through wilderness, flood, and drought;
> They worked, in the struggles of early days,
>   Their sons' salvation out.
> The white girl-wife in the hut alone,
>   The men on the boundless run,
> The miseries suffered, unvoiced, unknown –
>   And that's how the land was won.

In the early twentieth century scores of pioneer poems by many hands rang the changes on these hardships. Two important aspects of the legend are embodied in 'How the land was won': in the first verse (not quoted here) we are told that the land was won 'for us'; secondly, there is no differentiation of the settlers – they are all simply 'they'. This conflation is the more noticeable in Lawson since elsewhere he gives such particular detail about social conflict on the land. Nor can the co-operation among the settlers – in the stories he describes young men putting in crops for sick men and widows, and women caring for bereaved neighbours – find a mention here, since the pioneer legend prefers to see hardships overcome, if at all, by further individual effort. It is a sign of the attractiveness of the pioneer legend to nationalists that Lawson was ready to abandon so much to produce his simple compelling saga. Of course the Lawson of 1899 had abandoned much of his early radicalism, and in his disillusionment the struggle on the land took on an elemental, purifying quality, but changing personal views will not wholly explain 'How the land was won'. The pioneer legend is a literary mode or a type of history which shapes material in its own way. Writing on a different assignment in the same year he composed 'How the land was won', Lawson highlighted the gossip and bitchiness of country towns and hinted broadly that incest was frequently practised in the isolated selectors' huts. That would never do for the pioneers.

In Lawson's prose there is little explicit glorification of the pioneers, but here Lawson made his most powerful contribution to the pioneer legend with his description of bush women. 'The Drover's Wife' occupies an important place in the pioneer canon. There is a sense in which all his bush women are heroines because, as he insists time and again, the bush is no place for women. When her husband had money the drover's wife was taken to the city by train – in a sleeping compartment – and put up at the best hotel. For Lawson, women deserve the attention and comfort which this signifies, and which bush life denied them. While she waits for the snake, the drover's wife reads the *Young Ladies Journal*, but Lawson does not use the hard life of a country woman to deride the artificiality of the woman's journal world; rather, he accepts that as legitimate, and so emphasises the sacrifices of the women who are obliged to live a different life, and in many cases do the work of men. The theme of women as pioneers was taken up by G. Essex Evans, a Queensland poet of the '90s, in his 'Women of the West'. This, together with his other pioneer piece 'The Nation Builders', have frequently been reprinted in the children's literature and anthologies.

The work of Paterson and Lawson is described by Ward as the chief vehicle for spreading a democratic, collectivist, national mystique. How was it that these writers also celebrated the pioneers which meant frequently the squatters, who had been, and were still, the enemy of democrats and radicals? In *The Australian Tradition*, A. A. Phillips has noted how sympathetic writers of the '90s were in their description of individual squatters, despite the squatters being the class enemy. Phillips offers a number of explanations for this. He wonders first whether 'the triumph of human sympathy over social prejudice' reflected the breadth of feeling one would expect in any good writer. Scarcely so, he concludes, since in other areas, notably the description of Englishmen, the writers reveal severe limitations and create caricatures. The writers knew some squatters personally and this no doubt helped them to write individualised, sympathetic portraits. But more importantly, according to Phillips, the squatter was a bushman too, and had shared with his men 'the pride and expansiveness' that came with the escape from 'fetid slums and the tight little hedgerow squares' of the old world, into the vast spaces of the new continent where the strength of individual character as a man determined success or failure. He concludes that the democratic tradition embodied in the literature reaches deep back into the pastoral age. But we must remember that what squatters had felt, or others had felt about them, may well be different from their depiction in imaginative literature. The tradition of the pastoral age did not flow automatically onto the pages of Lawson and Paterson. The writers were making a tradition as well as reflecting one – how much they created and how much they reported has been one of the matters debated in the argument over *The Australian Legend*. We can extend Phillips's analysis and come closer to understanding these writers' attitude to the squatter–pioneer if we examine what influenced their view of the pastoral age.

Both men were disturbed and angry at the new harshness and poverty which drought, depression and strikes brought to the colonies in the

1880s and 1890s. They were cast into a world they did not like, and like many others before and since in this predicament they began to exaggerate the virtues of the world they had lost. Lawson's poem 'Freedom on the Wallaby' is well known. It was written in Brisbane in 1891 to support the shearers' strike and its last verse contains the much-quoted threat of violence: 'If blood should stain the wattle'. Less well-known is the previous verse:

> Our parents toiled to make a home,
>   Hard grubbin' 'twas an' clearin',
> They wasn't troubled much with lords
>   When they were pioneerin'.
> But now that we have made the land
>   A garden full of promise,
> Old Greed must crook his dirty hand
>   And come ter take it from us.

Those who know Lawson's usual description of the Australian country – unyielding, desolate, drought-ridden – will scarcely credit that he could describe it as a garden; domestic, fruitful, a symbol of paradise. Lawson's explanation for the lowering of wages and the assault on the unions is that Greed has invaded this garden. It was a theme he used many times. Sometimes Greed had invaded the countryside from the cities, on other occasions it was an unwelcome import from the old world into the new. In the poems the particular forms which Greed assumed were not always defined. The stories identified the process more explicitly. In the countryside it meant the increasing ownership of pastoral properties by banks and companies, and the replacement of resident proprietors by managers. Before this process began were the good times, and squatters of that time, or who have survived from it, are described as squatters of the 'old school'. In describing Black, the squatter who employed Joe Wilson, Lawson outlines their virtues: 'He was a good sort, was Black the squatter; a squatter of the old school, who'd shared the early hardships with his men, and couldn't see why he should not shake hands and have a smoke and a yarn over old times with any of his old station hands that happened to come along.' A. A. Phillips errs when he says Black is Lawson's only portrait in any detail of a squatter. There were several other good squatters – Baldy Thompson, Job Falconer, Jimmy's boss – and their goodness is carefully explained: they are resident proprietors of long standing, not managers for absentees. Job Falconer, for instance, was 'Boss of the Talbragar sheep station up country in New South Wales in the early Eighties – when there were still runs in the Dingo-Scrubs out of the hands of the banks, and yet squatters who lived on their stations'. Lawson's one detailed portrait of a bad squatter is that of Wall, the man who, until it was almost too late, refused to send his employees to fight the fire on Ross's farm. Until this last-minute repentance Wall was a hard man who had done all he could to make the selector Ross's life impossible. But he had not always been so: 'Men remembered Wall as a great boss and a good fellow, but that was in the days before rabbits and banks, and syndicates and "pastoralists", or pastoral companies instead of good squatters.' The pattern is clear: it is not only that managers for absentees are mean: all resident proprietors of the old days were good.

In Paterson's work there was much less overt social commentary than in Lawson's, but briefly around 1890 Paterson was a committed reformer, and in his poem 'On Kiley's Run' published in December 1890, he gives a clear picture of the world which Greed had disrupted and the new world it was making. The poem describes the 'good old station life' on Kiley's run. The squatter was resident, swagmen were welcome, there was plenty of good fellowship and horseracing with neighbouring stations, and relations between squatter and his men were excellent.

> The station-hands were friends, I wot,
>   On Kiley's Run,
> A reckless, merry-hearted lot –
> All splendid riders, and they knew
> The boss was kindness through and through.
> Old Kiley always stood their friend,
> And so they served him to the end
>   On Kiley's Run.

But droughts and losses forced the squatter into the hands of the bank, which finally took possession of the stock and sold the station. The new owner is an English absentee; a half-paid overseer runs the place, shearers' wages and all other expenses are cut, swagmen and drovers receive short-shrift – and the name of the run has been changed to Chandos Park Estate. Paterson felt this transformation very keenly, for at the end of the poem he adds, for him, a rare call to arms:

> I cannot guess what fate will bring
> To Kiley's Run –
> For chances come and changes ring –
> I scarcely think 'twill always be
> Locked up to suit an absentee;
> And if he lets it out in farms
> His tenants soon will carry arms
> On Kiley's Run.

'The Song of the Future', Paterson's classic pioneer piece, in its last section contains a similar lament for the old bush life and urges that the land be thrown open to all to reduce poverty and unemployment.

Men live by myth and golden ages have frequently been created. What is odd about this one is that it was placed in the very recent past. The democrats and land reformers of the 1850s had denounced the squatters as monopolists and tyrants: they were the lords who would make everyone else serfs if they could. In their defence the squatters had actually attempted, fruitlessly, to attach to themselves the name of 'pioneers' and so justify their claim to retain their lands. Thirty years after their political defeat, they were accorded that title, among others by the poets of democracy. How could they overlook the denunciations made so recently? A large part of the answer is simply that Lawson and Paterson, like most other people in the 1890s, knew very little of the struggles of the 1850s. John Robertson had given his name to the Selection Acts and had achieved legendary status, but he was not seen as part of a wider movement. The Australian born certainly did not learn of the land reform movement in school. Those who had survived from that era, like

Robertson himself and Henry Parkes, did not talk freely of their early struggles, chiefly because, one supposes, the bitter social and economic divisions of those years and the whiff of republicanism which hung over the reform movement were no longer apt for their present political purposes.

The Sydney *Bulletin* was republican, a constant derider of British aristocrats and Australians who fawned on them, and it had no qualms about disturbing the liberal consensus over which Parkes and Robertson had presided, but it too did little to inform its readers – among whom were Paterson and Lawson – of the democratic movement of the 1850s or to celebrate its triumphs. The *Bulletin* ran a very crude line on New South Wales history: it insisted that very little had changed in the colony since the convict days. The British had created an abomination in the convict system, and since its influence was still potent, New South Wales could never establish a truly democratic society until the British connection was severed. It wrongly attributed the flogging of criminals and other evils to the survival of the spirit of earlier times. Victoria, by contrast, had managed something of a fresh start with its gold rushes and the Eureka rebellion, whose anniversary the *Bulletin* wanted to celebrate as Australia's national day. Such a view of the past could not allow that there had been genuine and far-reaching reforms in New South Wales in the 1850s and 1860s. The history which the *Bulletin* promoted was Price Warung's *Tales of the Convict System*. This was the stick to beat the British with. The triumphs of Robertson over the landowners and squatters would not have suited its purpose.

We are now in a position to understand better why Paterson and Lawson were among the founders of the pioneer legend. Their work is suffused with a generalised nostalgia – ''Twas a better land to live in, in the days o' long ago' – but they also created a highly specific past which was free from the social evils of the present. Before Greed invaded the land there were humane employers and decent class relations in Australia. Having made that past, and as they made it, they elevated the early settlers into pioneers. That they could create this past so freely gives new meaning to the dictum that Australia had no history. For Paterson and Lawson, the 1840s and 1850s when the squatters were the popular political enemy might never have existed. No democratic tradition had survived from these years.

In broad terms, the creation of the pioneer legend can be explained by the growth of nationalism in the 1880s and the 1890s and the need to find new national heroes and symbols. Paterson and Lawson were attracted to the pioneers as nationalists, but also as radicals. They used the past to condemn the present. However, the pioneer legend quickly shed its radical overtones. Paterson's classic statement 'Song of the Future' is very simply rendered innocuous in anthologies and school readers by the omission of the last section which urges that the land be thrown open to all. In any case, the golden age of pioneering was, in some respects, rather uncertain in its political implications. Paterson's claim, though false, that there had been a time when land was freely available to all did relate clearly to the current radical demand for land taxes and breaking up of large estates. But the depiction of the old station life of hard work and mutuality between boss and men can serve the conservative cause, for clearly there were no unions or industrial arbitration or parliamentary limitations on hours worked on Kiley's Run. Reform movements which aim to purify and simplify government can appeal with some chance of success to golden ages; once radicalism is associated with state regulation and ownership, as it was in Australia from the 1890s, the ideal society needs to be placed in the future rather than the past. In finding a glorious past for Australia, Paterson and Lawson ultimately did more to help the conservative cause than their own. Once there is a valued past, the future is more confined. 'She is not yet' Brunton Stephens had written of the Australian nation in 1877. Because we are nationalists as they made us, we still enjoy the celebrations of Lawson and Paterson and we forget that as well as being an affirmation, their work marked also a retreat: the nation was no longer yet to be, it had arrived, and, more amazing still, its best days were already passed.

*

In 1904 Frederick McCubbin painted 'The Pioneers', a massive work in three panels which is the classic embodiment in art of the pioneer legend.

The first panel shows a settler and his wife on their first arrival at their selection in the forest; the second shows the selection established; and in the third, the 'triumphal stanza' as the *Age* described it, 'A country youth, with reverent fingers, clears away the undergrowth from the rough wooden cross marking the last resting place of the gallant couple. In the distance the spires and bridges of a glorious young city and the stooks of a rich harvest field tell of the joys that another generation is reaping from the toil of the once lusty pioneers now gone to dust.' The painting was, and is, enormously popular, and the *Age* successfully urged that it be purchased for the National Gallery. It described the work as a 'poem of democracy'.

The conservative implications of the legend have already been noted; in what sense is the legend, nevertheless, a democratic one? In the first place it accords historic status to the ordinary man – frequently the pioneers were squatters, but small settlers were also honoured with the title. The pioneer legend transformed the low status selector of the nineteenth century into a nation builder. The legend also proclaims that success is open to all since all may possess the requisite qualities of diligence, courage and perseverance. Secondly, the legend provides a simple, unofficial, popular history of the nation. When it was formed the standard histories were still organised by the terms of office of the various governors, to parallel the British histories which dealt with monarchs, the dates of their accession and death, and the chief events of their reign. Governors made some sense as organising principles for the period before responsible government, but in some works their comings and goings continued to be crucial events even after responsible government. In contrast to history as high politics and administration, the pioneer legend offered social (and economic) history and declared that the people had made the nation. The 'people' in the pioneer legend have always included women. Feminists may object that too often they are seen merely as helpmeets for men, but their complaint that women have been omitted altogether from Australian history is not true of the popular history fostered by the pioneer legend. There are Pioneer-Women gardens and memorials in Melbourne, Adelaide and Perth. In the celebration of state and national anniversaries, pioneer women have been honoured in special ceremonies and commemorative histories. The pioneer legend is a people's legend, in this sense it is democratic; its conservatism is not the conservatism of deference, but of communal pride in what the people have achieved.

Of democracy in the sense of a system of government, the legend has nothing to say, since it implies that politics were unnecessary or irrelevant to the work of pioneering. It is a further instance, then, of the Australian tendency to isolate politics from the heroic or the good. Paterson claimed his pioneers as worthy of Greece and Rome, but in fact he had abandoned the classical tradition which found its heroes in those who served the state. Kendall, true to that tradition, thought that an Australian democracy would want democratic statesmen for its heroes, but he was wrong, and he worked in vain on Deniehy and Lang.

The pioneer legend had a significant influence on the writing of formal history. It solved the problem which formal historians could never overcome satisfactorily: the embarrassment of the convict origins of the nation. The pioneer legend, by proclaiming the settlement of the land as the chief theme in Australia's history, found it easy not to mention the convicts at all. If you begin Australia's history with Governor Phillip it is very difficult to avoid the convicts, though some histories for children managed it. The first formal history to reflect the influence of the pioneer legend was James Collier's *The Pastoral Age in Australasia* (1911). This dated Australia's freedom from the opening of the pastoral lands west of the mountains and rejected the traditional view that the gold rushes marked the divide from the convict origins. Collier described the old society to the east of the mountains as static, unfree, with the settlers relying on governments for land, labour, stock, and markets. The new pastoral society was dynamic, independent, a wild free life that 'lifted the community to a higher plain, and started it on a new career'. He conceded that convicts were still employed but in a 'radically different' way, which was never explained. Stephen Roberts in *The Pastoral Age in Australia* (1935) celebrated the pastoral expansion in a similar way and from Collier borrowed the image of the protoplasm of the nation, long lying dormant, and in the magic year 1835 showing at last what form it was going to take. The theme is present too at the opening of Hancock's *Australia*: 'Wool made

Australia a solvent nation, and, in the end, a free one.' The concentration on the pastoral expansion meant that Sydney's merchants and trades went unexamined. So it was only recently that historians rediscovered the importance of the whale industry and the Pacific trade, which had been known to the older historians like Rusden (1883) and Jose (1899) whose approach was strictly chronological and who wrote uninfluenced by the pioneer legend. The pioneer legend, having first excluded convicts, eventually enabled them to be rehabilitated and given a place in the nation's history. Convicts could be regarded as pioneers. In this role Mary Gilmore depicts them in 'Old Botany Bay':

> I was the conscript
>> Sent to hell
> To make in the desert
>> The living well;
>
> I split the rock;
>> I felled the tree:
> The nation was –
>> Because of me.

By the early twentieth century a new meaning of 'pioneer' had come into common use. It was now also applied to people who were at present at work on the land, and particularly on new farms or at the edge of settlement. This extension of meaning occurred at a time of heightened concern for racial strength and purity and a new awareness of the vulnerability of the nation. Cities were now seen as dangers to national and racial health, and further development of the land was considered on all sides as essential for the nation's survival. The pioneer's struggle with the elements and the nation's struggle to survive in a more hostile world became fused. 'The people in the bush were fighting the battle of Australia every day and every year', said George Reid in 1909 at the foundation of the Bush Nursing Association which was formed to bring medical help to remote country areas. 'From a national point of view', the Association declared, 'the lives of pioneers and their children are of the utmost value to the State.' G. Essex Evans, one of the important makers of the legend, caught these new concerns in 'The Man Upon The Land'.

> The City calls, its streets are gay,
>   Its pleasures well supplied,
> So of its life-blood every day
>   It robs the countryside.

> How shall we make Australia great
>   And strong when danger calls
> If half the people of the State
>   Are crammed in city walls ...?

The concluding lines of the poem are its refrain:

> And the men that made the Nation are
>   The men upon the land.

The change of tense here illustrates nicely how the men upon the land gained in glory from the heroic status of their predecessors. Well before the Country Party was formed, its ideology had been made – by no means solely by country people – and the pioneer legend gave it added force.

After the landing at Gallipoli, Australians acquired a legend more powerful than either those of the bush men or the pioneers. In *The Australian Legend* Russel Ward has outlined the way in which the legend of the digger embodied aspects of the bush men's legend. A similar process occurred with the pioneer legend. *The Anzac Memorial*, published in 1917, carried a poem by Dorothy McCrae, 'The First Brigade', reproduced subsequently in the Victorian *School Paper* with the subtitle 'The Pioneers of Australia':

> They cleared the earth, and felled the trees,
> And built the towns and colonies;
> Then, to their land, their sons they gave,
> And reared them hardy, pure, and brave.

They made Australia's past: to them
We owe the present diadem;
For, in their sons, they fight again,
And ANZAC proved their hero strain.

The first celebration of Anzac Day in 1916 posed a problem for the compilers of the Victorian school calendar. Since 1911, 19 April had been set aside as Discovery Day. This was the anniversary of Cook's sighting of the Australian coast and was devoted to the celebration of explorers and pioneers. Since it fell so close to Anzac Day, it was suspended in 1916, but on Anzac Day teachers were encouraged to link diggers, explorers and pioneers together: 'The lessons and addresses on Anzac Day will, no doubt, include matter appropriate to Discovery Day, such as reference to the discovery, settlement, and development of Australia.' The connection between 'settlement and development' and the Anzac spirit took substantial form after the war in the soldier settlement schemes. Diggers were to become pioneers.

The subsequent history of 'pioneer' and the legend cannot be fully traced here. The legend still survives, though its foundations are not as firm as they were in the early twentieth century. It has suffered inevitably from the waning of faith in progress and the virtues of European civilisation. No-one now writes of the pioneers as Paterson did, though his pioneer verse and others' is still collected in anthologies. Historians have for a long time escaped the romanticism of Roberts' *Squatting Age* and have emphasised the clash between squatters' interests and those of the rest of the community. Paterson's golden age has received no help from them. The legend, which was made by creative writers, was eventually attacked by them. Brian Penton in *Landtakers* (1934) overturned the view that the squatter's life was exhilarating and free. His theme was the coarsening and hardening of a well-bred English emigrant as he coped with life in a 'gaolyard' and then on the frontier, with 'the grind and ugliness and shame of Australia'. Xavier Herbert's *Capricornia* (1938) is still the most devastating anti-pioneer piece in our literature. It confronts the legend explicitly. Herbert's Northern Territory society is brutal, chaotic, hypocritical and drunken. The book is an indictment of the white settlers of the Territory for the destruction which they brought to Aboriginal society and for their continuing exploitation of Aborigines and half-castes. 'The Coming of the Dingoes' is how Herbert describes the arrival of the white man in the Territory. Herbert was, in fact, the first to write black history in this country. Pioneers were the enemy to the original inhabitants of the land, and as sympathy with Aborigines grows and the brutalities of the frontier continue to be highlighted, the pioneers' reputation will suffer more. The growing concern with the environment will damage the pioneers still further as their ruthless exploitation of the land comes under closer scrutiny. And yet, sympathetic accounts of pioneering men and women continue to be written, among the most notable are Margaret Kiddle's *Men of Yesterday*, Patrick White's *Tree of Man*, and Judith Wright's *Generations of Men*. While not endorsing the crudities of the pioneer legend, these works nevertheless depict the pioneers as a creative, ordering force, whose work gives their lives a certain nobility and completeness. *The Tree of Man* describes in its first pages the arrival of Stan Parker at his uncleared land in a forest, a similar scene to that McCubbin depicted in the first panel of 'The Pioneers':

> Then the man took an axe and struck at the side of a hairy tree, more to hear the sound than for any other reason. And the sound was cold and loud. The man struck at the tree, and struck, till several white chips had fallen. He looked at the scar in the side of the tree. The silence was immense. It was the first time anything like this had happened in that part of the bush ...
>
> The man made a lean-to with bags and a few saplings. He built a fire. He sighed at last, because the lighting of his small fire had kindled in him the first warmth of content. Of being somewhere. That particular part of the bush had been made his by the entwining fire. It licked at and swallowed the loneliness.

We may come at last to see Stan Parker merely as a destroyer of the natural environment or as a labourer transforming himself into a small property holder, but so long as our spirit stirs in other ways at this scene the pioneer legend will not be without its force.

Popular history is still very much pioneer history, embodied in new forms now in the reconstructed pioneer villages and settlements which have proliferated throughout the country in recent years. What is conveyed by these is in some ways rather different from the classic pioneer statements in literature. The concentration is much less on the struggle on the land, partly because the encounter with the elements, which was central to the drama, cannot be reproduced. But the buildings and their fittings strike the visitor with a sense of the pioneers' achievement, in making their homes or farms or businesses where nothing was before, and with a sense of the pioneers' hardships in contrast to his own life. We noted earlier how the legend confines pioneers to their land and ignores their wider society. The pioneer villages carry this tendency to its ultimate by leaving out people altogether. We are shown empty buildings, disembodied achievement, and are told nothing of the social and economic factors which determined who had the chance to achieve what. Buildings cannot speak readily of social conflict; these pioneer villages are powerful contributors to the consensus view of Australia's past.

Early immigrants generally, as distinct from the first settlers on the land, are still honoured as pioneers. In New South Wales there is a Pioneers' Club, formed in 1910, and in South Australia a Pioneers' Association, formed in 1935, to keep their memory alive. These organisations define categories of membership by year of arrival of ancestor, construct genealogies and exercise a declining influence on the edge of the old state establishments. The pioneer–immigrants continued to be associated more with state than national loyalty. They were also honoured more frequently by those who wished to stress the British identity of Australia, and who saw its history as the winning of new areas for the empire. The British heritage these pioneers brought with them was as important as their accomplishments here. Pioneers as settlers on the land were more purely nationalistic heroes. At some times in the twentieth century – particularly in South Australia with its clear and clean foundation – pioneers as first immigrants may have had greater standing than pioneers as settlers on the land, but there is no doubt now of the latter's primacy. The two groups of pioneers are, of course, not totally distinct. The pioneer poem at the beginning of the Fifth Grade *Victorian Reader*, quoted above, is concerned chiefly with the struggle on the land, but the pioneers are identified clearly as British immigrants – 'We are the old world people' – and this is part of their virtue – 'Ours were the hearts to dare'. The pioneer legend has served local, Australian and imperial patriotisms.

The survival of the word 'pioneer' itself means much. The word originally applied to those in an army who went as pioneers before the main body to prepare the way by clearing roads and making bridges and so on. It was then extended to the initiator of any new enterprise or new undertaking who 'showed the way' for those who came after. In this sense it could well be used as Kendall used it in 'Blue Mountain Pioneers' for the explorers. In the new world, first in North America and then in Australia, the meaning was again extended to refer to first settlers on the land. But to whom or in what were the first settlers showing the way? Their aim was to occupy the land for their own use and to keep others out. The metaphor of showing or preparing the way was now being stretched further to make them pioneers in a very general sense; they showed the way to the generations or the nation which came after them, and benefited from their labours. In this way the word itself obscures the private interests which they had in acquiring the land and depicts it as a service, as something for which we should be grateful, thus embodying a central concept of the legend. Let any who doubt the significance of the word consider what would have to change before we consistently referred to the first settlers as, say, landtakers, which was Penton's term.

This paper shares Russel Ward's assumption about the significance of a nation's legends, or its dreaming: 'The dreams of nations, as of individuals, are important, because they not only reflect, as in a distorting mirror, the real world, but may sometimes react upon and influence it.' That the legend which Ward describes exists is unquestionable; he is misleading, however, when he implies that this was the only national legend. Ward claimed with very little analysis that Lawson and Paterson embodied the legend which he had described; what they in fact embodied was a great deal more complex and varied. We have already noted their favourable view of the squatters, which A. A. Phillips identified. Ward takes too little account of this in his attempt to stress the radical collectivist aspect of the legend. Phillips is closer to the literature in writing of 'The Democratic

Theme'. The anti-police aspect of the legend is not well reflected in Lawson, who nearly always makes his policemen good cops, sympathetic to the poor and outcast, and who wrote a poem celebrating the bravery of a police trooper. And both writers fostered the development of the pioneer legend.

Some of Ward's critics, over-reacting perhaps to his less guarded claims for the legend's influence, have attempted to deny its existence or force by citing social behaviour which runs counter to the legend. This is, of course, very easy to do, but when faced with this criticism Ward can retreat to very safe ground and declare that he was merely tracing the origins of the national legend which is not fully founded in fact, nor vastly influential. Those who feel that Australia has not been made according to the legend would be better advised to establish the other legends, stereotypes and symbols Australians have made or adopted. The pioneer legend is one such. It is a national rural myth, democratic in its social bearing, conservative in its political implications.

1978

NOTHING BUT BAD

AUSTRALIA WAS CALLED A PARADISE FOR WORKINGMEN IN the late nineteenth century. For a long time historians of the left and right wrote on the assumption that Australian working people enjoyed the highest living standards in the world. But such a view frustrates the purposes of a new generation of radical historians. They begin by putting black spots in their portraits of nineteenth-century society and then finding that colour, or more strictly that absence of colour, to their taste, they proceed to fill the whole canvas with it.

The term 'workingmen's paradise' seems to have been first used by Samuel Smiles, son of the father of the same name who taught Victorian workingmen the virtues of thrift and self-help. Smiles Junior came from a society where the working class was increasingly comfortable, thrifty and respectable, but on his visit to Australia he entered a different social order. Workingmen's standard of living was not only higher; their savings here put many of them onto the land or into their own house.

These impressions were confirmed by the calculations of Timothy Coghlan, the leading statistician of the nineteenth century, and by economic historians of recent times. Income per capita in the Australian colonies in the second half of the nineteenth century was certainly higher than anywhere in Europe and possibly also exceeded that of the United States. Smiles' account gives a false impression of the ease by which a workingman could turn himself into a farmer, though the gloomiest views of the Selection Acts are no longer tenable. On home ownership the Australian record was extraordinary. Graeme Davison in his *Marvellous Melbourne* calculates that 45 per cent of Melbourne householders owned or were buying their homes in the 1880s and that the proportion of proprietors among workingmen was only marginally lower than that in other classes. In the older city of Sydney the rate of ownership was lower; in the smaller capitals and country towns it was higher.

The new radicals do not directly dispute these findings. They give us the black spot treatment. They warn us that the figures of per capita incomes are only averages and so reveal nothing about how wealth was distributed. The skilled workingmen might have been well off but what about the unskilled labourer and the widow? Wage rates might be high, but lots of work was casual and seasonal so that men were not in constant work. Workers might have been buying their homes, but the cities were not without their slums and were slow to provide themselves with deep drainage.

All this is true. But the critics forget or want us to forget that the original claim was comparative – Australians were better off than people elsewhere. The figures on income levels in other societies are averages too, and will anyone suggest that wealth was more equally distributed in the United Kingdom or the United States than in Australia? Were the casually employed and the unskilled in the great cities of Europe and the United States better off than their confreres here? Did Sydney slums constitute a higher proportion of the housing stock than they did in London or Manchester? Did the harsh winters of Europe or North America cause less disruption to the economy than the mild winters of Australia? The critics wisely do not pursue these questions.

These writers are still traditionalists in one sense – they appeal to evidence. There is another element in the black school which writes history straight from their theories of capitalism and the state with scarcely a glance at Australia and the people in it. The ultimate expression of this is Alastair Davidson's account of the state in *A People's History of Australia* (1988). His chapter is entitled 'Big Brother Is Watching You'. To apply a term coined for totalitarian regimes to the liberal state in nineteenth-century Australia reflects a monumental inability to discriminate between cases, a common failing with these authors. Davidson's conclusion is that the regimentation of Australian society was so complete, the power of the state so strong, that people had 'no room for autonomy or a sense of self.' This should not be dignified as an error; we have left truth and falsehood behind and are in the realm of fantasy.

It must be said that the *People's History* as a whole is not committed to this view. Stuart Macintyre, who writes in the same volume as Davidson, knows that the liberal freedoms were real freedoms which enabled workers to develop trade unions and other institutions to protect and advance their interests. The editors, too, are committed to the view that the people 'are not powerless victims of their position,' but not committed enough to consign Davidson to the dustbin.

There is a more general ahistorical tendency in these volumes – the judging of past society by the standards of our own day. Since these authors are opposed to the inequalities of class, discrimination on the grounds of race, gender, etc, etc and the destruction of the environment, a wide field for denunciation lies open to them when they turn historian. Faced with the amazing phenomenon of eleven ships bringing convicts halfway round the world to found a new society, they can only regret that Governor Phillip did not order the production of an environment impact statement before they landed. I expect it will not be long before we have to read 'Before the first week of the invasion had passed, Phillip and his fellow marauders had sacrificed the lives of a thousand trees ...' If these authors had to deal with Attila the Hun, they would criticise him for the skewed gender balance of his horde and the total absence of social workers in his entourage.

History writing will always reflect our current preoccupations, but as a disciplined enquiry it is also committed to understanding past people in their own terms. Unless it does that, it can explain very little about the past. History as skittle alley, where people are set up merely to be knocked over, is a travesty. Great history writing has the poise and wisdom of great literature, not committed to the society it describes but understanding it better than it did itself.

There is room only for yes/no answers as these writers check the ideological soundness of past society. No one disputes that nineteenth-century society discriminated on the grounds of gender and race, but the extent to which it did so is of little interest to them. These discriminations are not unvarying forces; the forms they take will be affected by the total circumstances of the society in which they occur. On the treatment of the Chinese, for example, Andrew Markus some time since highlighted the difference between the Australian and Californian goldfields. In Australia the strong government presence and the wide respect for the rule of law meant that mob action against the Chinese was usually contained or nipped in the bud. By contrast, mob action and murder were quite common in California. For the rest of the nineteenth century the prejudice towards the Chinese already here was only mild; the hostility towards allowing further migration was intense. A general condemnation of the racism of our forebears misses that distinction which is vital in an assessment of the quality of nineteenth-century society.

The black school's lack of interest in understanding 'unsound' behaviour is most evident in their discussion of women and relations between the sexes. The late nineteenth-century ideal was that married women should remain at home, where she was to be in control, and not take paid work outside it. Men believed that by their exertions to make this possible they were raising the status of women. They were being kept from the harshness of the world and given a new autonomy as mistresses of the home, where they had always laboured but without being in charge. It is a rare writer on women's history – Pat Grimshaw is one – who will acknowledge that these arrangements did indeed raise the status of women. Of course the women-in-the-home ideology makes it harder for women to take the next step towards an equal role in employment and public life. But this is the way the world runs. One generation's idea is not another's. Unless a new era has dawned, our ideals will seem wrongheaded to our successors.

Needless to say, the black school cannot be relied on to describe what life was like for women when they were homemakers. The *People's History* says it will give the view *from* the kitchen sink; rather it gives us the advanced feminist view *of* the kitchen sink. Women at home, says Marilyn Lake, were under 'house arrest', kept prisoners by their men to cook, clean and minister to their comfort. What women themselves thought of their position is not explored. There was, in fact, a mutual respect in these companionate marriages – the woman for the labour, skills and dedication of the breadwinner; the man for those of the homemaker. The oral testimonies of the 1930s depression record this again and again. Amazing to relate, men and women could find contentment, even happiness, when the world was not made according to our formula.

None of this is to suggest that good history cannot be written by reformers. Intelligent reformers will want to understand the people and the society they hope to change. Those who have no interest in the past except to condemn it want not reform of our society but its total transformation. The ruling assumption of the new radicals is that liberal capitalism has been a disaster in Australia and only socialism can provide a decent and fair society.

The old radicals were also socialists but they were ready to acknowledge what had already been achieved by and for the common people in Australia. Compare Alastair Davidson's oppression fantasy with the final words of Brian Fitzpatrick's *Australian Commonwealth* where he describes the people making 'of Australia a home good enough for men of modest report to live in, calling their souls their own.' The older writers were also admirers of the working class. The dilemma of the latter-day socialists is that they despair of the working class who are criticised for being racist, imperialist, sexist and acquisitive. The *People's History* is addressed to them but much of it reads like a statement of grievance in a divorce petition. In these hands the history of the workers is demeaned along with everyone else's.

1988

HOW SORRY CAN WE BE?

I N 1897 JOHN FARRELL, EDITOR OF THE SYDNEY *DAILY TELEGRAPH*, wrote a poem to mark Queen Victoria's jubilee and sent it to Rudyard Kipling, hoping for praise and endorsement. Kipling lighted on the passage in which Farrell regretted the bloody excesses of the empire's conquests and took Farrell to task for his easy moralism. He declared:

> A man might just as well accuse his father of a taste in fornication (citing his own birth as an instance) as a white man mourn over his land's savagery in the past.

The critic only exists because of the deed he criticises. Let us call this the hard realist view of Australia's origins. It avers that it is morally impossible for settler Australians to regret or apologise for the conquest on which colonial Australia was built. It is the view that I share.

No-one has been putting this view publicly in the recent history wars over the extent of frontier violence. Keith Windschuttle, rightly sensing that accounts of violence towards the Aborigines have been used to question the legitimacy of the nation, argued not that violence was inevitable but that its extent had been grossly exaggerated. In the case of Tasmania, on which he has produced the first of a promised series of books, he concludes that only 118 Aborigines were killed (later increased to 120). To his mind, with this low figure, he has rescued the reputation of the British empire and its successor settler nation from their detractors. Compared with the Spanish in the new world, the British in Australia, he says, were restrained by Christian and Enlightenment values in their dealings with the indigenous inhabitants. Tasmania 'was the least violent of all European encounters in the New World'.

With his other critics, I believe that Windschuttle has a misplaced faith in the documents he uses as giving a complete account of what was happening on the frontier. The documents from which he draws the figure of 118 dead themselves speak of terrible deeds being committed in the woods, which by design were leaving no records. But even if Windschuttle were right about the number of those killed by direct violence, he cannot deny that forty years after the European settlement, all the Tasmanian Aborigines had either perished or had been removed to offshore islands. Empires – even good empires – believe in conquest and by any standards this was a complete and rapid expropriation. A people and their way of life had been destroyed. Compared to the starkness of that fact, how many had been directly killed by settler violence seems a matter of lesser consequence.

Again with his other critics (and one or two supporters) I am surprised at Windschuttle's lack of sympathy for the plight of the dispossessed Aborigines. A position of hard realism about the nation resting on conquest certainly does not require that we abandon sympathy for Aborigines as fellow humans. We must understand what Aborigines have experienced since 1788 if any policy-making in Aboriginal affairs is to be effective.

In the course of his argument Windschuttle claimed that Aborigines had no attachment to the land and that in attacking the settlers they were not defending their territory, still less conducting a war; they were simply wanting to acquire the settlers' goods. This was plunder and murder merely. Windschuttle's critics suspected that he was intent on demolishing the claim that present-day Aborigines had to the land or to compensation. So they thought it important not only to destroy Windschuttle's claims about land and resistance but also the symbolic heart of the book: the fewness of the deliberate deaths. There was much argument about the numbers.

At the Melbourne Writers Festival in August 2003 Windschuttle agreed to a debate with Robert Manne, who had edited a book of essays designed to demolish Windschuttle's Tasmanian book. I was in the chair. Among his other criticisms, Manne pressed Windschuttle hard on the numbers: even given his own methodology, could he be sure that Aborigines injured in a battle did not later die of their wounds? Windschuttle did concede that this was possible.

In question time one woman in the audience declared that she was sick of the argument about numbers. Even one death, she said, was one too many. This remark was met with spontaneous applause, which though not universal was nevertheless revealing. The woman and those who applauded believe that it was possible to dispossess the Aborigines without bloodshed. The woman did not speak of dispossession but she and her supporters were located in the Malthouse Theatre which stands on land that formerly belonged to Wurundjeri. Let us label this the liberal fantasy view of our origins. It avers that the conquest could have been done nicely. This view is quite widespread and influential and warrants close examination.

Liberal fantasy is prominent in the judgments given in the *Mabo* case in the High Court. The Court found that since 1788 the common law had not been properly interpreted: it should have respected the Aborigines' rights in their land. The Court did not rule that the invasion itself was illegitimate. On the contrary, it legitimised the invasion by declaring that the British Crown's proclamation of sovereignty over Australia could not be questioned in an Australian court. The error of the Crown and the courts was to assume that sovereignty meant that Aborigines could be summarily dispossessed of their lands. Justices Deane and Gaudron in a famous passage said this:

> The acts and events by which that dispossession in legal theory was carried into practical effect constitute the darkest aspect of the history of this nation. The nation as a whole must remain diminished unless and until there is an acknowledgment of, and retreat from, those past injustices.

This envisages that the nation could have come into being without a dark past. The darkness is only an 'aspect' of our history; there could have been a nation without it. But even if the law had been as the High Court now declares it should have been, the desire of the white invaders for Aboriginal lands would have been no less. The clash between Aboriginal hunting and gathering and European pastoral pursuits would have been as stark. What would have happened if the Aborigines on being fully apprised of the invaders' intentions had refused to negotiate any of their land away? – they would have been *forced* to negotiate. Even if each tribe had been persuaded to yield half their land, Aborigines would still have regarded the invaders' sheep as fair game and white shepherds would have misunderstood what was involved in their acceptance of Aboriginal women – two potent sources of conflict in the world as it really happened. It is very hard to envisage a settlement history without violence. It is a great conceit on the part of these two judges to think that a difference in the law could have tamed the force of European colonialism and given us a history with no dark aspects. From all that we now know of what the land meant to the Aborigines, they would not have yielded it without a fight. The judges insult them by thinking that it could have all happened peacefully.

From 1823 the law in the United States on Indian land was as the High Court says it should have been in regard to Aboriginal land in Australia. The United States had sovereign control over the whole landmass, but the Indians had the right of occupancy over their lands until it was extinguished. Indian land could officially only be yielded up by treaty. But the Indians were not free to make or not make treaties. They were pressured into treaty-making after they had been defeated in battle or in an attempt to save some of their lands from the onrush of the settlers, who did not wait for official sanction before pressing into Indian country. Under these treaties Indians in the east had to agree to be moved westward and the Indians in the west were confined to reservations. The treaties provided that on the reservations they should be supported in money or goods, but the Indian agents frequently robbed them of their due. Their reservations were always subject to incursions by settlers. If the Indians fought back, this was an 'uprising' that the US army would savagely suppress. The area of the reservations was regularly reduced and from 1887 reduced even further by the policy of allotting farm-size plots to each Indian family and opening the rest to the settlers. The process of Americanisation of the Indians required that children be forcibly removed from their parents and placed in boarding houses. The recognition of an Indian right in land did not save the United States from a 'dark aspect' of its history.

One might have thought that Henry Reynolds, the author of the classic work on Aboriginal resistance, *The Other Side of the Frontier*, would be proof against the liberal fantasy. Yet it sustains one of his later books, *This Whispering in Our Hearts*, which deals with those few colonists who opposed the disruption and destruction of Aboriginal society. One or two of these dissenters thought the Aborigines could be saved only if the colonists left. Most thought that colonisation could and should proceed by 'purchase, treaty and negotiation'. This view Reynolds endorses without considering how this process would have been implemented and what difference it would have made. The dissenters were all opposed to punitive expeditions. Reynolds himself is very definite that punitive expeditions were 'indiscriminate and disproportionate violence'. So the historian who celebrated Aboriginal resistance and wanted their battles to protect their lands honoured in the War Memorial now thinks that milder measures – a bit of deft police work, perhaps – would have been enough to make the Aborigines give up the fight.

The liberal fantasy has a strong hold on Kate Grenville, one of the best of our fiction writers. Her latest book *The Secret River* deals with the European settlement along the Hawkesbury River north of Sydney. The chief character is loosely based on one of her ancestors, a waterman on the Thames who was transported for thieving. In the modern way she has talked and written a lot about her project and hence revealed the impulses that drive her. She told the ABC:

> You want to go back 200 years and say to the settlers, 'Look, this is how the Aborigines are,' and to the Aborigines, 'Look, this is why settlers are behaving the way they are. Let's understand this. There's no need for all this brutality.'

Here is the liberal faith that conflict comes from misunderstanding. Actually, if Aborigines had earlier understood the settlers' intentions there would have been more violence and sooner. The settlers were fortunate in that the Aborigines at first welcomed them or avoided them or attempted to accommodate them.

Grenville wants there to have been peace, but she knows why there was war. In the book she gives a good account of the dynamics of conflict.

Her character is a good man who does not want to do the Aborigines harm, but in his dealings with them on his Hawkesbury farm he is perplexed, fearful and finally angry and desperate. He is a very good man, amazingly sensitive for an illiterate waterman brought up in a hard world. He also appears to have read the modern textbook accounts on Aboriginal society. So he realises that 'the blacks were farmers no less than the white men' and that hunting and gathering allowed plenty of time for 'sitting by their fires and laughing and stroking the chubby limbs of their babies'. On one occasion he beats his son for avoiding work and playing with the Aborigines. When the son remains defiant, he says, 'Do I got to get the belt out again, lad?' But his anger soon leaves him. On the transport ship he had learnt that repeated floggings did not work. He says to the boy 'Just joking, lad. I beat you once that were enough.' *Just joking?* At what date did a parent first say that after threatening to discipline a child?: try the 1950s in the United States.

Kate Grenville ponders what she would have done on the frontier and what sort of person that would have made her. The leading character in her novel is not an eighteenth-century waterman at all; it is herself. And so it is no surprise that the waterman, having joined in a massacre of the Aborigines that ends their harassment of the settlers, finds that the land he has possessed gives him no comfort. This is clearly meant as a parable of the nation.

Worrying over the conquest; wishing it were peaceful; feeling that somehow it has to be rectified if settler Australia is to be at peace with itself: these are the products of the liberal imagination. Its decency knows no bounds or thought. *Even one death is one too many.* This mindset has perverted Aboriginal policy over the last thirty years so that it has not been dealing with Aborigines as they are or may be and it raises expectations that cannot be met. The *Mabo* judgment was a great offender in this. Having denounced settler atrocity and called for a retreat from past injustices, it then proceeded to legitimise the invasion and declared that native title had been extinguished on all freehold and leasehold land.

Kate Grenville thinks that novelists, better than historians, can get into the heart and mind of past people. Depends on the novelist – and the historian. Between Kate Grenville and the historian Inga Clendinnen there is no contest. In her study of the first years at Sydney Cove, Clendinnen is not projecting herself back into the past; she knows that these people, settlers and Aborigines, are very different from herself. You need to work hard to understand them. One of the several novelties of *Dancing with Strangers* is Clendinnen's characterisation of the Aborigines as warriors and her cool appraisal of how violence worked in their society. When Governor Phillip orders the first punitive expedition against the Aborigines, she does not hasten to condemn him; she thinks he has correctly divined the sort of retribution Aborigines will understand. The expedition failed to find any Aborigines – which Clendinnen, not altogether convincingly, claims is what Phillip intended, reckoning that the threat of retribution would be enough.

Grenville is appalled by the plans for this punitive expedition. Aboriginal heads were to be cut off and brought back in bags. Her modern sensibility reels at this hacking at bone and muscle. Her historical enquiries into violence have obviously not been extensive. Europeans were still hanging, drawing and quartering their own when Sydney was founded. Grenville is rather coy about Aboriginal violence. We see the results as visited on the settlers but not Aborigines performing it. The settlers on the Hawkesbury follow what Aborigines are doing elsewhere through the pages of the *Sydney Gazette* and we are encouraged to think that Aboriginal violence is to some extent a media beat-up. However, the climactic European massacre of the Aborigines is rendered in close-up grisly detail.

The liberal imagination, appalled at European violence on the frontier, tends to cast the Aborigines as victims merely and not fine practitioners óf violence themselves. Violence was more central to their society since its practice was not allotted to a professional caste of soldiers; all adult males were warriors. Aboriginal warfare was endemic, usually with a small number of deaths, but occasionally Aborigines massacred each other. This is an account based on reports by the perpetrators:

Spears and boomerangs flew with deadly aim. Within a matter of minutes Ltjabakuk and his men were lying lifeless in their blood at their brush shelters. Then the warriors turned their murderous attention to the women and older children, and either speared or clubbed them to death. Finally … they broke the limbs of the infants, leaving them to die 'natural deaths'.

The writer is T. G. H. Strehlow, who grew up with the Arrernte of the Centre. His life work was to record and translate their songs. Of their warrior songs he wrote that the 'unbridled expression of blood-lust was relished by old and young'.

Kate Grenville cannot imagine how she would have behaved on the Hawkesbury frontier because, unlike the Hawkesbury settlers, she does not believe in savagery, European superiority and conquest. The pioneer settlers are not ourselves. Nor are the Aborigines whom the pioneers encountered the Aborigines of today. Settler Australians no longer hang and flog offenders or colonise other countries. Aboriginal Australians no longer abandon their old, kill their superfluous young and levy war against their neighbours. We are all a long way from 1788.

There is literally no place for settler Australians to stand to decry the conquest of this country. It all belonged to the Aborigines. The only honest approach is to recognise the conquest as conquest and not to give any utilitarian defence of it – like that the land under European control was able to provide food and fibre to the rest of the world, a view which Geoffrey Blainey advances. In the European world of the late eighteenth century acquiring new territory was perfectly legitimate; what dispute there was concerned the treatment of the people already there. An heroic moralist of today may say that the European conquests were wrong and attempt the impossibility of imagining world history without conquest. Better, if you must speak of right and wrong, to say that according to their lights the settlers were right to invade and the Aborigines were right to resist them. It is our common fate to live with the consequences of that conjunction.

*

The consequences were more varied than is commonly imagined. Here is a thumb-nail sketch of race relations since 1788, the work of an Aboriginal radical which would be assented to – except perhaps for the Nazi comparison – by many progressively-minded settler Australians.

When white men arrived in this country, they shot the blacks, poisoned their waterholes, murdered them, left, right and centre. Those that were left were rounded up like dogs and cattle and stuck in these places called Aboriginal reserves, which were nothing less than concentration camps. And there they stayed until very recently.

It is correct that there were two attacks on the Aborigines, but wrong to imply that the second followed hard on the first. After the first attack – the taking of the land and the crushing of resistance – the Aborigines were more or less left alone. The time between the two attacks was as much as a hundred years in the lands settled first in New South Wales.

The Aborigines, depleted in numbers more by disease than violence, remained on their own land. Unlike the American Indians they did not have to be put on reserves to stop their resistance. Many took work in the pastoral industry, which until 1900 was much more important than farming and sat more lightly on the land. The boss who hired them might well a few years previously have been shooting at them. The more remote the property, the more reliant was the pastoralist on Aboriginal labour and the less likely the Aborigines were to be paid wages. But where the white presence was slight Aborigines could retain more of their traditional life. As Ann McGrath wrote in *Born in the Cattle*, we can exaggerate the significance of the settlers to the Aborigines, ruthless and exploitative though the settlers were. As well as doing the regular work on the pastoral stations, Aborigines became drovers and shearers. The Shearers Union (later the AWU) was fanatical in its opposition to Chinese labour but allowed Aborigines (and Maoris) to be members. There were some reserves and missions, more important as refuges to the Aborigines where settlement was denser, but Aborigines were not confined to them; they were free to come and go.

Across the countryside Aborigines remained a presence. Some were ruined by drink and survived by begging and scrounging. Most made their own living and the good workers gained reputation and respect. On the missions Aborigines could be living in cottages as good or better than those of the working class. On the pastoral stations and near the towns they lived in humpies from which they might emerge in suits and hats. Aborigines were local notables and the giving of King plates to 'chiefs' continued and the deaths of the last of the tribe were commemorated. The tide of general opinion was becoming more hostile towards the Aborigines as an inferior race, but settlers on the land had their experience of particular people to temper their attitudes.

Aborigines of the first generation after contact have consistently been described as a mild, uncomplaining, generous people. This seems a puzzle: why would defeated warriors display these characteristics? In his Boyer Lectures W. E. H. Stanner, the great anthropologist, thought the mildness was a sort of anomie induced by homelessness, powerlessness, poverty and confusion. I think his essay on 'The Dreaming' provides a better explanation: the cosmology of the Aborigines cannot be destroyed by any disruptions in their life here and now. It is beyond time and circumstance. This attachment to what is unchanging meant that Aborigines were less inclined to quarrel with pain, sorrow and sadness. Their stoicism we may take to be an aspect of character, but as with the original Stoics it had its basis in philosophy.

After their homelands were taken from them, the Aborigines were, in the terms of the society that had overwhelmed them, a marginalised people, but in their own understanding they were, in a double sense, not a displaced people: they were on their own territory and what gave ultimate meaning to their life still continued. Their 'sense of oneness with Eternity', in Strehlow's words, 'made them more kindly, tolerant and helpful towards their human fellows everywhere'.

In this way we can understand the lack of resentment towards the settlers and the willingness to be of service to them. This is celebrated in the many stories of Aboriginal trackers finding lost children in the bush. Someone rides for the tracker who briefly becomes the leader and instructor of the settlers before returning to the humpy from which he was fetched. The stories having become legendary are a continuing reminder of the laissez-faire times between the first and second attack on the Aborigines.

The second attack began in the decades around 1900. The Aborigines presented no new problem to white society except that they continued to exist. By processes that had little to do with the Aborigines, the new nation had formed its ideals in and through the slogan White Australia. Once the nation had given itself that racial identity, the Aborigines became an anomaly. Much indulgence had been shown to the Aborigines in the nineteenth century because they were expected to die out; now there were growing numbers of mixed-blood people. The white nation seemed likely to have a permanent group of people of 'inferior' blood. Two solutions were adopted. In the more closely settled areas part-Aborigines were to be separated from their full-blood kin and encouraged to disappear into the wider community. This involved the shrinking and destruction of the Aboriginal communities on the reserves and missions and the removal of children from their parents. Where Aboriginal populations were larger they were to be confined on reserves (as far as was compatible with the need for their labour) and their interbreeding with whites forbidden. To control, confine and manage Aborigines in this way their civil rights had to be removed.

The second attack on the Aborigines disturbs me much more than the first. I am not shocked at a settler riding out to shoot Aborigines. He acted in hot blood to protect what was close to him, the lives of himself and his workers and the survival of his highly risky enterprise. Nor am I shocked that settlers and their men sometimes rode out together hoping to kill enough Aborigines to give themselves finally the security they craved. But I cannot be calm at police arriving at settled communities to drag children away from their mothers. This was cold-blooded cruelty planned by a distant Bureau in pursuit of the ideal of racial purity. Humankind has been very inventive in its cruelty, but cruelty of this sort did not appear until the early twentieth century. We are still struggling to come to terms with it.

Concern for racial purity was then general in European civilisation; it had a peculiar intensity here because Australia happened to form its national ideal when racism was at its peak and it had experienced and disliked migration from Asia. Its ideals of a progressive, egalitarian and harmonious society became fully mixed with the racial poison. Now that they have been untangled the nation should apologise to those that suffered – particularly to children forcibly taken from caring parents. I believe that more settler Australians would be ready to acknowledge this wrong and apologise for it if the proponents of apology did not urge apologies for everything.

So why does the second attack on the Aborigines warrant an apology and the first one not? Though the High Court judges in *Mabo* spoke of the Australian nation expropriating the Aborigines, this is not so. The settlers were English, Irish and Scots who invaded Aboriginal lands with the sanction of the British state. Only subsequently was the Australian nation formed by those settlers and their children. It is true that the nation was only made possible by this expropriation, which is why I consider it cannot be apologised for. Some might be tempted to point the finger at the British, but settler Australians are the beneficiaries of their deeds. The second attack on the Aborigines was an attack by the Australian nation (though the agents were the various state governments) in pursuit of a national ideal. I accept what Rai Gaita has argued that if a nation can feel pride at its past achievements it can properly feel shame (though not guilt) for its past misdeeds. Forcibly removing Aboriginal children was undoubtedly a misdeed. What finally makes the case for apology compelling in this instance is that some of the victims are still alive.

*

Civil and political rights were rapidly restored to Aborigines from the 1950s. Settler Australians showed their willingness to see Aborigines become equal citizens by the overwhelming assent they gave to the 1967 constitutional amendment. But just at this point Aboriginal policy took a new separatist turn. The new policy proposals were for self-determination, land rights, a treaty, even Aboriginal sovereignty. These were the fruits of liberal fantasy conjoined with Aboriginal radicalism, which fed on each other.

The liberal fantasy is that the conquest would have been acceptable had there been recognition of the land rights of traditional owners and negotiation with them. Hence the most urgent need of policy is to rectify these omissions which are the source of all our ills. But a treaty with the Aborigines would not be with a traditional grouping. The traditional groups numbered about 500 tribes, only a few of which survive.

The Aborigines are a group formed since the conquest from those tribes-people and their descendants who had the common experience of oppression and exclusion at the hand of Europeans. The failure of 1788 is to be rectified by dealing with a group that did not exist in 1788.

In the 1950s and 1960s, when assimilation and integration was the policy, differences between Aborigines were acknowledged. Some Aborigines, chiefly of mixed blood, were already part of the wider society. Their problems were not that different from those of the white underclass with whom they frequently intermarried. In remote Australia there were Aborigines living something like a traditional life who were to be induced or encouraged over time to move into settler society. But with the new policies of separatism, the Aborigines were regarded as a single group and whatever characteristics were ascribed to traditional Aborigines, were true for them all. That is, Aborigines wherever located and however distant from a full-blood ancestor, were considered to possess, and may well have come to believe that they did possess, traditional ties to land and a deep spirituality.

William Cooper, the pioneer leader of Aboriginal protest in the 1930s, referred to himself and his supporters as 'the *descendants* of the original owners of the land'. Now all Aborigines were simply the original owners of the land. The politics of identity eroded history.

The High Court in *Mabo* encouraged all Aborigines to think that they had been deprived of their land rights, but it indicated that traditional ties would have to be demonstrated still to exist for a claim to land under native title to be established. Many non-traditional groups attempted to present themselves as having traditional ties to land. An early indication that these claims were spurious was the ferocious battles between Aborigines over who constituted the groups and over what land they had a claim. After millions of dollars of public money had been spent on lawyers' fees, the Federal Court and then the High Court ruled that the Yorta Yorta in Victoria no longer had traditional ties to their land; they had been washed away in the tide of history. No other decision could have been reached, but the Yorta Yorta now have a grievance that they did not have before policy departed from need and all Aborigines were encouraged to think of themselves as traditional.

The *Mabo* decision and the *Native Title Act* which followed might be considered a treaty with Aborigines who still have traditional ties with the land. But proponents of a treaty do not regard it as such and the demand for a treaty with 'the Aborigines' continues. There are suggestions that a treaty should confer particular rights and privileges on Aborigines and provide them with compensation. The immediate difficulty with such a proposal would be to define who the Aborigines are.

An official definition already exists. It has three parts. An Aborigine has (1) to be a person of Aboriginal descent, with no particular proportion of this ancestry stipulated (2) to identify as an Aborigine, and (3) to be accepted by other Aborigines as an Aborigine. This definition is appropriately loose. Aboriginal communities in the more settled parts of the country have been very open and accepting.

But this looseness is now being exploited. People are claiming to be Aborigines partly in order to qualify for the benefits and opportunities specially provided for Aborigines. Tasmania is the state in which the number of Aborigines is rising most rapidly. Dr Cassandra Pybus, who knows the state and its records well, estimates that three-quarters of the people now identifying as Aborigines do not have an Aboriginal ancestor.

In 1997 Michael Mansell, the Aboriginal leader in Tasmania, brought an action in the federal court to challenge the right of eleven people to stand as candidates for the now defunct national Aboriginal parliament, ATSIC. He claimed they were not Aborigines. The judge was plainly unhappy at having to examine lines of descent; he was prepared to give the benefit of the doubt to people who had a strong family tradition that there was an Aboriginal ancestor. He excluded only two of the eleven. He said that today identity is much more social than genetic. In effect he relaxed an already loose definition. This might not matter too much when the issue is standing for ATSIC, but if under a treaty a class of people with special legal rights was being defined, this looseness would be unacceptable.

Cassandra Pybus, who gave evidence in this case, is sure that some people accepted by the judge have no Aboriginal ancestor. All their ancestors were settlers. The descendants of those who shot the Aborigines and took their land are now receiving benefits earmarked for Aborigines.

Many people do not recognise how well integrated many Aborigines are. When they think of Aborigines they think of tribal people in the outback, not people who have been living in the suburbs for three generations. In their partnering the Aborigines of the cities and towns are a less cohesive group than the Greeks in Australia or the Jews. A majority of Aborigines have partners who are not Aborigines.

Consider this household. The husband is an Aborigine of mixed descent; one of his four grandparents was Aboriginal. His wife is of English, Scots, Irish and Italian descent. Their oldest daughter in her late teens becomes interested in her Aboriginal heritage. Her siblings show no interest. She declares that she is an Aborigine and seeks out other Aborigines. There can be no objection to this; it is a free country. But is it seriously proposed that by treaty she should officially be declared indigenous, that she acquire special rights, and that she be given compensation for the loss of her ancestral land, language and culture? That this notion is entertained shows how far policy has departed from an assessment of need.

A treaty has been criticised as divisive. It certainly would be and in a more profound sense than is commonly realised. The division and the bitterness would begin with the act of defining who the Aborigines are. It would give members of the same family a different status.

In the 1980s the Hawke Labor government contemplated and then abandoned the idea of a treaty. Instead it proposed a process of Reconciliation which would begin in 1991 and be completed in time for the centenary of federation in 2001. Liberal fantasy was again at work. The premise of Reconciliation was that nothing significant had so far been done to right past wrongs and yet complete harmony was within close reach.

Reconciliation as a process was borrowed from societies where two groups had been at loggerheads if not at war. In Australia Aborigines had regained their civil and political rights thirty years previously; they enjoyed a large measure of goodwill from the settler Australians and huge sums of public money had been spent on their welfare and advancement. Aboriginal art and dance were widely appreciated; Aboriginal sportspeople were honoured. Traditional Aborigines had acquired the rights over their land. Assimilation and integration of other Aborigines – though those names could not be breathed – were proceeding rapidly.

Intermarriage was high and increasing. And yet Reconciliation presented Australia as a fundamentally divided society. We were compared to South Africa or the Middle-Eastern conflict between Jews and Palestinians.

The naming of the groups presented them as being a long way apart. There were indigenous Australians and non-indigenous Australians. This is an amazing formulation; 98% of the population is defined by what it is not. The use of the term indigenous for Aborigines had innocent enough origins. The Torres Strait Islanders do not want to be mistaken for Aborigines, though they want to share their status. Hence the mouthful term 'Aborigines and Torres Strait Islanders' had to be used. Indigenous was a simpler portmanteau term and simultaneously it was coming into use at the United Nations which also needed a generic term. But only in Australia was the settler population then defined as non-indigenous – there are not non-indigenous Americans or non-indigenous New Zealanders. 'Non-indigenous' implies a people without roots in this place; it elides the fact that settlers have been here for eight generations, that they have formed a distinctive polity and are not indigenous to anywhere else; they regard Australia as their home. On the other side it elides the fact that most Aborigines are descendants of settlers and the original indigenous population. The formulation in fact casts modern Australia as if it were 1788: one group has just stepped off the boat and confronts the traditional owners of the country. That's where the liberal imagination is fixated.

The process of Reconciliation enjoyed bipartisan support in the federal parliament. The Liberal and National parties had opposed Labor's dalliance with land rights and a treaty; it supported Reconciliation with the proviso that the Reconciliation Council was to consult widely before it committed itself to any document of reconciliation. The Council did produce a Declaration of Reconciliation, elegantly drafted by David Malouf and Jackie Huggins, which acknowledged Aborigines as original owners and custodians and that the land was colonised without their consent. It also offered an apology in these terms: 'as one part of the nation expresses its sorrow and profoundly regrets the injustices of the past, so the other part accepts the apology and forgives.'

To discover what the Australian people thought of the Declaration, the Council commissioned a poll and organised focus groups. On the issue of an apology, people were asked to agree or disagree with the proposition that 'On behalf of the community, governments should apologise to Aboriginal people for what's happened in the past.' This was a more comprehensive apology than envisaged by the draft where the apology was for 'injustices'. Fifty-seven per cent of people disagreed with the proposition; 40 per cent agreed. This was the strongest dissent that the pollsters encountered. The advantage of defining closely what should be apologised for was obviously not recognised. 'What's happened in the past' includes the European settlement of the country. Only hypocrites can apologise for that.

The apology survived in the final document, which was presented to Australian leaders at the Sydney Opera House in May 2000. Prime Minister John Howard produced a revised version of the document without an apology. He had always made clear his opposition to an apology of any sort. The government was prepared to express 'profound regrets' that past injustices had occurred but not to apologise for them. The government very firmly rejected the Reconciliation Council's plan to continue working on a treaty after 2001, which had passed without the spectacular results hoped for it.

The acute social problem that Australia faces is not the division between Aborigines and settler Australians. It is that many Aborigines in remote Australia live in communities which have appalling records on health, housing, employment and rates of imprisonment. These are Aboriginal communities; the few settler Australians who live there provide services to them. Decent liberal-minded people worry enormously about this social malaise, but they keep mistaking its cure; they think that the moment of reconciliation which they desperately seek is necessary to fix this problem. In fact their attitudes have been making it worse.

The Reconciliation Council which was formed to heal a social divide had added to its brief the addressing of what was called Aboriginal disadvantage. The Liberal and National parties supported Reconciliation on the basis that practical measures would be taken to improve Aboriginal communities, which they saw as more pressing than symbolic acts, still less a treaty. This is the approach that Prime Minister Howard later termed 'practical reconciliation'. Those who believed in the symbolism of a declaration of reconciliation or a treaty then argued in response that Aborigines cannot be whole people until past hurts are acknowledged. The difficulty with this argument is that among the most troubled communities are those that exist on their own land and, comparatively, have experienced little disturbance from settlers. Their health and life expectancy are appalling but they may still be initiating their young men.

The social situation in these communities has got worse over the past thirty years not better. Welfare without the usual work tests replaced employment at low wages; schools were built without ensuring that students attended them; health declined because of alcohol and drug abuse. Huge sums were spent on buildings and equipment that were trashed or never used. The situation was allowed to continue because of the commitment to supporting traditional life on Aboriginal lands, though there were few worthwhile jobs there. Generosity and respect in this generation have done more damage to Aboriginal communities than the indifference and neglect of the past.

Now in Cape York the erstwhile radical leader Noel Pearson is steering a new course. He has attacked welfare dependency; he wants to create real jobs for his people; and he plans to send the young away to get a decent education. He has identified as part of the problem the progressively-minded people in Sydney and Melbourne who walked across bridges as one of the symbolic acts sponsored by the Reconciliation Council. He complains that their soft-headness about social problems has been too influential on policy: the treatment of welfare as a right; of alcohol abuse as a symptom of malaise rather than something to be attacked in itself; and the willingness to excuse anti-social behaviour as the result of poor treatment in the past. Perhaps soon the progressively-minded people will be asked to apologise.

*

What does Australian history look like if we assume a close interaction between settler Australians and Aborigines and not distance? Here are some Notes Towards the Definition of an Integrated Australia.

The explorer Matthew Flinders, knowing the Aboriginal love of ceremony, put on a special display when he left King George's Sound after spending a month there in 1801. He ordered his marines ashore and put them through their drill. The Aborigines were delighted with the men in their red coats and white crossed belts; these 'red-and-white men', said Flinders, had 'some resemblance to their own manner of ornamenting themselves'. They followed their drill closely and one old man put himself at the end of the rank and using a stick imitated the soldiers' movements as they shouldered and grounded their weapons. When the anthropologist Daisy Bates visited King George's Sound over a hundred years later she found an old man who could still do the drill. He covered his torso in red and put white pipe-clay across the red and performed the movements as his father and grandfathers had taught him. The Aborigines had made of the drill a sacred ceremony with Flinders and his men being spirits returning from the dead. John Mulvaney in *Encounters in Place* writes, 'This Aboriginal application of ritual exchange, of formal ceremonial involving hierarchy, persons with special functions, particular dress, and display of regalia, has application to later developments' – like the enlistment of Aborigines into the Native Police and their enthusiasm for organised sport, especially cricket.

Aborigines were attracted to European food and tobacco – and this before their own society had broken down. Stanner witnessed this process in the Northern Territory in the 1930s. He reports in 'Continuity and Change' how one group of Aborigines tried to get tobacco and tea through another which had a supply because they had settled with Europeans: 'The encroachers used every claim of right they had – kinship, affinity, friendship, name-sake relationship, trade partnership – to get and keep a toehold.' This movement towards settler society was not intended as a break with their own, though that could be the consequence. Aborigines saw immediately the superiority of iron axes to their own stone ones. In a famous 1952 article, 'Steel axes for Stone-Age Australians', Lauriston Sharp argued that the new axes threatened the stability of Aboriginal society since the making and distribution of stone axes was intimately linked to the maintenance of kin relationships and no explanation of the new axes was provided in the Aboriginal cosmology. This view of Aboriginal society as a fragile structure is now discredited. The axes were not so disturbing – axes occur because of white man's Dreaming.

However, Aboriginal society had its points of tension. Older men took the young women as wives and the young men were left with none or with the older women. Young men and women wanting to escape this regime were attracted to settler society, which could not always protect them from the retribution of the old men. On Bathurst Island the Catholic missionary Bishop smoothed matters over by buying the young girls from the older men and then marrying them to young men. He became known, as his book telling of his exploits has it, as *The Bishop with 150 Wives*.

Henry Reynolds in *With the White People* tells of how much Aborigines contributed to the European exploration and development of the country. The explorers were not 'discovering'; they were following their Aboriginal guides. Bushman learnt their bushcaft from the Aborigines. Much of the work in the outback was done by Aborigines. Today, choose at random six white Australians and six Aborigines and examine their family history. Of the whites, two would be postwar migrants or their children, two could trace descent from late nineteenth-century colonists mostly in the cities, perhaps two would have ancestors who had done pioneering work on the land. But of the Aborigines all six would have ancestors who were stock-workers, shepherds, trackers, troopers, pearl-divers. Much of this was forced or semi-forced labour. However the priority for Aborigines was not good working conditions but a proper relation with the boss. Reynolds writes,

> Aborigines worked out of a sense of obligation – as a favour to particular individuals, not because they felt they should be 'industrious'. Work was not a matter of an unequal exchange between master and servant but merely one aspect of a reciprocal relationship. Long-term bosses were not seen as masters so much as *de facto* kin – as classificatory uncles or brothers.

Most modern Aborigines have Aborigines and settler Australians as their ancestors. The sexual congress between Aborigines and settlers ranged from rape to settled unions, though seldom to marriage.

The attractiveness of Aboriginal women to European men, both the lure of 'black velvet', and the stigma of acknowledging it, are the themes of Xavier Herbert's novel of the Northern Territory, *Capricornia* (1938). It honours the lack of hypocrisy of Tim O'Cannon, a railway ganger who lived openly with an Aboriginal wife and acknowledged his children. There is a similar character in *Coonardooo* (1929), Katharine Susannah Prichard's novel set in the north of Western Australia. Sam Geary has several wives and many children and cites the patriarchs of the Old Testament in support of his behaviour. Hugh Watt, his neighbour and the central character in the book, despises Geary and will not give himself to the Aboriginal girl Coonardoo whom he loves. She waits patiently, puzzled, wanting to give herself to him. Hugh's refusal leads to their mutual ruin and that of his station. The novel caused a scandal when it was published for allowing that a decent man could love an Aboriginal woman; it is still in print carrying the message that 'You had to keep in the life flow of the country – its land and its original people – to survive.'

The pioneer anthropologists Spencer and Gillen, who studied the Arrernte in Central Australia, coined the term Dreamtime. It was not a translation of an Arrernte word; it combined two words that seemed to have a similar root: the word for what is eternal and the word for dreaming. Hence Dreamtime. Stanner took out 'time' altogether, for this cosmology is everywhen. Hence The Dreaming. Some traditional Aborigines did not recognise it as appropriate for themselves, but it has become now the term used by modern Aborigines to discuss Aboriginal culture. It has also been used by settler Australians for their own world, as in John Carroll's *The Western Dreaming*.

T. G. H. Strehlow published his *Songs of Central Australia* in 1971. Barry Hill in his *Broken Song* defines its status and its double origin:

> Strehlow designed his book to sing and elucidate the soul of the first inhabitants and it does so with the lyricism of the *Song of Songs* and the gravity of the *Torah*. There have been other renderings of Aboriginal poetry, and they have been splendid reminders of the depth of the culture that has pulsed here so long, but no other book has been as embracing as Strehlow's, or more honorifically committed

to placing the 'first songs' of the 'first people' in the context of world poetry. In *Songs*, Aboriginal life breathes in the company of Greek and Anglo-Saxon, Norse and Hebraic utterance.

In the 1930s Margaret Preston studied Aboriginal design closely and urged that it be the basis of a truly Australian art. She was in touch with the Jindyworobak movement, which wanted to use Aboriginal words and concepts to make a truly Australian literature. These were both awkward appropriations. In the renaissance of Australian art in the 1940s and 1950s Drysdale, Nolan, Boyd and others regularly treated Aboriginal subjects. Geoffrey Dutton in *White on Black* reports that this unparalleled preoccupation went 'beyond national problems to the roots of human existence on earth, and what humans have left on earth'. In the 1970s when Geoffrey Bardon at Papunya gave the Aboriginal elders canvas, boards and paints, the wondrous designs and patterns that had previously been rendered in sand and on flesh could hang on gallery walls here and overseas.

Aborigines today are more devoted to Christianity than settler Australians. Christianity gave new meaning and purpose to part-Aborigines and was frequently the basis of community morale. When traditional Aborigines embrace Christianity, its key figures and episodes take on strange forms within The Dreaming. Tony Swain in *Aboriginal Australians and Christian Missions* found that the Warlpiri at Yeundumu thought that Adam, Moses and Jesus all lived on the one day, a likely outcome when a faith that is historically based enters a cosmology without time. But Christians too need timelessness for some purposes and Swain suggests that The Dreaming is a good rendering of Augustine's understanding that 'eternity is the "now" of God'.

Aboriginal protest is not located outside settler society. To speak their grievance Aborigines have to use the language of their conquerors and manipulate their concepts and values. They have always received help in this from settler Australians.

The Gurindji at Wave Hill struck for equal wages in 1966, a cause that Australians could understand and which was advanced by the presence at Wave Hill of Frank Hardy, the communist, who knew something about how to run a strike. I had always believed, on the basis of Hardy's own account in *Unlucky Australians*, that it was the Aborigines who gradually revealed to him that they were more concerned with pushing their rights to the land. But as Bain Attwood shows in *Rights for Aborigines*, land rights had long been the policy of the Communist Party. So this crucial new turn in Aboriginal protest cannot be set down solely as an Aboriginal initiative.

Tim Flannery in *The Future Eaters* argues that Aborigines and European settlers both mistook the land they came to. Both discovered that it was not as abundant as it appeared and had to make fundamental adjustments to their way of life. He considers the European adjustment has only just begun. I think the contrariness of the country – the droughts and flooding rains – was recognised by settler Australians sooner than Flannery allows. I remember my father saying when some disaster struck, 'We should give the country back to the blacks,' a sentiment which I know did not arise from a recognition of Aboriginal land rights. I could find no other reference to this saying and thought, as was possible, that my father had coined it. Then in Richard Broome's *Aboriginal Victorians* I found this Aboriginal song of the Depression years:

> White boy he now pays all taxes
> Keeps Jacky Jacky in clothes and food
> He don't care what becomes of the country
> White boy's tucker him pretty good
>
> *Chorus*
> Clicketa Boobilah wildy maah
> Billying etcha gingerry wah
>
> Now the country's short of money
> Jacky sits and laughs all day
> White boy wants to give it back to Jacky
> No fear, Jacky won't have it that way

Germaine Greer in *Whitefella Jump Up* and Inga Clendinnen in *Dancing with Strangers* have claimed that there is a similarity in Aboriginal and settler Australian humour. Perhaps this is so. How could it be so? Has it something to do with this bugger of a country?

When David Malouf was working on the Declaration for Reconciliation, he was for the most part improving on the standard talk about Aborigines and settler Australians. He had one novel idea that quickly disappeared because his clients could not understand it. His draft began with 'The people of Australia, of many origins, recognising the gift of one another's presence ...' That's not being sorry or forgiving at all.

2006

THE CONVICT LEGACY

WHAT TO ME SEEMS THE MOST CHALLENGING QUESTION in Australian history receives commonly a very confident answer. What effect did the convicts have on our national character? Answer: they made us an anti-authoritarian people.

The best antidote to this view is still an article written forty years ago by Henry Reynolds, before he turned his attention to Aboriginal history. He deals with the aftermath of convict transportation in Tasmania and, unusually in historical enquiry, argues with the simplicity and conclusiveness of a syllogism. In Tasmania the convicts represented a higher proportion of the population than on the mainland. If convicts are responsible for an anti-authoritarian attitude it should be particularly prevalent there. In fact, Tasmania after transportation was the most conservative, the most traditional and Anglophile of the colonies, the most un-Australian in outlook, with a working class submissive, unprotesting and apolitical. Therefore convicts cannot be responsible for anti-authoritarianism.

Reynolds had in his sights the classic work on the national character by Russel Ward, *The Australian Legend*, published in 1958. Long before Australian society generally accepted and even boasted of its convict foundations, Ward took pleasure in insisting that convicts are our 'founding fathers' and from them he derives our independence, anti-authoritarianism and the group solidarity of men, which became mateship. But he also outlined other factors which accentuated and embedded these characteristics. In the colonies generally and in particular 'up the country' where the old hands (convicts and ex-convicts) were concentrated, there was a shortage of labour, which removed from workers the fear of the boss. In the pastoral country outback, men wandered independently from station to station, not bound to one employer, known often by only a nickname and not needing references to land a job.

The sparseness of settlement and the isolation from civilised society led men to depend on each other. Their bonds were more intense because there were few white women in the bush; the pattern of these men's lives was to work hard, drink away their earnings, swear outrageously and find sexual release with Aboriginal women.

It is said that a good history book will carry the evidence to refute its own argument. Perhaps all these other factors that Ward presents were enough to produce the national characteristics? And so convicts can be dropped from the explanation? The Tasmanian case seems to support such a conclusion because Tasmania did not have a labour shortage, settlement was closer, and governments and the employing class exercised a firm control on the lower orders.

However, convict influence might be saved by arguing that Australia inherited convict characteristics but they needed certain circumstances in which to flourish. New South Wales had them; Tasmania did not. But doubt can be thrown on this supposition and with an argument that Ward half recognises. Australia in its foundation years acquired free British workers as well as convicts, and both came from a Britain where the old social bonds of deference were weakening with the disturbances brought by rapid economic growth and industrialisation. In the late eighteenth century the working people of the towns were known as the 'loose disorderly sort' and were notorious in Europe for their unruliness. By the early nineteenth century working people were beginning to organise to claim political rights, to be part of the nation and not merely to be the poor or the lower orders. If we find stroppy workers in Australia we don't have to look for convict influence.

William Howitt, a traveller to the goldfields in the 1850s, was alert for rude behaviour from the lower orders. In England he was a radical but a gentleman, and in Australia he travelled heavy and dressed as a gentleman. On one occasion a group of diggers threatened him and his son by continuing to play a game of cricket in which the stumps were pitched in the middle of the main road. The bowler hurled the ball just past the ear of Howitt's horse and the batsman struck it back so that it nearly hit Howitt's son in the face. Some mounted police had just ridden by and they had made no attempt to stop the game. Howitt quietly remonstrated with the men on the danger they were causing, but they heaped abuse on him and yelled, 'We do as we like here. You are not in England, remember.' These men were almost certainly fresh off the boat, as was Howitt himself. Though he was annoyed, he was calm in his explanation of their behaviour, which made no reference to convicts and their influence. He saw them as Englishmen crudely asserting their freedom after being held in more restraint at home.

It is possible in Britain itself to find a workforce with the 'Australian' characteristics but without any convict influence. The navvies who built the railways in the early nineteenth century were high-paid, roving men, often known only by a nickname, spending their monthly wages in a great burst of drinking and being a great terror to decent society. They were a tribe apart, with strong loyalty to each other: a navvy on the tramp between jobs would camp with other navvies, who were honour bound to contribute funds to see him on his way. Like the Australian sundowners, some of these trampers were suspected of never wanting to find a job.

Are we done with convicts? Not quite, because we need to consider the quintessential anti-authority figure, the Irish convict. Ward puts much stress on him. Since the Irish were rebels against foreign domination and tyrannical landlords, they seem natural candidates for contributors to Australian anti-authoritarianism. But this mistakes the nature of the anti-authority attitude we are discussing. We are not looking for explanations for open, violent rebellion. There has been little of that in Australia and when it did occur, at Castle Hill and Eureka, the Irish were prominent. We are looking for the origins of a street-smart, irreverent attitude, mocking or evading authority but with no sense of controlling or replacing it. The origins of this are English, late eighteenth-century, working-class, urban; not pre-modern, rural, Irish. The Irish were more communal and tribal, more combative and loyal, less interested in independence and swagger, and pleased to find a patron who would protect them: 'God bless you, your honour.'

The Australian national character is always presented as a marked departure from the character of the English. When Australians make these comparisons they are thinking of the toffy upper-crust Englishman in a bowler hat. When George Orwell described the English national character in 1940 he wrote of the working class and the lower-middle class – the very people who came to Australia:

> … another English characteristic which is so much a part of us that we barely notice it … is the addiction to hobbies and spare-time occupations, the privateness of English life. We are a nation of flower-lovers, but also a nation of stamp-collectors, pigeon-fanciers, amateur carpenters, coupon-snippers, darts-players, crossword-puzzle fans. All the culture that is most truly native centres round things which even when they are communal are not official – the pub, the football match, the back garden, the fireside and the 'nice cup of tea'. The liberty of the individual is still believed in, almost as in the nineteenth century. But this has nothing to do with economic liberty, the right to exploit others for profit. It is the liberty to have a home of your own, to do what you like in your spare time, to choose your own amusements instead of having them chosen for you from above.
>
> One thing one notices if one looks directly at the common people, especially in the big towns, is that they are not puritanical. They are inveterate gamblers, drink as much beer as their wages will permit, are devoted to bawdy jokes, and use probably the foulest language in the world.

Much of this is true of Australians and true of Australians who are no longer working class. The drinking, gambling and swearing are part of the national stereotype that Ward identified and explored; he did not recognise as part of the national character the desire for the back garden and the home of your own, but that has been highlighted by those who have labelled Australia the first suburban nation. Nationalists writing of national character look for distinctiveness of local origin; we are better off thinking that Australian characteristics are those of the English working class writ large.

Ward considers that the outback workers – shearers, stockmen, drovers – adopted in the purest form the national characteristics that interest him. Yet it was the city larrikins, whom he does not mention, that made anti-authority an art form and who set a style which has become nationally admired. Larrikins flourished in the last decades of the nineteenth century and at first were not loveable people. Their pushes operated openly; they blocked the footpaths, jostled passers by, made obscene remarks to respectable girls and women, and spat on the clothes of welldressed men. They beat up and robbed drunks and Chinese. But they were different from the roughs of European towns. The Melbourne journalist John Stanley James described them in this way:

> One marked difference between the Melbourne larrikin and his compeers elsewhere is his extreme boldness and contempt of authorities. In Europe, the 'rough' avoids the neighbourhood of police courts. He loves not to be known by magistrates or detectives. But here, the larrikin not only chaffs and annoys the policemen on his beat, but daily crowds the police court, and manifests the liveliest interest in the fate of male or female friends who may be on trial ... Another marked difference, which is in the larrikin's favour, is his generally better-fed and better-clothed appearance. The rowdy and thief in the old world, after all, lead a miserable life, and generally their profession does not appear to be a lucrative one; but here, in the first stage, they seem physically in good shape.

When tough measures against larrikins were called for, the larrikins were often found to be the children of respectable parents and in work. When they were prosecuted they could raise the money to employ a lawyer in their defence. The larrikin spirit is still a mysterious phenomenon. It was not the defiance of the damaged and excluded; it was the boldness that came from self-confidence, of young men who would not be confined. A prosperous working class, free of old-world condescension, had spawned in its native-born youth this baroque display of independence. In Sydney it was possible to argue that the larrikins were a residue from convict times, but larrikins flourished in all cities, particularly in Melbourne, the largest, which had only a faint convict heritage.

*

The strongest influence of the convicts is not to be sought in the anti-authoritarian attitudes in a segment of the people, but in the trauma of a nation which had to come to terms with its shameful origins. How was Australia to cope with the world's bad opinion? The one thing that everyone knew about Australia was that it was founded with convicts, which continued to make it morally suspect. As an 1850 British verse had it:

> There vice is virtue, virtue vice
> And all that's vile is voted nice.

The world would not forget the convict past, though Australians had themselves disowned it with the anti-transportation movement of the 1840s. When the crowd at the Sydney Cricket Ground invaded the pitch in 1879, an Englishman at the crease called out, 'You sons of convicts!' In 1942 Winston Churchill was tired of John Curtin's requests about the need for British reinforcements for Australia and blamed this panic on 'bad stock'.

For more than a century Australians observed a taboo of not mentioning the convicts. This covered the shame; it did not remove it. My exploration of the consequences of this repression is necessarily speculative, but there is no doubt about how raw the wound was. In 1899 a well-intentioned governor of New South Wales en route to take up his post sent this message ahead:

> Greetings, your birth stain have you turned to good.

There was an uproar; the governor had to retreat from such an offensive remark.

In the second half of the nineteenth century, as the national image began to take shape, Australia was presented by Australians in verse and picture as a young virginal girl, absolutely pure. The purity came from being free of old-world ills of caste, inequality and class prejudice; Australians were one people on a single continent living in harmony, with no civil strife, with opportunity for all, isolated from the rest of the world by the encircling sea, a nation made with no blood spilt (the battles with the Aborigines being entirely overlooked).

The best poem on these themes was written in 1883 by the Sydney journalist John Farrell. It concludes in this way about the British settlers of Australia:

> They found a gracious amplitude of soil,
> Unsown with memories, like poison weeds,
> Of far-forefathers' wrongs and vengeful deeds,
> Where was no crown, save that of earnest toil.
>
> They reared a sunnier England, where the pain
> Of bitter yesterdays might not arise:
> They said – 'The past is past, and all its cries,
> Of time-long hatred are beyond the main ...
>
> 'And, with fair peace's white, pure flag unfurled,
> Our children shall, upon this new-won shore –
> Warned by all sorrows that have gone before –
> Build up the glory of a grand New World.'

As was common, the poet depicts the flag as white, because this is the badge of peace and purity.

I think this stress on the nation's purity was the Australian response to the impure origins of the nation. You think we are polluted, the poets are saying to the world, but we are developing a nation that is superior to all others. The purity and the whiteness did not at first refer to race. This image was developed before Asian migration was taken to be a threat. It was not until the late 1880s that the nation-to-be was taking a racial form; the colonies first cooperated to limit Chinese migration in 1888. We can now better understand why that policy gets its name, White Australia, which first came into use in the 1890s. Whiteness was already established as a symbol of the nation; the purity of Australia was then distilled into a purity of race. Thereafter the slogan of White Australia carried all the hopes for the young nation: pure, progressive, enlightened.

Other nations excluded Asian immigrants but not under a slogan of the Australian type – a 'White New Zealand' or a 'White Canada' did not become the panoply of nationhood. Racial purity was more desperately sought and proclaimed in Australia. Around the world purity of race increasingly mattered, and on that test Australia could rate high; Australians boasted they were 99 per cent British, free of the mixture of other races. The insistence on this, the boastfulness about this, was the way to show the world that the convict stain was washed away. Except, of course, in racial thought blood went on counting; so in hitching Australia's destiny to a purity of race the Australians did not escape their origins – as Churchill's jibe about bad blood showed.

Purity of race is no longer a progressive cause, as it was in 1900, but democracy still is. In disowning the racism of White Australia, we can overlook that it advanced the cause of a more democratic Australia, in two senses. First, a racial identity obliterates the differences of class within the nation. All men are 'white men', a common bond of masculinity, which took on a moral dimension as a white man became one who was true-hearted, loyal, reliable. Secondly, racial exclusion had been demanded most vociferously by working people, their trade unions and the early Labor Party. Workers would be the ones to suffer most directly if cheap coloured labour became prevalent. The acceptance of their demand for the exclusion of Asians was a commitment from the nation to the dignity of labour and its proper reward.

Here is another speculative connection between convict shame and national history. The landing at Gallipoli has been honoured more and more fervently in recent years but the claim, made at the time, that the nation was born at Gallipoli is a puzzle to modern Australians. Did Gallipoli mean so much because it was a supreme test of Australian mateship? No. Did Australians honour it because they have a perverse delight in defeat? No. Gallipoli did make the nation because it freed Australia from the self-doubt about whether it had the mettle to be a proper nation. Australian soldiers had been put to the supreme test and they had come through magnificently. Landed at the wrong place, facing almost perpendicular cliffs, with the Turks firing on them from above, they got ashore and scrambled up and hung on. All the military experts proclaimed their success; the British, most importantly, praised them. Once that had happened the outcome of the venture, whether defeat or victory, did not matter. And what was the deepest source of self-doubt? The convict stain.

New Zealanders landed with the Australians but not in the first wave at dawn on 25 April. The feats of their soldiers led to a growth of national consciousness but no one ever said that the New Zealand nation was born at Gallipoli. New Zealand was not so desperate for the world's approval. Though a British colony with strong connections to its neighbours in Australia, she declined to join them in the Commonwealth in 1901, often giving spurious reasons for doing so because one of the strongest reasons could not, without giving offence, be mentioned: she did not want to join the *déclassé* Australians and be identified with their shame.

As the war progressed the Australian soldiers became more proficient and they played a large part in the final battles against Germany on the Western Front. The soldiers had cemented Australia's reputation before the world and Australia then had to accept its soldier, warts and all. Respectable people could be proud of him as a warrior for the empire; however, there were other aspects of his character – his refusal to show respect to officers, his tendency to larrikinism – which were harder to swallow but had now to be indulged. They became willy-nilly acceptable national characteristics because they were characteristics of the digger. Every Anzac Day both parts of the character were on display: the warrior in the formal celebrations in the morning; the drunk two-up player in the afternoon, when the police turned a blind eye so that the digger as larrikin could have free rein.

This is not Ward's account of how an anti-authoritarian attitude was accepted or tolerated by the nation at large. He claims that the attitude came from the outback workers and in the 1890s spread to the rest of the population, chiefly through the nationalist literature of Paterson and Lawson. In the long term this literature did have an influence but there were many people around 1900 not yet ready to embrace a shearer or a swagman as an iconic national figure. The bourgeoisie was more immediately and completely won over by the digger because he had suddenly made the nation and themselves respectable.

Ward explains that the nationalist literature had tidied up and ennobled the outback worker. The same thing also happened to the larrikin.

As the real larrikins were becoming less of a menace, C.J. Dennis published *The Songs of a Sentimental Bloke*, a series of verses about a larrikin who puts behind him the loutish behaviour of his push after he is smitten with love for Doreen. The book was an instant popular success when it was published in 1915. The larrikin had already been redeemed by love when his deeds in war put him in the pantheon. But the larrikinism still had a hard edge. Australian soldiers trashed and burnt the red-light district of Cairo, the Wazzir, before they left for Gallipoli. C.J. Dennis defended them in verse as innocents who had come from the 'cleanest land on earth', a claim that should not surprise.

It was part of their native carelessness; an' part their native skite;
Fer they kids themselves they know the Devil well,
'Aving met 'im, kind uv casu'l, on some wild Australian night –
Wine an' women at a secon'-rate 'otel.
But the Devil uv Australia 'e's a little woolly sheep
To the devils wot the desert children keep.

So they mooches round the drink-shops, an' the Wazzir took
    their eye,
An' they found old Pharoah's daughters pleasin' Janes;
An' they wouldn't be Australian 'less they give the game a fly ...
An' Egyp' smiled an' totted up 'is gains.
'E doped their drinks, an' breathed on them 'is aged evil breath ...
An' more than one woke up to long fer death.

When they wandered frum the newest an' the cleanest land on earth,
An' the filth uv ages met 'em, it was 'ard.
Fer there may be sin an' sorer in the country uv their birth;
But the dirt uv centuries ain't in the yard.
They was children, playin' wiv an asp, an' never fearin' it,
An' they took it very sore when they wus bit.

'Ave yeh seen a crowd uv fellers takin' chances on a game,
Crackin' 'ardy while they thought it on the square?

'Ave yeh 'eard their owl uv anguish when they tumbled to the same,
'Avin' found they wus the victims uv a snare?
It was jist that sort uv anger when they fell to Egyp's stunt;
An', remember, they wus trainin' fer the front.

Training for the front was the best of excuses but for a time the censor blocked publication of these verses. They did appear later in the war after the soldiers at the front had made the nation proud.

It was always something of a puzzle to observers of Australia to explain the high standing of working men and the prevalence of their values in the culture. The easy answer was to say the middle class was numerically weak. But in a capitalist society their values should be predominant whatever their numbers. So was it that they lacked the will to rule? I have suggested here that convict origins help to explain this puzzle. The bourgeoisie, sharing the shame of the nation, looked for respectability through White Australia and military prowess, and the forms these took had a strong proletarian cast; the working man was elevated by one and was the most notable embodiment of the other.

Australia has now emerged from the long era of repression about its origins. But it is still a distinctive nation because Australians are now *proud* of their convict ancestry. To find a convict ancestor is no longer a matter of shame but cause for celebration. This is a puzzle to the world at large, which thinks that slurs about ancestry will still hurt – witness the Barmy Army at the cricket who chant, 'You all come from a convict colony, a convict colony ...' Suppressed or embraced, convict origins must have an effect. At the very least a nation pleased about its convict ancestry cannot take itself too seriously.

Those who think that national character is an unnecessary, oppressive and dangerous contrivance will have found this whole discussion otiose. If you are tired of this old theme, read the poet Les Murray's treatment of it in 'Some Religious Stuff I Know About Australia' (in *The Quality of Sprawl*). Religion? And Australian national character? Yes. Murray suggests:

The ability to laugh at venerated things, and at awesome and deadly things, may, in time, prove to be one of Australia's great gifts to mankind. It is, at bottom, a spiritual laughter, a mirth that puts tragedy, futility and vanity alike in their place.

Murray finds the origins of this spiritual laughter in the underground traditions of working people's irony, of the poor who came to Australia from the old world. In line with the suggestions I have made above, he calls Australia a 'proletarian evolution'. But how does working-class irony become and remain a national attitude? It can happen in a nation which knows itself to be an oddity from the start.

2008

FROM SENTIMENTAL NATION TO DIVERSE DEMOCRACY

FEDERATION

Destiny and Identity

AUSTRALIANS KNOW LITTLE AND CARE LESS ABOUT THE origins of their nation. Historians have commonly encouraged them in this response by depicting federation as a business deal or a compact hammered out by hard-headed politicians looking after their own colonies. They find little here to inspire later generations.

This is a strange outcome because the people who devoted themselves to the creation of the federation regarded it as a holy or noble or sacred cause which would carry the people to a higher form of life.

Federation would supplant the mutual suspicion and hostility between the colonies with brotherhood, a widening of human sympathy which was the hallmark of moral progress. The petty and provincial concerns of colonial politics – the struggle over roads and bridges, the endless deputations to ministers begging favours – would be replaced by a politics that dealt with a national life and the fate of a whole people.

Federation itself – the means by which Australia was to become a nation – wore a progressive air. It represented so clearly a stage in social evolution from simple to complex forms. It was by federation that men envisioned that the British empire, the Anglo-Saxon race, the English-speaking peoples and finally the world, would be united. Tennyson, the poet laureate, sang of 'the parliament of man, the Federation of the world'.

In looking for the motives for Australian federation, historians usually are far too instrumental in their thinking. The Commonwealth government was given power over various subjects and the puzzle of why federation occurred is reduced to ranking these in order of importance. Was federation chiefly to secure a customs union, or a united immigration policy, or a national defence? To federalists none of these things was sacred; the whole forty-two powers given to the Commonwealth did not together make federation sacred. It was the making of the nation, apart from anything it might do, which was sacred.

Because federation was a sacred cause, poetry was considered the most appropriate medium to express its rationale and purposes. It was poetry's role to deal with what was noble, profound, and elevating. There are innumerable federation poems by hundreds of different hands. The nation was born in a festival of poetry. Historians have noticed the poems, but haven't quite known what to do with them. Most of them are valueless as poetry. One leading scholar who produced a bibliography of federation sources decided that it would be kinder to his readers to leave it all out. He thus removed from consideration the best guide to the ideas and ideals which inspired the movement. You are not to be spared, but I will be very selective in my quotations.

The poets considered that God or destiny intended Australia to be a nation. The evidence for this was in the first place physical. They forgot Tasmania (which was inconsiderate since it was always keen about federation) and saw the nation-to-be as a single geographical unit, a whole continent with only natural boundaries. This was a special benediction. Other nations had man-made frontiers; Australia's were the sea. A common word for the sea in this role was 'girdle' and in its verbal form 'girdled' or 'girdling' or 'girt'. 'Advance Australia Fair', written by Peter McCormick in 1878 and now the national anthem, uses 'girt' and assumes the implications of the sea boundary do not have to be spelled out, recording merely 'our home is girt by sea'.

The social uniformity within the continent also marked out Australia for nationhood. The people were of one blood or stock or race; they spoke the same language; they shared a glorious heritage (Britain's), the most celebrated part of which was political freedom which had been extended in Australia to all men so that the country was the freest on earth.

The best federation poem, written very early (1877), does not argue that Australia should be one, but assumes it and deals instead with the ideal becoming real. It is the most powerful expression of the idea that union was Australia's destiny. The author was James Brunton Stephens, a headmaster at a Brisbane state school.

His federation poem was called 'The Dominion of Australia: A Forecast':

> She is not yet; but he whose ear
> Thrills to that finer atmosphere
> Where footfalls of appointed things,
>   Reverberant of days to be,
> Are heard in forecast echoings
>   Like wave-beats from a viewless sea,
> Hears in the voiceful tremors of the sky
> Auroral heralds whispering, 'She is nigh'.

The middle part of the poem develops an elaborate comparison between the silent force carrying Australia to its destiny and the underground rivers which some experts assumed must run under the parched lands of the outback and which one day might be released to make the desert bloom:

> So flows beneath our good and ill
> A viewless stream of Common Will,
> A gathering force, a present might,
>   That from its silent depths of gloom
> At Wisdom's voice shall leap to light
>   And hide our barren feuds in bloom,
> Till, all our sundering lines with love o'ergrown,
> Our bounds shall be the girdling seas alone.

When Henry Parkes opened his campaign for federation in his famous speech at Tenterfield, he quoted from this poem. He did well to quote from Stephens' poetry rather than his own. At the time he launched his campaign he was revising the proofs of his next book of poems, *Fragmentary Thoughts*. In the preface he said with his usual mock humility that he would be happy to be judged no great poet, but lest anyone dare to make that judgment he reproduced a letter from his friend Lord Tennyson which praised his efforts, how guardedly Parkes probably did not notice.

In Brisbane a few days before his Tenterfield speech, he had refused to disclose his federal plans to the *Courier*'s reporter but had been very willing to discuss poetry. He passed the proofs of his poems to the journalist for his opinion. He declared Stephens to be the best poet in Australia, a compliment Stephens returned in his review of *Fragmentary Thoughts* which contrived to be favourable without pronouncing definitely on the quality of the poems.

In his new collection Parkes rehearsed a standard theme in 'The Flag':

God girdled our majestic isle
    With seas far-reaching east and west,
That man might live beneath this smile
    In peace and freedom ever blest.

He was a much better phrase-maker in his speeches.

As federation became a firm proposal, it met opposition as well as the old indifference. The poets identified the forces which frustrated it as selfishness, greed, and faction, by which they meant a sinister political combination. Men were damaging the union already created by God. The symbols of this divisiveness were the customs houses on the colonial borders, which were hated not as a commercial inconvenience, but as a moral outrage. So to reveal the Australian nation, men had to repent and return to God. In a Christian culture this was a powerful theme. It was best expressed by William Gay in his sonnet 'Federation' written in the early 1890s:

From all division let our land be free,
    For God has made her one: complete she lies
    Within the unbroken circle of the skies,
And round her indivisible the sea
Breaks on her single shore; while only we,
    Her foster children, bound with sacred ties
    Of one dear blood, one storied enterprise,
Are negligent of her integrity. –
Her seamless garment, at great Mammon's nod,

> With hands unfilial we have basely rent,
>
> With petty variance our souls are spent,
>
> And ancient kinship under foot is trod:
>
> O let us rise, united, penitent,
>
> And be one people, – mighty, serving God!

Deakin quoted Gay's sonnet to conclude his great speech that launched the 'Yes' case in Victoria in 1898.

According to the poets, the prospects for the new nation were unrivalled. Australia had no ancient feuds, no privileged caste, no bar to anyone making money from its abundant resources; a land of freedom and opportunity. Always imagined as female, Australia was young, pure, virginal. The themes are present in 'Advance Australia Fair', though again rather minimally. Australians are young and free; the land is rich in opportunities – golden soil – which are open to those ready to work: wealth for toil.

There was a constant insistence that no blood had been spilt in this land. This is a puzzle to us who are now so conscious of the violence done to the Aborigines. In part the claim could be made because the slaughter was simply being forgotten, though the forgetfulness was more complete in the early twentieth century than in the nineteenth. It was possible to know well enough what had happened on the frontier and still see Australia as pure. In *Fragmentary Thoughts* Parkes wrote of the Australian flag: 'It bears no stain of blood and tears./ Its glory is its purity.' In the same volume is a poem that gives a chilling account of the murder of an Aboriginal boy by settlers on the Hawkesbury in 1794. He was tied hand and foot, dragged through a fire until his back was horribly burnt, and then thrown into the river and shot:

> Loud talk ye of savages
>
> As they were beasts of prey! –
>
> But men of English birth have done
>
> More savage things than they

The two thoughts remain unconnected. It was easy not to make the connection when Aborigines were not seen as part of the future nation since they were dying out and in any case unworthy of its citizenship. Furthermore, when they spoke of no blood spilt, the poets had in mind the European experience of warfare ravaging the land and being constantly renewed.

The best poem on Australia as a new world free from all the ills of the old was written by John Farrell. He was a brewer turned journalist and poet. In the late 1880s he was editor of and chief contributor to a radical Sydney newspaper which supported land nationalisation along the lines of Henry George's single tax:

> We have no records of a by-gone shame,
> > No red-writ histories of woe to weep:
> > God set our land in summer seas asleep
> Till His fair morning for her waking came.
> He hid her where the rage of Old World wars
> > Might never break upon her virgin rest:
> > He sent His softest winds to fan her breast,
> And canopied her night with low-hung stars.
> He wrought her perfect, in a happy clime,
> > And held her worthiest, and bade her wait
> > Serene on her lone couch inviolate
> The heightened manhood of a later time.

The sexual theme was never more explicit. The men worthy to take Australia, the 'manful pioneers', only leave Europe when freedom has dawned there:

> They found a gracious amplitude of soil,
> > Unsown with memories, like poison weeds,
> > Of far-forefathers wrongs and vengeful deeds,
> Where was no crown, save that of earnest toil.
> They reared a sunnier England, where the pain
> > Of bitter yesterdays might not arise:

They said – 'The past is past, and all its cries,
Of time-long hatred are beyond the main ...
And, with fair peace's white, pure flag unfurled,
   Our children shall, upon this new-won shore –
   Warned by all sorrows that have gone before –
Build up the glory of a grand New World.

The new Commonwealth did not seem designed to build up a grand new world since it was to have limited powers. In the 1890s Australia was gaining a reputation for progressive social and economic legislation, but this was and would remain chiefly the responsibility of the states. Only at the last minute was the Commonwealth given power over old-age pensions and interstate industrial disputes.

It was in the name of the federation that the delegates most clearly expressed their sense that Australia represented a new dispensation. The name 'Commonwealth' was suggested by Parkes at the 1891 convention and was taken up enthusiastically by Deakin who lobbied the delegates on its behalf. After being narrowly adopted by the convention's constitutional committee, it won general acceptance in the convention and outside it because it embodied an Australian view of the nature of government. The state existed not to aggrandise an elite or to embark on conquest, but to serve the common weal, the common good. It was this view of government which was to make the Commonwealth much larger than its formal powers implied.

The entry which won the New South Wales government prize for a poem celebrating the inauguration of the Commonwealth deals with its name. These are its best lines; the poet was George Essex Evans:

Free-born of Nations, Virgin white,
   Not won by blood nor ringed with steel,
Thy throne is on a loftier height,
   Deep-rooted in the Commonweal!

On 1 January 1901, and for the days before and after, the newspapers gave over a large part of their space to poetry. There was Evans' prize-winning poem; a new poem by Brunton Stephens whose 1877 work was now very well known; and the words of the anthem sung at the inauguration which had been written by John Farrell who had celebrated Australia as a grand new world.

These poets are now almost entirely forgotten. The poets of the turn of the century who are remembered, honoured and read are Banjo Paterson and Henry Lawson. They have helped to define the Australian nation. They were newcomers in the 1890s. The critics, while acknowledging the appeal of their work, regarded it as light, ephemeral verse. Paterson's poems had sold in the thousands, but would anyone keep the book on their shelves? He lacked the nobility, the profundity, and moral elevation thought proper to poetry. Brunton Stephens was generous about Paterson's achievement, but could not believe that poems about racecourses and backblocks life would endure. He regarded William Gay as the true, new poet of the 1890s. Evans conceded that Paterson was a master of the bush ballad, but thought Stephens would always be acknowledged as the founder of the national literature. Of course, no-one in the 1890s ever imagined that a whole nation could come to treasure a Paterson poem about a Snowy River horseman and a Paterson song about a sheep-stealing swagman.

Historians examining what part nationalism played in the creation of federation find it hard to imagine the founding fathers reciting 'The Man from Snowy River' and assume that nationalism's role was small. They overlook the whole school of nationalist poetry which flourished from the 1870s, whose leading practitioners were in a double sense the established poets of their time. Their reputation stood high and they were encouraged and supported by leading colonial politicians who became founding fathers of the Commonwealth. When Griffith took to translating Dante he sent his efforts to Brunton Stephens and Essex Evans for their professional criticism. The flier advertising Gay's book of sonnets carried endorsements from Parkes, Barton, and Deakin. When Gay produced a book of essays on federation he attracted contributions from Deakin, Inglis Clark, and Griffith.

The nationalism of these poets was a civic nationalism, concerned with the state and the principles and values it should protect and advance;

its symbol was female, a young virginal goddess in the classical tradition. The nationalism that grew from Paterson's verse was social and masculine, concerned to honour men of the outback and their values. It was the civic nationalism, now lost to sight, which inspired the federation movement. It was dignified, earnest, Protestant, not raffish, Irish-Catholic or working-class.

I don't think I can talk safely for much longer about the idealism that underlay the movement to federation. You hard-headed realistic Australians will want to know what was the true driving force of the movement. It can't be poetry.

Australian historians who doubt the force of national feeling in federation have looked to economics to reveal the selfish motive behind it. They overlook the motive that is quintessentially selfish and integral to nationalism, the desire for identity and status. As the Italian patriot Mazzini declared: '... without a country you have no name, no identity, no voice, no rights, no membership in the brotherhood of nations.'

The federalist who was most revealing about this was Samuel Griffith, the chief draftsman of the Constitution. Griffith came to Australia as a boy of eight. His father was a Congregational minister who gave his bright son a good education, hoping he would follow him into the ministry. But Griffith would not be bound by his parents' narrow puritanism. His ambition was to become pre-eminent in the law, rich, and famous. There was no open rupture with his parents; the young man kept his exploits with women and drink secret and outwardly conformed. He took to drinking when he was at university in Sydney; at home in Brisbane during vacations he went with his parents to teetotal meetings. From the start there was something unruffled in his progress. Until his father died he attended the Congregational Church and then he switched to the Anglican. Religion did not mean much to him. He invested far more in the masonic lodge, whose codes he studied as assiduously as the law and where his advancement was equally rapid.

He was a man of principle, a legal philosopher in politics who could not rouse a crowd, but could argue a case from first principles. He pursued his personal ambition in politics with the same rectitude, as if he were taking only what was his due. As premier he directed the government's legal business to himself and brought his political career to an end in 1893 by getting himself appointed Chief Justice, but only after Parliament had increased the salary.

He liked the trappings as well as the substance of success. At twenty-one he designed the coat of arms that he hoped would be his; at forty-one he secured it when he was made a Knight of the Order of St Michael and St George. One of the jobs of Queensland's Agent-General in London was to lobby the Colonial Office for honours for Premier Griffith. After gaining his knighthood, Griffith wanted to be promoted to Knight of the Grand Cross. Once he was Chief Justice, he set his sights on being in addition Lieutenant-Governor. On formal occasions he delighted in wearing all his badges and ribbons. He was always well dressed; a tall, spare, dignified figure.

On great occasions, when Griffith was called on to detail the advantages of federation, he spoke, quite uncharacteristically, in a personal and heartfelt way. He said, 'I am tired of being treated as a colonial.' Even when the English were being considerate, he continued, they could not hide their disparagement of the colonist. In the eyes of the world, Australians were nothing but children while they remained as colonies. As a nation, they would meet the rest of the world as equals and the status of every Australian would be raised.

As premier of Queensland, Griffith was well aware of the difficulties involved in inter-colonial co-operation and the advantages union would bring. He was a conscientious administrator. Yet at the deepest level, he wanted federation not so that public affairs might be handled differently, but so that he might be someone different. His assiduous application and lobbying for honours could not prevail against one barrier: there would have to be an Australian nation before Samuel Griffith ceased to be a colonial.

Griffith wanted to constitute an independent Australian nation which would remain in the empire, but without being subordinate to Britain; the only link to Britain would be the crown. Britain would be an equal and an ally and all the people of the empire would share a common citizenship. This was the arrangement not formally achieved until the passage of the Statute of Westminster in 1931. Legally, Griffith could not produce that outcome in 1901, but he had it in mind as he drew up the Constitution. When Australia became independent, the Constitution did not have to be changed.

Griffith took great satisfaction from the fact that immediately the Commonwealth was established the colonies were to be reconstituted as its states. So the word *colony*, the badge of inferiority, would no longer be used by Australians talking of themselves, nor, Griffith hoped, by other people, particularly the English, in talking about Australia and its people. In England *colonial* meant second-rate or at least suspect.

Australians laboured under a double handicap because *Australian colonist* also suggested 'convict', or the descendant of convicts, or the associate of convicts and their descendants. The Australian rule was not to talk about the convicts – unless to insult New South Wales in intercolonial feuding – but Australians knew that the world had not forgotten. They were very anxious to find and parade signs that the stock had not degenerated despite this taint. Victories over England at cricket were very comforting.

Australians were annoyed and sometimes angry at British disdain, but they could not easily reject or ignore Britain. Most of them admired Britain and its civilisation and wanted British interest and approval. By the late nineteenth century there was more British interest in the colonies than thirty or forty years before when the colonies were widely viewed as an encumbrance, but old attitudes persisted. Simple ignorance abounded. People in Britain did not know the names of the various colonies or their location. Letters arrived with bizarre addresses: 'Melbourne, near Sydney, Victoria'. Visitors to England were asked where they learnt to speak English.

In the 1880s the leading colonial politicians, among them Samuel Griffith, were brought into a new relationship with British ministers and officials as they sought to influence the empire's defence and foreign policies. The men who were accustomed to govern their own societies were cast into the role of lobbyists and petitioners at the metropolis. Frequently they found it a frustrating and humiliating experience. They felt themselves very much the colonials. 'We are children,' said Griffith, 'dependent on a superior people.' They thought the British did not care enough for them. If their submissions were rejected, their first response was to assume it was because they and the people they represented were mere colonists.

The leading politicians gave as one of the advantages of federation that the colonies would speak with one voice and more notice would be taken of them as a nation. Britain would no longer ignore them. Australians would benefit from this increased stature and strength, but so in a very particular way would they as their representatives and spokesmen. They would cease to be colonial politicians. They might be Australian statesmen. It was notable that the founding fathers, having declared that they must limit Commonwealth power and keep the states strong, immediately transferred to the Commonwealth on its inauguration.

The man who hoped to lead the new nation as prime minister was Henry Parkes, an intention clearly indicated by the frequency with which he disclaimed it. He was the best-known politician in Australia and the only Australian politician well known in Britain, but he still knew the hurt of being colonial. It was part of his success as a politician that he could fuse his own pursuit of a greater glory with the emancipation of a whole people. In the series of speeches with which he launched his campaign for federation he promised to remove humiliation and slight and bring dignity and pride:

> Instead of a confusion of names and geographical divisions, which so perplexes many people at a distance, we shall be Australians, and a people with 7000 miles of coast, more than 2,000,000 square miles of land, with 4,000,000 of population, and shall present ourselves to the world as 'Australia'.
>
> We shall at once rise to a higher level; we shall occupy a larger place in the contemplation of mankind, the sympathies of every part of the world will go out to us, and figuratively, they will hold out the right hand of fellowship. We can not doubt that the chord awakened by such a movement will be responded to in the noble old country where our forefathers' graves are still. All England has awakened with sympathy to this movement through its press.
>
> We shall have a higher stature before the world. We shall have a grander name. These are the desires that make nations.

The committed federalist leaders – Parkes, Deakin, Griffith, Barton, Inglis Clark and others – were pursuing a sacred ideal of nationhood. They can be thought of as both selfish and pure. Selfish, in that the chief force driving them was the new identity and greater stature they would enjoy – either as colonists or natives – from Australia's nationhood. Pure, in that the benefit they sought did not depend on the particular form federation took. In a sense any federation would do. They knew of course that interests had to be conciliated and other ideals not outraged; they shared some of these themselves. But they were not mere managers or lobbyists; underneath all the negotiation and campaigning there was an emotional drive. Those who only considered economic and provincial interests when they contemplated federation understood this quality in the federalists. They called them federation-at-any-price men, enthusiasts, or sentimentalists.

It might be objected that these enthusiasts were only a minority. Sometimes the test for the role of national feeling in federation has been how widespread it was. So relatively low turnouts for the choosing of convention delegates and at the referendums have been used to indicate that national feeling played a small part in federation. But the role of national feeling is not to be measured by taking the pulse of the community at large. Nationalism has always possessed one section of the population first – whether poets or intellectuals or a new middle class or local officials of an empire. They become passionate for the nation while the mass of the people remain attached to their chiefs, villages, or provinces and can see no benefit in creating a new government. Nationalism in its creative phase is a minority movement.

The practical people, the hard-headed men, saw no need for federation. If the colonies needed to take more joint action, let them co-operate more closely. If the border customs houses were a nuisance, let a customs union be formed. It was the nationalists who wanted a nation and it is to them we owe our federation.

2001

Why Did the Colonies Federate?

When I was a university student, historians commonly looked to economic forces to explain events. It is that view of federation that I have been contesting. Now historians are very interested in race and national identity. This has led to the claim that the chief purpose of federation was to establish the White Australia policy.

At first glance, this claim has a lot going for it. The first substantial measure the new federal parliament passed was the *Immigration Restriction Act*, which was the legislative basis for the White Australia policy. In supporting the measure, Alfred Deakin, the attorney-general and deputy prime minister, asserted that the chief motive for federation was the desire of the Australian people, acting together through a national government, to protect their racial purity. These were his words:

> No motive power operated more universally on this continent or in the beautiful island of Tasmania, and certainly no motive power operated more powerfully in dissolving the technical and arbitrary political divisions which previously separated us than did the desire that we should be one people and remain one people without the admixture of other races.

Deakin was well placed to speak about the federation campaign because he had devoted himself to it throughout the 1890s. He led the campaign in Victoria. The only other man who had done more for the cause was Edmund Barton, who led the campaign in New South Wales. Deakin is an attractive character. He was a profound scholar of the religions of the world; he sought nothing for himself out of public life; he was free of the cruder forms of race prejudice; he was the best of the enlightened progressive liberals who made the Commonwealth. He was also a clever politician, and these eloquent words turn out to be totally misleading.

This is the conclusion reached by Ron Norris, who subjected this claim of Deakin to very close scrutiny in his book *The Emergent Commonwealth*. Norris looked first at the conferences and conventions which were responsible for the writing of the constitution. At none of these meetings was immigration an important issue. Amid all the arguments advanced for why the colonies should federate, control of immigration simply did not rate. The new Commonwealth was to have power over immigration, but even here there was no sense that this was a matter crying out for national attention. In the 1891 constitution the Commonwealth was to have exclusive power over immigration; in 1897–98 the states and the Commonwealth were both to have power. The founders were envisaging that immigration could go on being a matter controlled by the states; only later would Commonwealth action be necessary.

In the referendum campaigns, extravagant claims and extravagant fears were peddled. Again, the need for national action on immigration did not rate. During the campaign, a Chinese hawker in South Australia was discovered to have leprosy. There was an outcry about this, but no one used the case to show that a national government was needed to take strong action against the Chinese.

The reason for this almost total lack of interest is obvious. The colonies had each passed more or less uniform laws against the Chinese in 1888, which went close to prohibiting Chinese immigration. Some colonies had widened the net in the 1890s and moved against the Indians and Japanese as well, using the device of a dictation test, which was the method used by the Commonwealth in 1901. The problem of Asian immigration had already been solved.

Had it not been solved, it is difficult to imagine that the Chinese would have been allowed to take such a prominent part in the federal celebrations in Melbourne in May 1901. The Chinese merchants of Little Bourke Street put up an arch and used it to get the street decorations extended to their quarter. Two days before the opening of the new federal parliament, 200,000 people watched a Chinese procession pass through the city streets.

So why the swift action against Chinese and other Asian immigration as soon as the parliament assembled?

The ministers who were sworn in on 1 January 1901 had to declare a policy on the vexed issue of the tariff. This was a pressing matter. The inter-colonial trade barriers could come down only when the Commonwealth established what uniform duties were to be collected at the ports. Barton's government was protectionist, but for the first election it declared for only moderate protection. The opposition leader, George Reid, was campaigning for free trade.

The tariff was divisive and tricky. The new government wanted to go to the people with a popular rallying cry, and in particular with something on which it could compete successfully with the Labor Party, the new third party, which was neutral on the tariff. Workingmen and their unions had always been in the forefront of the demand for a White Australia, and the Labor Party had a White Australia at the top of its platform.

This explains why the Barton government went to the people at the first federal election promising to legislate for a White Australia. The results of the election pushed it to honour that promise. Protectionists and free-traders were close to equal in their parliamentary strength. The balance of power would be held by the Labor Party. Some of their members were protectionists, some free-traders – but all would support a government which was legislating for a White Australia.

The government had to pretend it was responding to some real need on the immigration front. It called for figures on the level of Asian immigration. Ten persons had invaded South Australia since 1899; 133 had swarmed into the Northern Territory, but 151 had left; and 304 Japanese had descended into Queensland since 1898, but 864 had left. Though clearly there was no pressing need, the defining of the nation by the composition of its people made a fitting opening to the Commonwealth's career.

Much more decisive in ensuring a White Australia was the government's decision to phase out the use of Pacific Islanders as indentured labourers on the Queensland cane fields. This was announced by Barton in his policy speech and became the chief issue in the federal election in Queensland. The system had been a matter of contention in Queensland for years. It had been marked down for extinction and then reprieved. Labor in Queensland was fiercely opposed to it but had no influence, since a grand coalition of all Labor's opponents ruled the colony.

The sugar planters had supported federation, since it would open an Australia-wide market for their sugar, but had hoped that any move against their labour force would be delayed. Barton's immediate move against it outraged them and the Queensland government. The last labourers were to be returned to their islands by 1906. The Commonwealth placed a duty on imported sugar to protect the industry, and an excise was placed on local production, which would be lifted if the planter used white labour. It was a great victory for White Australia when it turned out that white labour on award wages could grow sugar in the tropics.

The origins of the term 'White Australia' are obscure. It was certainly coined in the context of an immigration policy directed against Asians. But from our previous discussion of the national poetry, it should be clear why White Australia was such an effective slogan: it caught the pure and virginal themes already present in the national ideal.

The Chinese were seen as a threat to this. Their blood was not British blood. They were inevitably going to be treated as inferiors and, hence, introduce a caste barrier into Australian society and rob it of social harmony. The Chinese would take work at low wages and threaten the high standard of living of the working class. The anti-Chinese agitation popularised the national ideal and gave it, of course, a much stronger racial element. White was not merely a symbol; it was the colour of the citizens' skins.

Let us return to Deakin. If we think of federation instrumentally, as an arrangement designed to achieve certain objects, then we will say that the desire to exclude the Chinese had little to do with it. But if we think of federation as the realisation of a national ideal, then the exclusion of the Chinese is very definitely part of the story. The agitation against the Chinese gave new power and cogency to the ideal of a pure, pristine, unsullied, united Australia. And that ideal led the federalists onwards. They did want to 'be one people and remain one people without the admixture of other races'.

2016

BOXING AND HONOUR

WHEN ALBERT FACEY WAS WORKING ON THE CONSTRUCtion of the Wickepin–Merredin railway, he challenged his foreman to fight because the foreman had cast a slur on his mother. He had called Facey a bastard, literally an illegitimate person, the child of a woman who was not married. Facey had no great love for his mother but he would not stand to hear her respectability questioned. He had a magnificent victory over the foreman who was a well-known bully. The fight was the talking point among the gang for weeks.

It was generally believed that a man should be able to look after himself, which was why fighting amongst boys was half encouraged. In using fists for fighting, Australians were carrying on a British tradition. The British thought fist fighting was a much more open, direct and manly way of settling differences than, say, using knives which some European people did. In Australia the men who regularly settled their disputes by fighting were construction workers, shearers, timber workers, men who worked and lived with other men, particularly in the country and outback.

Until the middle of the nineteenth century gentlemen in Australia and in England had used a highly regulated form of violence to settle their differences: the duel with pistols. With the end of duelling, gentlemen had to be content with 'cutting' their enemies in the streets (refusing to acknowledge them) or voting to keep them out of their clubs. But as the duel disappeared from the highest ranks, some of its features reappeared in the fist fights of working men. Quite frequently, like the gentlemen, they were fighting for their honour. Facey certainly was. Protecting your own honour involved also protecting the honour of those with whom you were closely connected – men fought to defend the reputation of family members, girlfriends, and their mates. Bullockies fought to protect the good name of their beasts.

As in duelling, the insult or the offensive behaviour did not lead directly to the fighting. One party proceeded to call the other a name which could not be allowed to pass without dishonour – with the gentlemen the most common, offensive word had been 'liar'. The term for this process which led to the final challenge and its acceptance was 'calling out'. In Lawson's story 'Telling Mrs Baker' Ned Baker went to the pub which employed the barmaid who had lured his brother to destruction and 'called the landlord out'. This does not mean he called him out to fight; he called him names which forced the landlord to fight. The challenge to honour went to the heart of a man's integrity. To keep self-respect and the respect of others, he had to fight.

If Facey had lost the fight with the foreman, his mother's honour and his own would still have been upheld. What had to be demonstrated was that he had been prepared to put himself at risk and, if need be, take a hiding. So fights settled disputes not only by establishing who was in the right – that would have occurred only if might was always on the side of right. They settled them in the sense of ending them. After the fight the two men were meant to shake hands and so acknowledge that the other was a worthy person, one of the brotherhood of real men. It was common for two young men to fight over a girl and after the fight to be best of friends. The fight was not to determine who should have the girl. It was to put an end to the accusation that one man had stolen the girl from the other.

There were clearly advantages, or temptations, in being a good fighter – you could stand over and insult other men. Either they would not dare to fight you or they could be easily beaten if they did. But might did not prevail in quite so straightforward a fashion. Firstly, a man who used his fighting ability to dominate others acquired the reputation of a bully. Once someone was discovered who could beat him, that loss destroyed him. Secondly, a man who was not a particularly good fighter might be protected by someone who was. 'This bloke's a mate of mine, anyone who touches him has to deal with me.' Or, 'Are you calling my mate a liar?' Henry Lawson's brother Charlie, a regular truant and the despair of his parents, was always wanting to fight on behalf of Henry, who refused to fight because he thought it was wrong. Thirdly, if a fight was too one-sided, someone else might challenge the winner so that he would not have things too easy.

At the annual picnic and sports day at Box Ridge in western New South Wales, fighting, or the threat of it, was handled so that right would prevail. There were no police in the town and the citizens themselves kept order. If anyone looked like causing trouble, he was surrounded by twelve men and given the option of behaving or fighting any one of them. If he beat him, he would have to fight another and so on until he had beaten all twelve. Since the odds were stacked so heavily against the disturber of peace, there was usually no trouble at the picnics. But why didn't the twelve men simply threaten to run the offender out of the picnic ground or out of town? They did not want to claim any unusual authority: this was the man-to-man way of carrying out the general will. True to the code of honour, they were willing to expose themselves to danger to preserve the picnic.

Men challenged and fought because they thought it was manly to do so; what they were fighting for was to be treated, as they would say, as men – not to be insulted or pushed around. Of course most of them had to work for other people and obey their orders – and bosses would not usually accept a challenge to a fist fight. Working men could live with this so long as the boss was a fair, straight-dealing man, that is, his 'bossness' should be the only barrier between them. Being a boss should not be an excuse to be superior or rude or arbitrary. Bosses who understood this did best.

Aside from everything else, fights were part of the sporting life of the country and outback. The cry of 'Fight' at a shearing shed or the tents of a construction site brought a crowd to watch, barrack and bet. Before organised team sports were established, individual tests of skill and strength were the only sport. Nearly all men were doing hard physical work and there was no clear line between work and sport. The sporting contests were work under different names. Men who worked with an axe clearing land entered log chopping competitions at the agricultural shows. Wheat lumpers at the railway station stacks issued challenges to beat their record feats. When travelling was by foot or on horseback, men were always in training for foot races and horse races. Shearing was simultaneously work and sporting contest. The scoreboard showing the number of sheep shorn by each shearer was updated daily and 'to ring the shed' – to shear the most sheep – brought the sort of fame which only sporting heroes enjoyed. The sporting records of the shearing game – the ringers and the best daily tallies – were carried in the heads of all the players.

Even when organised sport came to the country it could not at first sustain a regular round of competition. There would be a town cricket and football team which would play teams from other centres by arrangement. At the opening of the 1907 season, the captain/coach of the Narrogin football club met many of the players for the first time. The local paper reported that there were some good individual performances, but teamwork was lacking. At a later match in the same season the paper regretted that it could not give a detailed account of the play because the teams did not have uniforms and it was impossible to learn the names of all the players. A few years later Facey joined the Wickepin team on the day of its match against Narrogin and learnt the rules during the first half of the game.

Team sports could only be well established as travel became easier and people had more leisure in common for practice and play. A log chopping competition could be staged without allowing time for practice, or learning rules, and without uniforms. Until World War I individual contests had bigger followings and aroused more interest in the country than team sports.

Boxing came to the country in an organised way in the 1890s, when travelling boxing shows would set up at the agricultural shows. The promoters put on exhibition matches and encouraged local young men to try out against the pros. They were delighted when locals fought to settle a difference in their ring. The success of the show depended on local participation and if this was slow in coming, it was helped along by one of the pros pretending to be a local. The boxing tents connected the everyday world of fighting with the big time, because a local who did well might be recruited for the show and from there could go on to fight in the Sydney and Melbourne stadiums. Fighters whose days at the stadium were over ended their careers in the boxing tents. It was a hard routine, fighting every day and packing up and moving on at night.

Facey complained that he never got enough sleep when he was travelling with Mickey Flynn's boxing troupe. He'd been recruited after he had beaten their heavyweight champion at the Narrogin Show.

During Facey's boyhood and youth, boxing as an organised sport of championships and prize fights had a great revival. For most of the nineteenth century it had been illegal to stage a prize fight. The law regarded the fighters as doing each other grievous bodily harm and the rules of boxing certainly allowed a great deal of harm to be done. Men fought with bare fists for an unlimited number of rounds. A round ended when one man fell. The fight ended when one man could fight no more. Seconds and backers did not let the fighter decide when this was; they propped up exhausted men to keep their chances alive.

Prize fighting went on despite the law. It was connected with pubs, bookmakers and fight-fixers and had a largely disreputable following. Only those in the know could attend prize fights because the location had to be kept secret. Fooling and dodging the police was part of the fun of attending. In 1879 in Victoria news of an impending big fight became so well known that the two fighters were taken to court and bound over to keep the peace. The fighters and spectators then went to Echuca and, eluding the police, staged the fight on the north bank of the Murray in New South Wales. Legend has it that Ned Kelly, on the run from police, was one of those to congratulate the winner. Kelly himself was a notable boxer, having become champion of north-east Victoria by beating Wild Wright in twenty rounds. The bare-knuckle boxing era in Australia ended in 1884 when a fighter died in Sydney just after he left the ring, which was a circle of spectators in the scrub. His opponent was convicted of manslaughter and sentenced to twelve months' hard labour.

Prize fighting revived with the adoption of the Marquess of Queensberry rules, which had been drawn up in London in 1867. The marquess lent his name to the rules to give them more chance of being adopted. He wanted to rescue prize fighting from seediness and secrecy and restore its reputation as a noble and manly sport. The new rules required the fighters to wear padded gloves. Rounds were limited to three minutes and the number of rounds in a fight were to be fixed at no more than twenty. A fighter who was knocked down was given ten seconds to be back on his feet or he lost the fight. Previously when a fighter was knocked down, the round ended and he had thirty seconds, the gap between rounds, to recover. The new rules made fighting a test of skill and not simply of endurance. They took some time to gain acceptance because old fighting men regarded them as sissy.

The first championship fight in Australia under the new rules was held in a Melbourne hall in 1884. From then on, boxing grew rapidly in popularity and respectability. The championship fight between Burns and Johnson in Sydney in 1908 drew a crowd of fifty thousand, as many as went to the Melbourne Cup or the Victorian football final. Just as on Cup Day, crowds gathered outside newspaper offices and post offices around the country to hear the outcome by telegraph. Two months after the event a traveller came upon two contract clearers in the bush in Western Australia and the first thing they wanted to know was who had won the fight. Facey extended his tour of the east to take in Sydney so that he could see it. He was one of the lucky twenty thousand who got inside the stadium; thirty thousand remained outside.

The Marquess of Queensberry rules had some influence on the fights among working men. They still fought with bare fists, but the three-minute round was generally adopted and there was great stress on fair play. The Marquess of Queensberry rules reaffirmed the ban on hitting an opponent who was down (which dated from 1743), on kicking, gouging, biting and hitting below the waist (which dated from 1838), and added a prohibition on wrestling.

The new acceptability of boxing allowed police to turn a blind eye to properly conducted fights and even to encourage them as an alternative to roughhouse brawling. At Barcaldine in Queensland the sergeant of police himself conducted the fights which were held on Sunday mornings in the stock yard. Harold Lewis, the author of *Crow on a Barbed Wire Fence*, fought there in 1913. He was only nineteen and the man he had challenged was a seasoned fighter. His mate Ted was worried that he would get badly hurt and asked the policeman if he knew that under the Marquess of Queensberry rules a fight had to be stopped when a fighter clearly could not win. The policeman replied: 'I am the Marquess of Queensberry around these parts.'

Not everyone would accept that boxing was now a legitimate sport. The wowsers – the group of Christians who were having such success in closing pubs – demanded that the governments ban prize fighting. They made great efforts to stop the Burns–Johnson fight. In this campaign they made no headway. When they condemned governments for allowing crowds to gather to cheer violence and bloodletting, governments replied that boxing was taught in Christian boys' clubs like the YMCA and the Boys' Brigade. Some priests and ministers did the teaching themselves. The Reverend Hulton Sams, championship boxer from England, preached to shearers in the backblocks of Queensland and in the next instance stripped off his minister's robes and offered to go a few rounds with any takers. On one occasion he refereed an amateur boxing match at Longreach in Queensland with the Catholic priest as timekeeper. When one of his decisions was greeted with boos, he shut up the protesters by offering to fight them.

Boxing appealed to those Christians who wanted to get rid of the idea that a Christian was a milksop and that religion was only for women and children. They wanted Christian men to be strong and manly and ready to use fists or rifles in a good cause. Their version of Christianity was given the nickname 'muscular Christianity'. Manliness was its central idea which meant physical strength and clean, wholesome living. Boxing seemed to them, and to all its other defenders, an excellent, manly sport because it required great physical fitness and great self-control – a man had to accept punishment but still fight fair. Manliness became such a shared ideal that even the opponents of prize fights said they were fully in favour of it. They said they had no objection to boxing as such; prize fighting was something different because men fought for money and crowds wanted viciousness and knockout blows and not just a fine sporting display.

The desire to foster manliness strengthened as the nation became more concerned with defence. The opponents of prize fights were criticised as traitors – they were hindering the development of the very qualities that Australia would need to survive. While the wowsers were denouncing blood lust and violence in the boxing stadiums, both political parties had decided that there must be compulsory military training for all young men, and this was introduced in 1911. Australians were preparing to meet the threat from Japan, which had conquered a European power, Russia, in 1905.

It was a common belief that a nation was not truly formed until men had died in its defence. There had to be a baptism of blood. Thereafter nations had to behave like men of honour, ready to spill their blood rather than accept insult or disgrace. Australia had not yet faced its trial. When the colonies had federated in 1901 Australians were fighting in South Africa against the Boers, and for some this was blooding enough. But doubts about whether Australia had what it took remained; just how strong they were was revealed by the relief and ecstasy which greeted the Australians landing at Gallipoli.

In the twenty years before World War I, as nations hastened to arm themselves, some people thought that the big, decisive battle would not be between nations, but between races. Europeans knew they were the superior race, but there were more black, brown and yellow people in the world than white and when they harnessed their resources they might be formidable. The victory of Japan over Russia made the fantasy of race war into a real fear. For Australia, a tiny nation insisting that it must be white in the face of the teeming populations of Asia, the decisive battle looked very much like being a race war.

These concerns help to explain why there was such an interest in the Burns–Johnson fight in 1908, for this was a white–black contest. Johnson was an American negro, the coloured champion who, like other blacks, had not previously been allowed to enter championship bouts against the master race. Burns was a white man from Canada who was defending his world championship. The two fighters genuinely hated each other. Johnson was quick footed and brutal in the game of words which preceded the fight and outclassed the white man. This clever, well-read black man, who was a musician as well as a fighter, gave no sign of recognising that he belonged to an inferior race. The Australian public, disgusted by his flashiness, was desperate for Burns to win to uphold the prestige of the white race.

Johnson nearly knocked Burns out in the first round of the fight and was never troubled by him. He fought not to win but to humiliate Burns.

He taunted him and took time off to talk to the crowd. His seconds told him to watch Burns and not the crowd: 'I see him, oh yes, though he is so small.' When he decided to finish Burns off, the punishment was brutal. The fight was stopped in the fourteenth round. There were a few cheers from the winner but most of the crowd were stunned and silent.

It was hard for white people to find any comfort in the result. They could tell themselves that negroes were closer to the apes and hence had tougher physical frames, but boxing, as its defenders always insisted, required also intelligence and skill. They could say that Burns, though smaller and outclassed, had fought on bravely and so had upheld the honour of the white race – but in a war of races, whites wanted to win.

Facey does not mention that the fight was a contest between black and white. He was disappointed by it, but not because the black man won. He was disgusted because both fighters were nasty and spiteful: 'It wasn't sport at all.'

1992

MAKING VOTING COMPULSORY

I N DEMOCRACIES THE PEOPLE ARE SOVEREIGN; THEY CREATE the government that is to rule them. That is the theory. In Australia that has not been the practice. The people in their sovereign power do not create governments; the people are forced to take part in the creation of governments. From 1911 it was compulsory to enrol for federal elections. From 1924 it was compulsory to vote in federal elections.

Compulsory voting is firmly enforced. Those who don't vote are asked for an explanation. If it is unsatisfactory, they are fined. If they are unable or unwilling to pay the fine, they are sent to gaol for one or two days. After the 1993 federal election, forty-one people were sent to gaol.

The first Commonwealth elections in 1901 were conducted on the franchise of the different states, using the state electoral rolls. A uniform Commonwealth franchise was set in 1902. It included votes for women (at that stage law in only two of the states) and in other respects was more generous than state law. The electoral rolls of the states clearly could not be used for the next Commonwealth election. The Commonwealth had to create its own.

The new Commonwealth law did not make enrolment to vote compulsory, but the government was worried that too few people would enrol. It was anxious to get the people involved in their new Commonwealth. The government decided itself to enrol the people. The prime minister got the agreement of the state premiers for the police to be used for the job. Over several months in 1903, policemen went from house to house, to every house in the island continent, collecting names for the first Commonwealth electoral roll.

To use the police for this job was not unusual in Australia. The police were the only officers of the colonial governments who were located in every district. Those omni-competent governments turned the police into omni-competent administrators. They collected statistics, inspected dairies, checked on school attendance, and buried paupers. In some states they had also collected names for the electoral rolls.

The police did a good job. But of course they missed some people. The lists went on public display and if your name had been missed you could apply to be included. Few bothered to check; people assumed that it was the job of the police to secure them the vote. On election day there were always some people complaining that they had been denied the vote because their name was not on the roll.

The mistakes were not simply due to the police. The lists were re-done every year, but before they had been collected and printed thousands of people had moved house. The population was very mobile. Much of the work in the country was seasonal and in the cities a large proportion of the population moved house every year.

The electoral office wanted to make people responsible for reporting changes in their address. It recommended that enrolment become compulsory. The Labor government of Andrew Fisher passed a law for compulsory enrolment in 1911.

To get the new system started the police were called in again. They visited every house and got each elector to fill in an electoral card with their personal details. The cards were now to form the master roll. When electors moved house, they had to send in a new card. If they did not do so, they were to be fined.

But how would the electoral office know if people had moved house? They appointed spies. In cities and towns they were the postmen; in the countryside the police. They sent regular reports of comings and goings to the electoral office. They also distributed electoral cards to newcomers on their beat and encouraged them to send them in. When the electoral office got reports from their spies, it checked to see if newcomers had sent in their card. If they had not, they were asked to explain why. If they did not offer a good excuse, the electoral officer fined them. In 1923, 27,000 people were fined; in 1924, 38,000.

Once government had taken the responsibility of enrolling the people, it was only a small step to force the people to supply the information to make the government's records as accurate as possible. It was only another small step from compulsory enrolment to compulsory voting.

In 1911 several politicians were ready to take it. They asked what the point was of getting everyone on the roll if they did not bother to vote. If parliament was ready to force people to do their civic duty as regards enrolment, why not force them to perform the higher duty of voting?

In Australia no new matter of principle was involved in moving from compulsory enrolment to compulsory voting. It was said again and again that the second was the 'natural corollary' of the first.

So the idea of compelling people to vote was born. Its birth was not related to changes in the proportion of people voting. Compulsion was discussed as an option in the federal parliament in 1911. At the 1910 federal election, the proportion of people voting had jumped to 62 per cent from 51 per cent in 1906 and 50 per cent in 1903. People thinking about this issue were not focusing on changing turn-out figures, but on the huge numbers of citizens who, if left to themselves, would never enrol or vote.

The idea of compulsion was born in Australia. It was not copied from anywhere else. There were a few European countries that had attempted compulsion in the nineteenth century, but these were not the spur to action. There was, and is still, no precedent for compulsory voting in the English-speaking countries with which Australia usually identifies itself.

The idea was generated in minds that accepted a commanding role for government. Government could produce a near-perfect electoral roll and it could complete the job by engineering a near-perfect turn out. Governments could do anything – even make apathetic men and women into citizens.

Compulsory voting was adopted first in Queensland for state elections. In 1914 the Liberal government in Queensland faced almost certain defeat at the 1915 elections. Labor looked set to win a majority of seats for the first time. The Liberals considered that one of their disadvantages was that Labor was better at getting its supporters to the polling booths. It decided to make its supporters turn out in equal force by making voting compulsory. Again, this move was not related to overall turn-out figures. At the previous election 75 per cent of the people had voted, a quite respectable figure, and the best for state elections around that time.

Labor in Queensland did not oppose the introduction of compulsory voting. It went on to win the 1915 election, which made it think quite well of it. Compulsory voting quickly became part of Labor's national platform. Just at the time the two political parties were becoming divided over military conscription, they were coming to an agreement that voting at elections should be compulsory. The advantage to the parties of compulsory voting was that they would not have to spend money and effort in getting people to the polls. 'Getting out the vote' would become the government's business.

At the 1922 federal election the turn-out fell to 58 per cent after being above 70 per cent for the previous four elections. The Nationalist government was returned and took no action on compulsory voting. In June 1924 at the Victorian state election the turn-out was only 50 per cent and the Labor Party for the first time became the largest party in the parliament. This was more worrying for the Nationalists. A week later Senator Payne, a Nationalist backbencher, introduced a bill for compulsory voting into the federal parliament.

The backbencher was not acting alone. The parliamentary Nationalist party supported the move. The government, however, did not want to take responsibility for the change. It reached an agreement with the Labor Party that compulsion would pass rapidly through the parliament as a private member's bill.

In introducing the bill, Senator Payne spoke of compulsion making Australia more democratic. If democratic government was meant to represent the people, it would be improved by representing all the people: 'We must force those who live under that form of government to see that it is democratic, not only in name, but in deed.' There was very little discussion. No leading members of the government or Opposition took part. Only one member spoke strongly against the measure as a denial of liberty. No votes were recorded; the bill passed both houses on the voices. It took only fifty-two minutes in the House of Representatives and eighty-six minutes in the Senate for compulsory voting to become law.

Australian voters accepted compulsion and turn-out figures rose to above 90 per cent. Compulsory voting was adopted for state elections in Victoria in 1926, in New South Wales and Tasmania in 1928, in Western Australia in 1936, and South Australia in 1942.

At the first federal elections held under the compulsory voting law, a Mr Judd refused to vote because as a socialist he could not support any of the candidates, who were all capitalists. The High Court held this was not a valid excuse and that he had to pay his fine. All such excuses have been rejected by the courts. Objectors have been told they have to vote even if they do not prefer one candidate over another and even if they don't know enough about the candidates to distinguish between them.

The defenders of compulsory voting dismiss these protests as 'grandstanding'. Though the law declares that voting is compulsory, all that can be enforced is attendance at the polling booth and the acceptance of a ballot paper. No one has to vote against their principles or conscience.

In the 1990s there was a movement within the Liberal Party against compulsory voting. It was now commonly accepted that the poor were the least likely to vote if voting were voluntary and so compulsory voting aided the Labor Party. In 1993 the Liberal Party of South Australia won an election with voluntary voting in its platform. It introduced a bill for voluntary voting but it was defeated in the Legislative Council by the Labor Party and the Democrats.

The Liberal Party was by no means united on this issue. In the 1990s a Liberal government in Victoria, controlling both houses, made no move against compulsion. Under voluntary voting there is the possibility that the Liberal Party might do better, but the certainty is that it would have to spend much more money on elections in order to get out its vote. Public funding for elections is made on the basis of the number of votes a party secures. Unless those rules were changed, voluntary voting would give the parties less government funding.

There is no broader movement against compulsion. Opinion polls record that over 70 per cent of the people are in favour of compulsion. If all those people voted voluntarily that would be a respectable turn-out. However, compulsion remains not because there is convincing evidence that Australians would not vote under a voluntary system, but because it suits the interests of the parties. The parties are fortunate to have a compliant electorate. The Australian people want to be compelled to vote.

Those who write and comment on politics are overwhelmingly in favour of compulsion. In defending compulsion, they make a distinctively Australian contribution to political philosophy.

They argue that with compulsion governments have to pay attention to the interests of everyone and particularly of the poor, which they could ignore under voluntary voting. They claim that to move to voluntary voting would 'disenfranchise' the poor. This is amazing double-speak. To allow people the freedom to vote or not would be to take the vote from them!

The writers and commentators are scathing about the low turn-out for American presidential elections and boast that in Australia governments have greater legitimacy because all the people take part in their creation. They do not think their case is weakened because the people are compelled to take part.

To the objection that compulsory voting is a denial of liberty, they argue that governments regularly make citizens do things: serve on juries, pay taxes, fight in the defence of the country. Of course governments compel citizens, but compulsory voting relates to another issue altogether: how governments themselves are created. Are citizens to be forced to create governments?

These arguments have been developed in a society where the value placed on personal liberty and the responsibilities of citizenship has shifted markedly from that in other English-speaking democracies. The existence of government is taken for granted and the people can be forced to be citizens.

2002

LABOR'S PART IN AUSTRALIAN HISTORY: A LAMENT

T HANK YOU FOR YOUR WELCOME. I AM VERY CONSCIOUS OF the honour the national university has bestowed in making me the Allan Martin lecturer for this year.

For most of my life I have voted for the Labor Party and I may do so again. I have voted for the Labor Party, but I do not have the instincts of a proper Labor man. I do not think that Labor parliamentarians should be compelled to vote as caucus directs; I do not believe that Billy Hughes who left the Labor Party in World War I and Joseph Lyons who left it in the Great Depression were, as the party called them, rats; I think the Labor Party's elevation of anti-conscription into a shibboleth was damaging not only to the party but to the nation.

Tonight I will be lamenting these aspects of Labor's career. You may think that lamenting is not the proper business of a historian – should we not explain what happened and not waste time on regrets? If you think this, let me say that I have an excellent precedent in the proper Labor people who have written histories of their party and who have wasted a lot of time on endorsement and praise. If you think, rightly, that is a cheap shot, then consider my lecture of lament as a way of establishing more precisely what Labor has in fact done to this polity.

I am continuing a theme begun by my revered supervisor and professor, Allan Martin. The most influential paper he wrote was an attack on the place that Labor had been accorded in Australia's history by the academic historians. It was entirely characteristic of Allan that he refused to allow this paper to be published. In the 1960s it circulated in manuscript copied and recopied on that shiny, slimy and unstable paper the first photocopiers used. I saw and devoured a copy as a post-graduate student in Adelaide. The paper was in Allan's words a 'thinks' piece and this probably explains why he did not want it published. It did not meet his rigorous standards of demonstration and proof. I am offering you a 'thinks' piece this evening. If we upheld Allan's standards, it would never be published.

Allan's paper contested the claim that Labor was the first real political party in Australia; that it was responsible for every good thing that happened in Australian politics after its formation in 1891; and that it alone was the vehicle for the realisation of Australia's progressive destiny. Allan urged historians to climb down from this metaphysics and allow (in his words) 'humanity and purpose to people unfortunate enough not to belong to the chosen race' – a rare note of sarcasm in his cool prose. I'm not so niggardly in my own writing. Nor would Allan accept the view that Labor's success was the result of the working class being large and the middle class, small.

Much of his own academic work was devoted to elaborating and validating the claims made in this subversive paper. He was the first to understand the inwardness – one of his favourite words – of the politics before parties in New South Wales. What he called faction politics operated from about 1860 to the 1880s. Then the system began to break down and parties began to emerge, the protectionist party and the free-trade or liberal party, which were operating when Labor appeared on the scene in 1891. That put paid to Labor as the first party. Allan made a close study of the reforming free-trade government of George Reid in the 1890s. Reid relied on Labor support but that maestro was far from being a creature of the Labor party and his reform agenda was his own. With his colleague Peter Loveday, Allan directed a major work on the emergence of the party system in Australia from 1890 to 1910. In these years Labor was one party in a system of three and this study was interested in establishing among other things how much influence it had – even to ask this question was to subvert the claim that Labor was solely responsible for the progressive legislation of this era.

Because of this work, academic historians can no longer write about the Labor Party as they once did. On the whole their sympathies are still with the left, but academics along with everyone else now find it hard to invest the Labor Party with a special virtue and any sort of pre-eminence.

There are still true believers in the party itself. Graham Freudenberg, who wrote speeches for Labor leaders Calwell, Whitlam and Hawke, has written: 'More than any other political party in the world, the Australian Labor Party reflects and represents the character of the nation which produced it.' The same sentiment was expressed by Paul Keating, whose speeches were not written by Freudenberg: 'We are the people who make Australian history. We are the ones who nominate the heroes, we anoint the heroes of Australia, our party sets the ethos of Australia.'

Freudenberg also wrote the official history of the Labor Party in New South Wales to celebrate its centenary in 1991. He identified his subject as an indigenous Australian institution, a response to Australian conditions, in the most profound sense native born. He then notices that most of its founders were British born, that the intellectual influences operating on it were Henry George and Edward Bellamy, Fabianism and socialism. George and Bellamy were Americans; Fabianism was English; socialism was European. A true native product! Freudenberg should have acknowledged, which few scholars still do, that the very notion of a labour party was British. Britain provided the models and inspiration for the craft unions that operated in Australia from the 1850s, for the new unions of the unskilled in the 1880s, and for unions creating a labour party in the early 1890s. In a dependent, loyal colony, Britain was the legitimator of working men entering politics on their own account.

In Britain the Labour Party was an institution of the industrial cities of Scotland and the north of England and grew fairly slowly outside its heartland. In Australia there was not a large industrial working class on which to base a working-class party – and yet the Labor Party grew much more rapidly here than in Britain. It made a spectacular debut in New South Wales in 1891, winning thirty-five seats out of 141, a quarter of the assembly, and immediately held the balance of power. It became the model for the parties in South Australia, Queensland and Victoria, which did well, but not this well. By 1910 there were Labor governments holding a majority of seats in the parliaments of New South Wales, South Australia and in the Commonwealth; by 1911 in Western Australia; by 1915 in Queensland. Labour in Britain did not have a majority in the House of Commons until 1945.

How is this phenomenal success to be explained? Paradoxically the class party from Britain flourished here because class mattered less. In Britain the Labour Party was and was seen to be the party of the working class, a group quite rigidly separated geographically, in status and style of life from the rest of the population. In Australia there was not this sharp break between workers and the rest, that terrible abyss which haunted the minds of the English lower-middle class. In Australia the working class and a good deal of the middle class sent their children to the same state schools, were members of the same friendly societies and the same mechanics institutes. In Australia the workers were more self-confident and respectable; the bourgeoisie less cultivated and fearful. So long as Labor had policies that appealed to them, there was less to inhibit those outside the ranks of the unions and manual workers from supporting the party. Labour in Britain was the party of the working class; in Australia the party of those who worked, and on this basis could be persuasively presented as both a class and a national party. Most importantly Labor could attract the votes of those who worked harder than the working man – the small farmer. Getting his vote widened Labor's geographical reach and enabled it to build majority support across the electorate. Here I am following in Allan's footsteps and explaining Labor success without having to posit a large, assertive working class.

In New South Wales, where the party had its great initial success, there were other factors working in its favour. Though, as Allan demonstrated, the free-trade and protectionist parties preceded Labor, they did not predate it by much. Politically conscious working people were supporters of either protection or free trade, but they had not had time to become rusted-on supporters of the free-trade or protectionist parties. We know how hard it is to change old political allegiances. In Britain Labour struggled against the workers' attachment to the Liberal Party, which had long supported causes dear to working people. In Victoria and in New Zealand, Labor support grew slowly because radical Liberal parties had won the trust and allegiance of working people.

The parliaments in the Australian colonies were rough-houses compared with the parliament at Westminster and of all the Australian parliaments that of New South Wales had the lowest reputation. Since manhood suffrage was introduced in the 1850s, disreputable men had gained seats and parliamentary proceedings lost their gentlemanly tone. Respect for parliament evaporated very quickly. In the Supreme Court in Sydney in 1861, the chief justice at the top of society and a criminal at the bottom shared a joke at the politicians' expense. The criminal was being tried for escaping from gaol. Before the case began, he asked that he be given another judge because it was the same chief justice who had given him the harsh sentence that put him in gaol in the first place. The criminal said the chief justice might have 'prejudicial feelings' against him. The judge, thinking he had said 'political feelings', replied, 'Why should I have political feelings against you. Are you a member of parliament?' To which the criminal replied, 'Not yet.'

The 1880s were the heyday of drunks and demagogues in the New South Wales assembly. In a *Bulletin* cartoon from this time, a man in a bowler hat approaches a man sitting on a park bench who is dressed in top hat and tails.

'Excuse me,' says the first man. 'Are you a member of parliament?'

'Certainly not,' replies the man in the top hat. 'I am a gentleman.'

Thus it was impossible to say in Sydney that working men had not the breeding or the learning to enter the parliament. That was a place where all the old standards had already been flouted. The respectable tradesmen whom Labor selected for parliamentary seats, many of them teetotallers, were a cut above the sort of popular candidate who had been elected previously.

I have been explaining why a British institution flourished in a new setting. The Labor Party did so well, so quickly that you can see why Graham Freudenberg was tempted into calling it an indigenous movement. So where is the lamentation? It begins now. With rapid success came high expectations, then disappointment and anger, crisis and disruption. As Labor resolved its crises it adopted policies and practices which, in my view, still have a baleful effect on the polity. I will discuss the consequences of the first two crises: the split in the early Labor Party of New South Wales, and the split in the federal party over conscription in 1916.

The first crisis produced Labor's unique discipline: the control of the parliamentary party by the movement outside and the control of individual parliamentarians by the caucus. This was the system developed in New South Wales within two years of the party's formation. The times were unique. In 1890 the trade unions, after growing rapidly and scoring notable victories, stumbled into a general strike and were defeated. Trade unionists were appalled at the government assisting employers by protecting non-union or scab labour. Humiliation for organised workers and governments openly wielding force against them was not meant to happen here. There was briefly among the working class that galvanising anger that comes from a sense of betrayal. The unionists were now determined to form their own party, a project they had been toying with for some time, and with its outstanding success expected that it would immediately make a difference.

After its first election Labor held the balance of power. Holding the balance of power, of course, does not give all power. How much power depends on the state of the whole game. If the third party is divided by an issue which separates the other two; or if its demands are opposed by the two majors, then its power will not be substantial. The Labor members faced both these problems. They were themselves divided over free trade and protection, the issue that produced the two-party divide. The old hands in the parliament soon used this to embarrass and confound the newcomers. Labor tried to fix the problem by declaring that free trade and protection should be decided by the people at referendum. But then in 1892 the protectionist government of George Dibbs prosecuted the leaders of a bitter strike at Broken Hill; the men were found guilty and were imprisoned. There was no indication that the free-trade party would have acted more benignly but the labour movement demanded that its parliamentarians join with the free-trade Opposition to vote Dibbs out. Some members refused because Dibbs was a protectionist, the doctrine they favoured. This was too much for the organisation. The government was locking up its union brothers and its parliamentary party could not stop or punish the perpetrators. The labour movement virtually started its political party again with the distinctive tight discipline. It called the new body the Solidarity Labor Party. Those who would not accept its rules left the party or were thrown out. This New South Wales system was slowly adopted by the Labor parties in the other colonies and immediately by the federal party on the inauguration of the Commonwealth.

Other labour parties have carried into politics the principle of solidarity, which unions had learnt was essential for success in a strike. The Australian party carried solidarity to an extreme. Its principle is fundamentally at odds with the notion of parliament as a deliberative assembly with members responsible to their electorates. But it is no surprise that early Labor had no respect for parliamentary tradition since these newcomers suddenly seemed able to control parliament for their own purposes and the parliament in question was that of New South Wales, which had already debased itself.

In the short term the tight discipline did benefit the party when it was one player among three, but in the long term it was a disaster for the party. When divisions were strong within the party, the discipline did not hold it together but forced the contenders asunder. Three times the federal party split – in World War I over conscription, in 1931 over how to cope with the Depression, and in the 1950s over communism. After each split the party took a long time to recover, which explains why the party which allegedly embodies the Australian ethos ruled Australia so infrequently.

With each split the party came to believe more firmly in the necessity and virtue of solidarity so that Labor seemed sometimes to believe more strongly in solidarity than in its program. With each split the organisation came to distrust politicians more, though its aim continued to be the production of politicians. Thus it was constantly seeking new ways to control, marginalise and humiliate its own representatives.

The party faithful and its faithful historians do not question the benefits of Labor's discipline. They never link the unique discipline of this Labor Party with its unique tendency to split. In their eyes the splits are evidence of the necessity of the discipline; it has led to the uncovering of so many traitors.

According to Labor lore the people who have been thrown out or left the party are rats who deserted to the conservatives. This is wrong on two counts. First, there has not been a conservative party in Australia for the rats to join. It is a conceit of the Labor Party that all who are opposed to it are conservative. Second, the rats did not join any pre-existing organ-isation. Billy Hughes and the other supporters of conscription formed a National Labor government, which governed briefly on its own with Liberal support and then merged with the Liberals to form the Nation-alists, with Hughes remaining as prime minister. Lyons, the treasurer in the Labor government during the Depression, became the leader of a new body, the United Australia Party. The anti-communists who left in 1955 became the Democratic Labor Party. There are some rats that not even the Labor faithful can describe as deserting to the conservatives – most notably those in the Depression who supported the plan of Jack Lang, premier of New South Wales, not to pay interest to British bondholders.

It is in the treatment of Hughes, the prime rat, that the Labor faith-ful perpetrate the grossest distortions. In the governments that Hughes led after the split, he promised that no part of the Labor edifice would be touched; he declared in fact that he was still a Labor man. He had not left the party; the party had left him. While Nationalist prime minister he created new government-owned enterprises, Amalgamated Wireless and the Commonwealth Oil Refineries. He even managed to persuade the Nationalists to put to the people a constitutional referendum to give the Commonwealth power over monopolies. Labor opposed it because it did not go far enough and the measure was lost. Hughes lost the prime ministership in part because his new colleagues thought that he was still too much the socialist. And they were not mistaken. In 1919, as National-ist prime minister, Hughes declared he was still a socialist.

What Labor's distorted view of Hughes reveals is its unwillingness to face the truth: that its discipline has driven out of its ranks genuine social democrats. Labor believed much too readily that if you were not within its ranks you must be with the capitalists. A looser discipline might not have prevented the split in World War I but it might have avoided the other two. It would more certainly have led to a party that kept more of its talent and attracted more talent to it. As it was, the social democratic cause in this country was led not so much by a party as by a tribe, fratri-cidal within and hostile to everyone without.

Remember this is a history lecture. I am not talking about today's party. I don't know how to talk about today's party. I am still in mourning over the loss of Qantas and the Commonwealth Bank.

Labor's opponents envied the efficiency of the Labor machine and its ability to mobilise thousands of volunteer workers at elections. They were still operating under the old system of having to pay their campaign workers in money or in kind. But they were genuinely appalled at Labor's exacting of a pledge from its candidates to vote as the majority of the caucus directed. They used this practice relentlessly in the electorate to attack Labor, but seemingly with little effect since Labor's vote continued to rise. In the early Commonwealth, Deakin, the leader of the radical Liberals, governed with Labor support. This was the continuation of the alliance between middle-class reformers and working people, which had been standard in Victoria. Deakin could agree with most of Labor's immediate objectives but he could not agree to take the Labor pledge, which would bind him to its platform and the caucus view of how he should vote on every issue. He had to think of whether he could join the Labor Party, because he himself thought that for good government the three-party system would have to be reduced to two, and his party was the smallest and shrinking under the Labor advance. The Labor movement outside did not like to see its parliamentarians cooperating with any other groups, and since Labor looked set to win a majority of seats, it did not have to worry about Deakin's scruples. Deakin finally had no alternative but to merge his radical Liberals with the free-trade party and present a united opposition to Labor.

This fusion occurred in 1909. It made Deakin prime minister, with his old allies the Labor members on the Opposition benches, and behind him his former free-trade opponents. Just after the fusion was accomplished the first speaker of the House of Representatives, Frederick Holder, died. He had been an independent speaker in the Westminster style, dissociating himself from the parties and with the parties agreeing not to run candidates against him in his electorate. The way to continue this practice was to allow all members a voice in the selection of the next speaker. Deakin as prime minister would not risk this. He was afraid that Labor would caucus and produce a block vote for its candidate. Instead he called a caucus of his supporters and the candidate they chose was installed as speaker. Labor members had a high old time denouncing

Deakin's rule by caucus. The Labor leader Andrew Fisher offered a free vote if Deakin would allow the same. Deakin pushed on with his candidate. It was not one of his great moments.

That was the end of the independent speakership. Speakers thereafter always came from the governing party; they changed when governments changed. Speakers made little attempt to hold themselves aloof from the party battle. Labor speakers always and Liberal speakers sometimes actually attended party meetings, where tactics in the House were discussed. In the 1990s Leo McLeay ran Keating's campaign to unseat Hawke while occupying the speaker's chair. In no other Westminster-style polity has the speakership been so debased.

This was the first case of Labor's opponents imitating Labor's discipline. Plainly if the Labor ranks were highly disciplined, non-Labor could not afford to allow too much leeway to their own members. Nevertheless, for a long time Labor's opponents continued to present themselves as the defenders of parliamentary government as against the Labor machine, which regarded parliament simply as the body to implement the Labor platform. This was an important distinction for Menzies and the Liberal Party he founded. Don Chipp gives a touching account of the trepidation with which he approached Menzies to tell him that he could not vote for a government measure and finding the old man quite relaxed and indulgent. Nowadays, though Liberals are not pledged to vote with the party, defections are very rare. Both major parties are committed to showing no division among their ranks. Neither wants the floor of the House to be the place where decisions are made. This does not mean of course that backbenchers are without influence; they may oddly have more influence because leaders are desperate for rebellion not to be officially registered.

Party discipline now controls Question Time. Backbenchers of the governing party no longer use this opportunity to prod and rebuke their own ministers. Grown-up people read out questions written for them, which are designed to allow ministers to boast of their achievements and to rubbish the Opposition. Question Time is a party battle. This is not Question Time as I remember first hearing it. I checked on this by taking down the 1959 Hansard and opening it at random. I was looking at Question Time of 10 March 1959. I was then sixteen and Menzies was prime minister. The Liberal backbencher Malcolm Fraser asked a Liberal minister whether it was true that wool was to be replaced by synthetics in the manufacture of army uniforms and blankets. The Liberal backbencher James Killen asked a minister whether he had the power to prevent the export of koala bears. Mr Riordan, a Labor member, asked the minister of territories whether it was true that a widow in the Northern Territory was being prevented from mining on her own freehold land. Clyde Cameron, later a Labor minister, asked Prime Minister Menzies quite unaggressively whether he had followed up his (Cameron's) suggestion that Aborigines residing on mission stations should receive the benefit of social service legislation in the same way as other people. I had remembered correctly – a general probing of the administration from both sides of the House.

There is a view that the unusually tight discipline in both Australian parties reflects something of the Australian character and, in particular, the low standing of its politicians and an instrumental approach to politics. John Howard considers that division is death in Australian politics and one hesitates on such a matter to question the judgment of a prime minister who has won four general elections. I am blaming Labor for the move to unusually tight party discipline on both sides. Howard does not; he seems simply to regard it as a necessity. Perhaps Australians now do see political parties as sporting teams whose members should all be kicking in the one direction. They see stability in government as requiring unanimity in the party. They might not be able to imagine a system in which a party supports a government but the party members not in the cabinet query and vote against measures that the cabinet brings to the parliament.

This is the system that operates in the mother of parliaments at Westminster. It is a matter of regular report that a government's majority on this or that measure dropped as its supporters absented themselves or voted on the other side or that a measure was carried only with Opposition support. The House of Commons still matters in a way that the House of Representatives does not. Voting on the other side is not described in Britain or anywhere else as far as I can see as 'crossing the floor'. That is the term reserved for *joining* the party on the other side. In Australia we are so unused to people voting against their party that we use a term for it that elsewhere means a complete switch of party allegiance.

Imagine a Labor government in Australia taking the country to war with a third of the party voting against the war in parliament and the decision being upheld by the vote of the Opposition. Impossible. That shows how far our polity now differs from Britain's, where Tony Blair took the country to war against Iraq in this fashion.

Australia had a Labor government at the time of the first Gulf War. Bob Hawke was keen to support the war but faced strong opposition from his left wing. He spent hours arguing with them. These divisions were not aired in the parliament. He did not need their support or their votes because the Opposition supported the war but he wanted to preserve Labor unity. Only after the war had begun was there a full debate in parliament. In his memoirs Hawke very revealingly says he *allowed* a debate. I was incensed at this and then I found in the debate that one of the left dissenters *thanked* the prime minister for facilitating a debate. Clearly neither the prime minister nor his critic thought that parliamentary sanction was essential for the upholding of the decision to go to war. Barry Jones, that awkward conscience of the party, pointed out that the House of Commons and the American Congress had their debates *before* the decision for war was taken. The left dissenters spoke against the war in the House but they did not vote against it.

The government sent two naval frigates to the war. The left extracted a promise from the prime minister that this would be the limit of the commitment and that there would be 'No Conscription'. In 1991 the issue that had torn the party apart in 1916 still mattered. I now go back to the second great crisis in Labor's history and its consequences.

The issue on which the party split in 1916 was conscription for service overseas, that is, for service on the Western Front in France; but the deeper cause was the dissatisfaction of radical trade unionists with the parliamentarians and the Labor governments they had run. Again it was dissatisfaction with seeming success that caused the crisis.

The trade unions had founded the party but soon after they almost faded away, broken by losses in strikes and severe economic depression. That left the parliamentarians in charge and they shaped the program that brought Labor's outstanding electoral success. In the early twentieth century the unions began to grow again as prosperity returned and as they were given official encouragement under the new arbitration system. The new generation of union leaders was contemptuous of the sobriety and caution of the Labor governments and of the concessions that the parliamentarians had made to win the support of the farmers and the small local branches in suburbs and country towns. They had the warrant of Labor's name for wanting the party to be based on the working class and to deliver more to the working class. They developed the view, which has been poisonous in Australian Labor, that the Labor program was not immediately and fully implemented because the politicians preferred the comfortable and quiet life. That view successfully blocked the thought that the Australian people might not want the Labor program to be immediately and fully implemented.

The tension in the party was reaching breaking point when Labor returned to office just on the outbreak of war. In the second year of the war Billy Hughes became prime minister and in 1916 he decided that conscription was necessary to reinforce the Australian troops. At this point the movement outside took its stand against the politicians. The Labor platform allowed for compulsory military training of boys and young men, a policy that Hughes had championed and Labor had implemented in office, but it was silent on the issue of conscription for overseas service. However, the organisation resolved against conscription for overseas service and made it plain that any politician who supported this measure would be punished. Hughes failed to shift them from this position so he decided to appeal over the heads of the organisation and to put the issue to the people at referendum. The Australian people voted narrowly against conscription, a great victory for the Labor machine-men, which they took to indicate that the time for a true Labor Party was dawning. They expelled Hughes and all the pro-conscription politicians from the party. But then Hughes, leading his new party, the Nationalists, had a landslide win against Labor in the general election of 1917 on the cry that he was determined to win the war and Labor was not. This was the first landslide against Labor. Never again did the party look, as it did before the war, to be on the brink of taking command of Australian society.

Among the anti-conscriptionists in the union movement, some were opposed to the war; more had doubts about the war and Labor's support for it. Who can blame them? The slaughter was appalling and of all the things the Labor Party was formed to do, no one had envisaged that it would be sending thousands of young men to fight and die for the British empire in Europe. The war put huge strains on all governments. On a Labor government it was immense. It was Labor's ill fate in Australia to have peaked too soon. The labour parties in Britain and in New Zealand were divided over the war but these divisions were not fatal because they were not running the war.

In the referendum campaign, opposition to the war or even doubts about it could not be mentioned; there was still general support for the war and a Labor government was prosecuting it. An argument had to be developed that made conscription wrong even for a war you supported and even when a mass mobilisation was required. The anti-conscriptionists developed the argument that conscription was an invasion of human rights; in no circumstances could a government compel a person to fight and kill. By the end of the war Labor had fully internalised this argument and wrote it into its platform. Conscription for overseas service was already wrong; conscription for training now became wrong; conscription for the defence of Australia was wrong. Even on the invasion of Australia the government should do no more than call for volunteers.

I need hardly point to the contradiction of the Labor Party adopting this extreme libertarian position. The people who believed in compulsory unionism and the nationalising of industry became the great advocates of individual freedom when the survival of the country was at stake. Solidarity in strikes but not against an invader!

Because of Labor's opposition to conscription, social democracy and soldiering became separated in World War I. Hughes told the anti-conscriptionists to stick with him and see the war through and then Australia would be at Labor's feet. That could not be. We see a hint of what might have been on the first Anzac Day. Hughes, the umbrella repairer now Labor prime minister, celebrated with the king and queen at Westminster Abbey. George Pearce, a former carpenter, the Labor minister of defence who had organised the army for Gallipoli, led the celebrations in Melbourne, the capital. By the next Anzac Day Hughes was leader of a Nationalist government and his standing as the 'Little Digger' brought votes to Labor's opponents.

In Australia, alone of all the major combatants in World War I, the government did not mobilise its population to fight. It called for volunteers and went on calling for volunteers ever more shrilly until the war ended. Conscription of course would have silenced the recruiting drum and stopped the circulation of white feathers. Since Australia's soldiers had volunteered to serve they had a greater claim on the nation. The Returned and Services League became a power in the land, more supportive of the Nationalists than of Labor. Labor complained about the RSL, but it was its own anti-conscription victory that had given the RSL its status. Labor's win against conscription also bequeathed to the nation the great bitterness between those who had served and those who had not.

Labor's policy after the war was to keep its distance from the empire and its European entanglements and concentrate on the defence of Australian territory. The policy of anti-conscription had been developed to limit involvement in the empire's wars, but if Labor was no longer to rely on the empire, why would it hobble Australia's own defence effort with the principle of no conscription? But it is futile to consider anti-conscription as a policy relating to defence. It had long since ceased to be that. It became instead the test of the genuine Labor man; the issue that had unmasked all those Labor rats.

Reality broke in upon the party with the outbreak of World War II. It accepted that there could be compulsory training and conscription into the militia for the defence of Australian territory, but on no conscription for overseas service Labor would never yield. Once the enemy overseas was no longer in Europe but instead occupying the islands to the north of the continent, from which it was bombing Darwin, the case for yielding seemed overwhelming; but still not to the Labor Party. Labor, taking office just as Japan entered the war, resisted all urgings to create one army that could fight anywhere. It persisted with two armies, one of conscripts that could fight only on Australian territory and the other of volunteers who could go anywhere – with all the inefficiencies that this entailed.

Meanwhile American conscripts were being sent across the Pacific to defend Australia and to prepare for the counter thrust against the

Japanese. It was the American general Douglas MacArthur who told Prime Minister Curtin that he would have to abandon Labor's policy. MacArthur did not want to take Australian conscripts north against the Japanese; he wanted to preserve all that glory for the Americans. He was concerned at the stories appearing in the American press about Australia's odd policy on conscription, which threatened his capacity to attract troops and supplies to this part of the world.

Curtin had great trouble persuading the party to change its policy. Four state branches supported and two opposed, which gave him a narrow majority at the national conference. He failed to get agreement on one army. He had to settle for conscripts serving in MacArthur's South-West Pacific zone, but not the whole of it. The equator was set as the northern limit. In Borneo, if the Japanese could stick north of that line, which bisects the island, they would be safe from Australian conscripts.

The concession to the cherished policy was very grudging and it was to be temporary only. After the war, no conscription for overseas service was reinstated even though the Japanese advance had shown up its absurdities.

Arthur Calwell led the opposition to Curtin on the change of policy. 'To me geography does not matter,' he declared. 'Whether the compulsion is for the South-West Pacific or for Europe, it is still military conscription for overseas service, and, therefore abhorrent to the traditional democratic principles of this country.' He had fought against conscription in World War I and he lived long enough to lead Labor's case against conscription for the Vietnam War when he invoked anti-conscription as the great Labor tradition, overlooking the fact that the party had not been able to maintain that policy in World War II.

The Vietnam War certainly gave new life to anti-conscription and with more point, since opinion was divided on the war itself and the conscription was partial only (depending on birth dates) and so did not embody the equity of universal service. But I fear that anti-conscription in its pure form – when you oppose conscription even for wars you support – still has a hold on the Labor Party.

It might be urged that this does not matter much because we can defend ourselves with superior air and naval forces and we don't require a large army. But we have trouble maintaining the numbers even in our very small army, which is now being used more regularly. Earlier this year Admiral Chris Barrie, a former chief of the defence force, urged the introduction of conscription because he could see no other way of maintaining a credible force. He gained almost no support. The Liberal minister of defence ruled it out. The Labor spokesman said he favoured only voluntary national service. The defence experts pointed to the burden that training large numbers imposes and that a modern army requires fewer men with more skill. I am always surprised at this argument because many European nations with high-tech armies have maintained conscription in our own time.

One of the opponents of Barrie's suggestion said it would be 'politically devastating'. There's the rub. I am not advocating conscription now. I am pointing to the odd burden this polity carries: what is regarded as a standard option elsewhere is here highly problematic. That is Labor's mark upon the polity. It is a burden on Labor itself – it wants a more independent Australia but its ancient faith prejudices it against the full mobilisation of Australia's resources in defence, which is what independence could well require. With the left, I can doubt whether the American alliance will always protect us; but I doubt more the left's commitment to defend Australia in the absence of the alliance.

I hope my laments have not got too much out of hand. I hope that I have explained how the things I regret came to be. My regrets in summary are these: The Labor Party has cared too much for itself and not enough for the central institutions of the polity. Its discipline has damaged itself, the social democratic cause and the quality of the parliament. Though it wants a more independent Australia, it cannot yet think clearly about what that might entail.

Those who have lived within the Labor tribe have loved it. They think it is the essence of Australia. But I doubt whether it was the ideal vehicle for fully realising the social democratic potential of this place.

This is my tribute to Allan Martin.

2006

DEEDS OF COURAGE

THE STUDY OF POLITICS, ASPIRING TO BE A SCIENCE, cannot explain those moments when the universe wobbles and shifts in its course because imagination and daring have taken over. I am not referring to the huge disruptions of revolutions and coups but to deeds of political courage in stable political systems whose operations look as if they might be reducible to a science. I collect these minor miracles, treasure them indeed, to ward off the bleakness of regularity. It is an occupational hobby because my trade is history, which is a continuous defiance of social science.

There are deeds of political courage that fizz and burn and have no lasting effect – or only a delayed effect. I leave these to other collectors; my collection is made up of deeds performed by those in power and which have a lasting consequence. This is political courage allied to statecraft and not to defiance, prophecy and martyrdom.

My Australian collection begins early, at Sydney Cove in 1789, the second year of the convict settlement. The nature of this anomalous society is still not well understood. Since the population consisted of convicts and military, it is assumed that the military controlled the convicts. This is not so. The military had no intention of demeaning themselves with such work. The convicts controlled the convicts. It was convict overseers who had the difficult task of getting their fellow convicts to work. Governor Arthur Phillip had no one else to call on.

In the second year at Sydney Cove food supplies were shrinking and starvation loomed. Desperate to stop robberies, Phillip created a police force and, as with all other offices, staffed it with convicts. These convicted felons were given authority over free men, the sailors and the soldiers; in particular, they were to detain any who were wandering around the camp at night. After several months the head of the military and lieutenant-governor, Robert Ross, raised a furious objection when a soldier was detained. Phillip had trouble eliciting his reasons; he was almost apoplectic with rage and could only repeat that the power given to the convict police was an insult to his corps.

Ross had given Phillip great trouble. He did not want to be in New South Wales and thought a settlement in such a barren, perverse place could end only in disaster. He objected to the military being involved with the convicts and complained that Phillip ignored him. Fortunately for Phillip, Ross did not get on well with his officers, not all of whom shared his views. When the convict-police business blew up, Ross announced that he was coming with two of his officers to complain, to which Phillip countered by asking him to bring them all. Neither of these projected meetings took place; Phillip yielded so far as to alter the rules for the police so that they could detain soldiers only if they were actually committing a robbery. Then he sent Ross to take charge at Norfolk Island and so put an end to the military threat to his rule. There Ross operated three systems of law: one for the soldiers, one for the seamen and one for the convicts.

Ross is the ordinary man who allows us to see how extraordinary were Phillip's faith and vision and how extraordinary was the society that Phillip shaped. Of course by all ordinary standards the convict police-force was a moral absurdity and its instructions an insult to the honour of the military. If Ross had been in charge, the settlement could well have been abandoned, or if it survived it would have been run with attention to distinction between soldiers and convicts. Phillip thought of a single law and was prepared to risk a military backlash to maintain it. He established the pattern of making convict status as unimportant as possible, which was the key to the easy escape Australia had from its convict origins.

*

Britain faced a dilemma with its convict colony: its people were British and hence entitled to some form of self-government, but it was scarcely prudent to allow a convict colony to be governed by ex-convicts, for it was they who for many years composed the majority of the free population. The settlers who had come free had an easy answer to this problem: give power to them and exclude the ex-convicts. But to men in Whitehall that smacked of oppression, especially as some of the ex-convicts were wealthy and respectable people. The wise, English response to this dilemma was to do nothing and muddle through – and hence keep the power in the governor's hands. There could be a nominated council to guide him, which would include a few free settlers, but the governor and his officials should have a majority.

So matters stood in the time of Governor Richard Bourke, the liberal Irishman who ruled from 1831–1837. The reforming Whig government in Britain had appointed him, and being inclined to liberal measures it thought about an elected assembly for New South Wales and then got cold feet. But it did give Bourke permission to replace the military juries in the criminal courts with civilian juries of the English sort. Over this matter Bourke took a great risk and brought upon himself a determined campaign to unseat him.

The governor proposed that so long as they met the property qualifications, ex-convicts should sit on the new juries. The free settlers were outraged, partly because of the dishonour of having to share a jury box with ex-criminals but more for what this presaged; if ex-convicts could sit on juries what could stop them getting the vote and hence controlling the colony when finally it was granted an elected assembly? They sent home to England stories that the governor's favouritism towards convicts and ex-convicts was making the place ungovernable – a good line to run in England, because convicts were thought to have too easy a time of it in Australia and the British government always feared that its convict colony would break out in rebellion.

Bourke pushed on with his jury measure. All the free settlers on the nominated council opposed it. So, secretly, did some of his officials who were councillors, but they had to vote with the governor. The voting was equal; the governor then used his casting vote to pass the measure. This was *force majeure*; the enlightened despot had rammed the rights of ex-convicts down the throats of the free settlers. He was made to pay. In a symbolic act of defiance, the magistrates – all free settlers – elected as their chair an opponent of the governor's measures, who happened to be the colonial treasurer, one of the governor's own officials. Bourke retaliated by sacking the treasurer from his executive council. The Colonial

Office in London told him to reinstate him. Bourke, rather than accept this humiliation, resigned. But his work was done, for the key transition to a free society had been managed. When in 1840 voting rights for an assembly were discussed, the free settlers did not quarrel with ex-convicts having the right to vote. Transportation was being abandoned, so the ex-convict party would no longer have new recruits to draw on.

*

The new assembly, which operated from 1843, went under the name of the Legislative Council. Britain, still cautious about self-government for New South Wales, allowed for the election of only two-thirds of its members; the rest were nominated by the governor. The council was the lawmaking body but it could not constrain the governor; he and his officials were still the government. And so it happened that in 1851 it fell to British officials, particularly to Colonial Secretary Edward Deas Thomson, to determine how the gold discovery was to be managed, which makes more remarkable the decision to allow anyone to dig for gold.

Geoffrey Blainey, as in other matters, was the first to highlight the oddity of this arrangement. Goldfields don't have to be opened up to all comers; they have been worked by slaves and serfs. The Australian finds could have been leased or sold to large companies, which is what the large settlers of New South Wales would have preferred. They urged the government to send soldiers to clear out the first diggers. The government may have been able to do this if there had been more soldiers and fewer diggers. The number of diggers grew because Edward Hargraves, who claimed to have discovered the gold, did not keep the discovery secret, as is usual, so that he could work the find himself; he publicised his find in the hope that there would be a rush and he could claim a reward.

Thomson decided that the diggers would have to remain but they would be controlled by a system of licence. But how to get men who were already winning gold to take out a licence? He gave that job to John Hardy, an English gentleman, Cambridge educated, and with plenty of colonial experience as a police magistrate. His instructions were to expel diggers who did not take out a licence and to recruit respectable diggers as special constables to control the rest. The courage of John Hardy lies in his refusal to obey his instructions.

The force Hardy had to back his rule was small: ten mounted policemen, whom he had handpicked in Sydney. At Bathurst, the nearest town to the gold find, there were more police in reserve and at Sydney the military was on alert. He soon announced that he would have no need of this extra support because his authority was firmly established. He had been firm, genial and flexible. He allowed men who had not struck gold to work on for a week without a licence; if they then did not take out a licence Hardy had his police destroy their cradles (which he had no legal power to do). He was pleased to find that men who had found gold were keen to have a licence as a protection against interlopers. Settling disputes between miners became one of Hardy's chief occupations, something not envisaged when his instructions were drawn up in Sydney and a tribute to the standing his fair-mindedness had brought him.

Though Hardy had established imperial authority over a democratic gold rush, his masters in Sydney noticed that he had not appointed respectable diggers as special constables and insisted that he should do so. He sent back an explanation of why this standard English procedure would be counterproductive: the special constables would be laughed at and defied. Authority worked better in this topsy-turvy community when it was official and bedecked in a uniform. This was the lesson he had drawn from his experience in the bush and he had the fortitude to stick to it. He had divined that odd Australian conjunction: a social democracy willing to accept paternal authority.

*

Three examples so far, and all indicative of how liberal was the rule of British officialdom in Australia. When the colonies were granted self-government in the mid 1850s there was very little for the local liberals to do, which is why colonial politics soon settled into the mundane business of building roads, ports and railways. There was a struggle to get access to the squatters' lands but here too Britain had given liberals their chance, because it had refused to give squatters freehold to their lands and had granted only a lease. Governor Bourke had suppressed another fruitful source of conflict when in 1836 he granted public money on the same basis to the three great divisions of Christianity: Anglican, Presbyterian and Catholic.

One far-sighted British secretary of state, Earl Grey, had feared that with self-government the Australian colonies might treat each other as foreigners and start erecting tariff barriers on their borders. To prevent this he proposed a federation scheme, which the colonies jointly spurned. Grey's fears were amply realised, so that after thirty years the colonies had to work out how to come together and create what Grey had wanted to preserve: an Australian common market.

The great difficulty in federation was that although the benefits of free trade within Australia were widely acknowledged, there was fundamental disagreement over what the policy of the new nation should be towards the world: was it to be free trade, the New South Wales policy, or protection, which was Victoria's? The claim that Henry Parkes was the father of federation has a solid basis, for it was he who proposed that instead of trying to settle this quarrel all sides should agree to create the nation first and let the new national parliament settle the nation's trade policy. This was a bold and dangerous policy for Parkes. In New South Wales he led the free-trade party, now in the 1880s under assault from a new and vigorous protectionist party. In his great federation speeches in 1889–90 – not the first one at Tenterfield, which is a poor thing – he declared that trade policy was a trifle compared to the business of building a nation. The leader of the free-trade party had declared his party's shibboleth to be a *trifle*! That alarmed many of his followers. Parkes was confident that finally he could carry his party, but he was wily enough to know that he would need allies from the opposition benches. He was successful in enticing Barton, one of the prominent protectionists, to sign up to his federal proposal on the basis he had foreshadowed: Barton would go into a federated Australia with no guarantee that protection would be the policy of the new nation.

This agreement across the party divide in the mother colony was enough to allow Parkes to call a convention and get a constitution written. But then the doubts and hostility of his followers and the need to court the new Labor Party, which was hostile to federation, forced Parkes to drop his scheme. He died before federation was achieved, but it was later achieved on the basis he had established. To leave trade policy to the first parliament became a foundation principle of the later federal movement – so obvious, but unimagined until that old charlatan-cum-visionary conjured it up.

*

Parkes had declared that the nation in effect already existed, for did not 'the crimson thread of kinship' run through them all? He was referring to the British blood of the colonists, and Britishness was and remained a key part of the Australian identity. All the government schemes to recruit migrants to Australia brought out Britons. That changed after Australia faced the threat of invasion in World War II. In 1945 the Labor government of Ben Chifley planned a massive migration program in order to boost population and so make Australia better able to defend itself.

The government contained the first federal minister of immigration, Arthur Calwell, who was an admirer of the United States and its success in integrating migrants from all over Europe. He was ready to look to Europe for migrants, though he promised that nine out of ten migrants would still be British. Calwell was himself a fierce defender of the White Australia policy and knowing that the bulk of the Australian people shared his views he wanted the Europeans to be as little 'woggy' as possible. The light-skinned Scandinavians featured largely in the government's plans but sadly their governments were not interested in promoting migration. All the government's planning came unstuck because of the shortage of shipping. The only ships available were those being used by the United Nations to ship persons displaced by war to the new world. Calwell, in Europe, decided to take these displaced people. He cabled home to Chifley for permission and received it. The cabinet was not consulted for the very good reason that it would have opposed this move. Already there was opposition to the departure from an exclusively British migration.

Calwell had the great disappointment of never being prime minister, but he had more influence on the course of Australian history than most men who have held that office. He was not alone in wanting a large migration scheme but it was he who at a crucial moment took the great risk of launching it as overwhelmingly a European scheme, ditching his nine-out-of-ten Britons promise. He came home and organised the first large-scale government advertising and public-relations campaign to ensure that Australians accepted what he had done.

*

As the minister for immigration, Calwell administered the White Australia policy with an inhumane zealotry, and as leader of the Opposition in the 1960s he stood ready to defend this bastion of old Australia as Liberal governments contemplated dismantling it. The Liberal minister for immigration, the champion cyclist Hubert Opperman, put to the Menzies cabinet in 1964 a proposal to allow migration from Asia; the old man opposed it and it failed. After Menzies left, Opperman tried again in 1966; he had the support of the new prime minister, Harold Holt, and a limited measure to allow entry of Asian people was accepted.

The minister and the prime minister deserve some credit for making the change but its constant advocate and its architect was the head of the immigration department, Peter Heydon. His was such a cautious approach to change that it is a surprise to learn from Peter Ryan, who knew him well, that this civil servant was large, ebullient and almost indiscreet with his political gossip. Heydon had been a diplomat in Asia and knew the damage to Australia that the White Australia policy caused. He knew too that there was a danger for the government in advocating its removal. The change, which he crafted and which the Holt government carried through parliament, was presented as almost no change at all, but once the law was amended the number of Asian people admitted to the country was much larger than reform advocates had dared to hope.

The process of change can be disappointing to those who always want fireworks. Whitlam very publicly shifted migration to a non-discriminatory basis in 1973, though he admitted not many more Asian people. The symbolism of this change was central to the nation's new view of itself, but the breaking of the taboo had been done by his predecessors and had required more persistence and courage.

*

The deeds I have discussed so far clearly have my approval. My seventh example is one in which I was a disappointed participant.

Soon after Bob Hawke and Paul Keating came to power in 1983 they began the deregulation of the economy, something which they had not intended to do and of which they had given no warning. They puzzled and dismayed their party, which had always thought that an unregulated capitalist economy was not in the public interest. The Liberal Party, after a fierce internal struggle, was openly committed to deregulation and wanted it to be carried further by the sale of government enterprises. Hawke and Keating won elections by ridiculing this policy: they were proud of having floated the currency but, they said, it was ideology run mad to sell off flourishing enterprises like Qantas and the Common-wealth Bank. These two enterprises were the creations of earlier Labor governments and they stood for Labor people as good in themselves, and as a symbol that businesses could be run for public benefit and not for private profit. I voted for the Hawke–Keating government to protect Qantas and the Commonwealth Bank. It was a matter of principle for me: I would never fly on a private airline; I would never use a private bank.

But Hawke and Keating could not resist the new logic of economic rationalism. They decided that they had to sell off government assets. They took this policy to the Labor Conference in 1988 and were rebuffed. The party, having accepted so much, was going to protect the Labor icons. Then the government, which meant Paul Keating, first as treasurer and then as prime minister, sold them off anyway, bludgeoning the party into agreement. The Liberal Party played the honest part in all this; since Labor had adopted its policies, it gave the government its support (which was necessary to get measures through the Senate).

I was in the dustbin of history, the victim of a very bold outfit. Keating was bolder than Hawke. Don Watson tells of his skipping down a corridor after one of his coups boasting that Hawkie would never have done it. John Edwards reports that his boss felt there was no job in the world that he could not do, which Paul Kelly cites as a sign not of boldness but of hubris. This government was almost too bold or took its followers too much for granted (which is Barry Jones's view). Other governments have disappointed their party followers by not doing what they had promised or not doing all that their party platform promised; this government summarily undermined the party's foundation principles and so may have done it fatal damage – or perhaps damaged it only for the purposes for which it was formed, and it can develop others. As to the effects of the Hawke–Keating deregulation, I and other sceptics have to admit that it has provided the basis of our new prosperity, though in the dustbin I still harbour private doubts about what global capitalism might finally do to a small nation. Will Qantas survive, for starters?

*

John Howard was a supporter of a deregulated economy before Hawke and Keating. He has acknowledged their part in creating the prosperity from which his government and the country have benefited, and he complains that while the Liberals supported Labor's economic reforms, they have opposed his. His courageous deed consisted of going to an election promising to introduce a new tax, the GST. He took a huge risk but won the election and hence defied the common sense that people won't vote for new taxes.

What is most commonly remembered in regard to Howard and the GST is that he promised never ever to introduce one. John Hewson, as the Liberal leader, went to the 1993 election promising a GST, which allowed Paul Keating to defeat him and survive as prime minister, though Keating as treasurer had wanted to introduce such a tax. John Howard, facing Keating in 1996, promised that he would not introduce a GST. A journalist, believing that the mutability of public affairs should be controlled by promises in perpetuity, asked, 'Never ever?' which forced him to reply, 'Never ever.' When he decided nonetheless to introduce a GST, he gave the people every chance to defeat the proposal, since it was put to them at an election. The people accepted him and his tax.

You have to be that rare bird, a historian of federal–state relations, to appreciate the full significance of the GST. It is a Commonwealth tax but the large revenue it raises goes to the states. Our federation was unbalanced financially from the outset because customs duties, a chief source of revenue for the states, passed to the Commonwealth. Every attempt by the states to raise their own form of indirect tax has been frustrated by the High Court. Then in World War II the Commonwealth, with the sanction of the High Court, blackmailed the states into giving up their income tax. Without the standard forms of direct and indirect taxes, the states were left as mendicants of the Commonwealth. The GST has given the states their own indirect tax whose returns grow with the economy, something which every expert has advocated for decades and which seemed highly unlikely ever to be realised. I pick it as the prime minister's most enduring legacy.

*

My list has encompassed the deeds of colonial governors who had a large discretion and of governments responsible to a wide electorate. What is interesting about the deeds of the elected governments is that none of them, except the last, was put as a proposal to the people at an election. Parkes had just won an election on the free-trade cry when he announced that free trade was a trifle compared to the making of a nation; Calwell took European refugees on the run; Holt began dismantling the White Australia policy once he had taken over from Menzies, who had certainly not signalled any such change at the previous election; Hawke and Keating had directly opposed at elections the policies they then adopted.

I find all this very heartening. I am happy not to have too much transparency in our politics; the hold of the people is the loose one of punishing for serious mistakes. For all that our system appears to push politicians into short-term considerations of survival, in fact it is a very open one allowing plenty of room for creative leaders who are willing to take risks. Part of the skill of a good leader is knowing when the odds of failure have lengthened. Part of the magic of good leadership is that dangers melt away in the face of it.

2007

THE COMMUNIST THREAT

THERE IS A PROFOUND AMBIGUITY IN THE TREATMENT OF communism by left historians of Australia. In their writings on the Communist Party and old communists, they treat them respectfully, if not reverentially. However, when discussing the movements to counter or suppress the Communist Party they declare there was nothing there! – the party was tiny and without real influence; those who opposed it were alarmist, paranoid or kicking the communist can for electoral purposes. Why is it that they are allowed to take the communists seriously and the opponents of communism are derided for doing so? They warm to the communists for their thoroughgoing radicalism and yet are surprised that they provoked a savage response. What do they expect? Agreement? Silence?

At first this ambiguity appears to be absent from Andrew Moore's study of the Old Guard and its predecessors, the secret armies organised in New South Wales in the 1920s and 1930s to counter the communist menace (*The Secret Army and the Premier*). Dr Moore is a serious historian whose sleuthing has given us the first full and reliable account of these shadowy organisations. Although he has no sympathy at all for the Old Guard, he is concerned to understand the world as they saw it. He reports that they were men of integrity who genuinely feared a communist revolution. They discussed it in their private letters and not just to alarm the public. Dr Moore is also an orthodox Marxist for whom the possessors of wealth are automatically 'the ruling class'. Since the communists were planning to appropriate private wealth and end class rule, it was perfectly understandable that the leaders of Sydney's business world should fight back with organisations like the Old Guard. The '20s and '30s were also, as he reports, a tempestuous time in New South Wales politics when to fear a breakdown in civil order was not altogether fanciful. Yet, despite all this, Dr Moore encourages the common view that the response to communism was exaggerated, an over-reaction touched by paranoia.

This may well have been so. For readers to judge how far it was so, they need to know something of the operation of communists in New South Wales in the 1920s and early 1930s. On this matter Dr Moore is mostly silent. He informs us of communism indirectly through the fears of its opponents, his procedure being to cite their attacks on communists and invite his readers to see them as absurd. It was absurd, no doubt, for anti-communists to denounce communists as 'unkempt, unwashed, unclean', a parallel to the left's depiction of capitalists as obscenely bloated figures in top hats. But was it absurd for anti-communists to claim that communists took their orders from Moscow, were cunning and unscrupulous, exercised great influence over the labour movement, and were planning a revolution? To answer that we should at least be told the following:

1. With encouragement from the Bolshevik Consul, a communist party was formed in Sydney in 1920. In 1922 it was officially recognised by the Comintern, based in Moscow, as the Communist Party of Australia (section of the Communist International).

2. The leader of the Communist Party was Jock Garden, who was secretary of the Trades and Labour Council, the chief executive, that is, of the peak council of the trade union movement. Nearly all the other members of the Council executive followed their leader and became communists. The Labour Council affiliated itself to the Red International of Labour Unions. In 1922 Garden visited Moscow where he met Lenin and announced that communists would come to power in Australia through controlling Labour Councils (as he did Sydney's) and through them the trade unions. In the annual report of the Labour Council in 1924 Garden proclaimed:

> Every day the Communist issue in politics becomes more and more the main issue. The shadow of Communism is over the Labour movement. All efforts to banish Communism and the Communists are bound to fail. The good old times of playing at politics are gone. Revolution has stepped upon the stage.

3. In the early 1920s the commitment within the labour movement to socialism as an immediate goal was stronger than it has ever been before or since. The socialisation of production, distribution and exchange was adopted as the Labor Party's objective in 1921. Since communists shared the same goal, it was difficult for socialists within the Labor Party to regard them as the enemy, especially since they half feared that parliamentary action would not bring the millennium. There was hence a great deal of sympathy for the communists, which they were very ready to exploit. In 1923 the New South Wales Labor Party Conference, on the motion of Jock Garden, granted affiliation to the Communist Party. The following year this was revoked on a vote of 160 to 104, the size of the minority indicating that the issue was far from being settled.

4. From 1929, following a new policy directive from Moscow, the Communist Party ceased to work within the Labor Party and instead set up 'front' organisations, that is, bodies devoted to some particular cause with broad support which the communists would control by tight organisation and hiding their true purposes. The most successful of these 'fronts' were the Militant Minority Movement, which worked in the trade unions with the aim of creating a revolutionary situation through a general strike, and the Unemployed Workers' Movement, which claimed a membership of 68,000 in 1934.

5. The parliamentary leader of the Labor Party from 1923 was Jack Lang, who had little sympathy for socialism and was a fierce anti-communist, but nevertheless attracted the support of the left in the extra-parliamentary party by a seemingly determined attempt to abolish the Legislative Council. At first the left thought it had found a parliamentary leader who meant business. To secure his place he was voted parliamentary leader by the Conference and given extraordinary powers to control the party. Lang needed this extra-parliamentary support because his parliamentary colleagues, who normally elect the leader, were deeply dissatisfied with him. One of the machine men working to keep Lang in office was Jock Garden, who had now left the Communist Party. During

Lang's second premiership from 1930, which coincided with the onset of the Depression, he was increasingly reckless and demagogic, and the extra-parliamentary organisation became more insistent that socialism must be the immediate goal of the party. A minority of socialists within the party openly urged revolution and the dictatorship of the proletariat.

*

There were thus good grounds for the claims made about communists which Dr Moore invites his readers to pass over with a smile. The communists as yet had no deep penetration into the unions, but they clearly had some purchase there. To have captured the Trades and Labour Council was an outstanding and, for their opponents, a very disturbing success. Some unions, unhappy with this leadership, disaffiliated from the Council, but the big unions remained.

In the battle for the control of the Labor Party, particularly complex and vicious at this time, the communists and their sympathisers were significant players. The ultimate outcome, of course, could not be known. Nor could an outside observer know whether Lang was in charge of his party or whether he had become hostage to the increasingly militant socialists within it.

There was plenty of alarm within the Labor Party at the extent of communist influence. Here is the young Dr Evatt, campaigning as an independent Labor candidate for Balmain in 1927 after having his official pre-selection revoked by the communist-backed executive:

The great Australian labour movement is seriously menaced by a small but determined body of men lacking in moral or religious scruple, who are gradually filling many of the key positions in the ALP. It is no answer to contend, as has been plausibly done, that the actual number of open and avowed Communists is small. That is perfectly true, but beside the point. At the last state elections the Communist party had to fight in the open against Australian Labor candidates, and its nominees were overwhelmingly defeated, as witness my own electorate of Balmain, where I myself polled 60 votes to every one recorded for the Communist candidate. Defeated in open contest these men resolved to seize control of the ALP by the less honorable but more effective method of organisation from within. Already their success has surprised themselves, and demonstrated the truth of Lenin's saying, 'that a small minority, if sufficiently unscrupulous and persistent, can capture most political parties' … The situation may not be so clear in the other electorates, but the issue is perfectly clear in Balmain. It is this – whether the labour movement is to remain Australian in spirit and ideals, or whether it is to be secretly controlled by a Communist minority who are out to degrade, disintegrate, and destroy the labour movement of Australia.

On all sides, belief in the stability of society had been eroded by the Bolshevik success in Russia in 1917. The fact that a tiny group operating in the capital had seized a whole nation made communists everywhere sanguine and their opponents wary. The Old Guard never feared that large numbers of Australians would be won over to communism; its plans were devoted to ensuring that if there was a breakdown in civil order, however caused, communists should not have the chance to take advantage of it as they had done in Russia. Its task would be as much to maintain essential services as to attack communists directly. The fact that the communists were few, which the historians retrospectively inform anti-communists was reassuring, was not the point. It might have been more reassuring if the communists had organised openly on their own behalf and left other organisations alone. It was their failure to do this which led them to be judged cunning and unscrupulous. For the communists themselves, small numbers were not deterring. Lenin, after all, had counselled a small, tightly knit party and Marxist theory predicted crises and collapse in capitalism, which would give communists their chance. The hopes of communists and the fears of anti-communists were perfectly matched.

*

To plan a private military operation to protect liberal democracy may threaten the object that is to be saved. The leaders of the Old Guard were very well aware of this. They insisted that their movement was purely defensive – they would not stir unless there was a breakdown in civil order and/or an attempt at revolution; they hoped the civil power would not need their aid; they would act only in support of the constituted authorities. As Dr Moore justly notes, though they felt the impatience with liberal democracy which could lead on to fascism, they were moved more by what he calls an Anglo-Australian conservatism: an attachment to the British empire as a world-civilising force, to the monarch and parliamentary institutions with (though Dr Moore does not say this) the rights and liberties they guaranteed. The Old Guard had no novel agenda of its own to impose and in this was unlike that other anti-communist organisation, B. A. Santamaria's Movement.

The Old Guard considered all loyal citizens could support its aims and planned to enrol them 'irrespective of creed, party, social or financial position'. In Sydney the membership was small and from the elite; in the country, however, it was widespread ranging from pastoralists through small-town businessmen and tradesmen, to rural workers. The RSL club rooms were important recruiting grounds and a nucleus of organisation. These people were organised in a military hierarchy by district. Altogether there were 25,000 members in the country with substantial representation from every region and town, as compared with 5000 in Sydney. In the country the organisation was sometimes known simply as 'The Country' and it embodied in a new form the old determination that Sydney should not rule New South Wales.

The Old Guard must be distinguished from the much better known New Guard which secured its place in history when one of its members spectacularly up-staged Premier Lang at the opening of the Sydney Harbour Bridge. The New Guard was a movement of young turks, second echelon businessmen who rejected the Old Guard's purely defensive stance. They took the offensive, organised openly, paraded in public, broke up communist meetings and claimed the right to eject Lang from office. Its leader, Eric Campbell, was a fascist. The New Guard had a large membership in Sydney, but very few in the country. Dr Moore rates its military capacity as very low compared to the Old Guard which was a formidable force. The Old Guard was dismayed at the growth of this offspring, fearing that it would create the disorder which the communists could exploit.

*

The existence of two rival private armies leads Dr Moore to ponder whether our democratic history has been as quiet and untroubled as sometimes it is depicted. To strengthen this theme he makes a half-hearted attempt to show that the possessing classes in Australia have always over-reacted to working-class movements and denied their legitimacy. Of course the reverse is true. There was no social environment more conducive to the growth of working-class institutions than Australia in the late nineteenth and early twentieth centuries. The trade unions had legal protection and widespread community support, including frequently that of employers. Once the arbitration system was established (1904) they were fostered and protected by an organ of the state. The Labor Party won control of the national parliament as early as 1910.

If workers are liable to be sacked, bashed or shot if they form a union and yet unions are still formed, we have truly repressive owners and determined workers – and the very weak union movement of the United States. Given that employment relations under capitalism are so unequal, if unions become stable and widespread, this is *prima facie* evidence that employers are being restrained by society at large or are restraining themselves.

Certainly when working-class organisations began to be formidable, employers began to oppose them – in response to co-ordinated bodies of trade unions they formed employers' associations; in response to the Labor Party they attempted, for a long time unsuccessfully, to form a mass-based party to oppose it. It was only from 1917–18, as Dr Moore's researches make clear, that they began to dabble in paramilitary organisations, that is from the time syndicalists were threatening to dispossess capitalists through a general strike, and communists by revolution.

*

Why the resistance to communism should take the form of an unofficial militia is not a question which interests Dr Moore. For him the operation of liberal capitalist states are all alike and possess no mysteries. The owners of the means of production are quite simply the ruling class. One might have thought that if this is so, a word or two might have been given to explain why periodically the government of New South Wales was in the hands of the party organised by the working class, which in 1930–32 was led by a premier who was proposing to replace the currency with a device of his own and was refusing to pay interest on the overseas debt. Is Dr Moore suggesting that who controls the state is of no consequence or perhaps that Jack Lang was, according to the Marxist formula, actually the chairman of a committee running the affairs of the bourgeoisie?

The fact that the anti-communist militia was unofficial indicates how far the possessing class was from being a ruling class. From the time of the introduction of democracy to New South Wales in the mid-nineteenth century, men of wealth had found it difficult to get seats in the Legislative Assembly and increasingly had less desire to be associated with the rowdy low-bred fellows who composed it. With the formation of parties around the turn of the century, they were more closely associated with the organisation of the parties opposed to Labor, but still not very likely actually to hold a seat in the House. The colonial parliament, unlike the British, was not a gathering of the elite.

In the United Kingdom the body developed after World War I to cope with civil disorder and any attempt at revolution was the Supply and Transport Organisation, which drew on volunteer labour, but was organised officially and secretly by the British Cabinet and placed under the Ministry of Transport. It was used in the railway strike of 1919, the miners' strike of 1921 and the general strike of 1926. Dr Moore argues with some reason that this body was the model for the paramilitary organisations formed or proposed in Australia in the 1920s and of the Old Guard. However, he does not consider why in New South Wales the organisation was *unofficial*. What reasons can be suggested for this difference? That in New South Wales there was not a single governing class, surviving the changes of the party in office, ready to act against a militant working class; and the owners of wealth, rarely participating directly in government, felt they could only exercise control if they now took matters into their own hands. In short, there was no reliable political and military establishment. Having no institutional buttresses, the wealthy had to look for support to the volunteer efforts of those citizens they could persuade to join them. To be effective, especially in the country, they had to practise no social exclusion and press no agenda of their own.

Dr Moore considers the Old Guard an indication of the ongoing power of what he calls the ruling class; it more clearly demonstrates their comparative weakness. They had the power to defend the existing liberal democracy – but that's what nearly everyone else wanted. The width and depth of Old Guard membership in the country is one of the conclusions of his study which Dr Moore highlights. He does not see this popularity in any way threatening his claim that the Old Guard was a 'ruling class' organisation. According to him, those members outside the ranks of the ruling class did not realise where their true class interests lay!

The Old Guard in its composition and purpose was similar to the National Guard of the states in the United States. Had the Australian democracy had this form of protection, there would almost certainly not have been private armies. The polity of the Australian states was a hybrid: British in form but without an establishment; democratic in essence but without a regularised popular force at its command. One can understand why the state appeared vulnerable.

*

Like all good scholarly history, Dr Moore's work can be drawn upon by those who do not share its author's world view – as I have done here. Indeed, Dr Moore's scholarship is in danger of getting the better of his ideology. The more he uncovers of the Old Guard's operations, the less dangerous and disturbing it seems. Every working paper he cites reveals a cautious, level-headed, unalarmist organisation. The secrets of the Old Guard turn out not to be shameful secrets. Consider the instruction that went out to members in its last days. As the Lang government struggled to stave off bankruptcy, the Old Guard detected the shape of the crisis it had long expected – the massive numbers of the unemployed, deprived of their government dole, would riot or become an effective force under communist leadership. The orders for mobilisations were therefore revised – everyone should not only have a rifle at the ready but set aside money to feed the unemployed.

In his final chapter Dr Moore goes to great length in an attempt to demonstrate that Governor Game in dismissing Premier Lang was acting under orders from the Dominions Office in London. There is absolutely no evidence to support this; all the evidence he cites points in the opposite direction. Dr Moore has the odd idea that a British-appointed governor of a state with responsible government was the representative of 'British interests'. Governor Game in fact followed the British constitutional tradition of the Head of State supporting his government while it had a majority in the House. To the outrage of the Sydney bourgeoisie, he agreed to the creation of extra members for the nominated upper house to improve the government's chance of controlling it – and this while Lang was repudiating the British debt.

Governor Game dismissed Lang when he was refusing to comply with federal law that he pay the federal government the amounts it was paying to British bond holders on his behalf. Lang had challenged the law in the High Court, which had upheld it. He had withdrawn the state funds from the banks and to keep them out of the clutch of the Commonwealth stored them in the Treasury, guarded by members of the Timber Workers' Union. How was the Commonwealth government to get him to pay if he and state taxation and treasury officials refused to comply? Dr Moore has one doubtful piece of evidence, which he uses with due caution, indicating that the Commonwealth was contemplating enrolling members of the Old Guard as special peace officers to storm the state taxation offices. No doubt Dr Moore is correct – force of some sort would have been needed if Lang and his officers had stood firm. The Governor's dismissal of Lang made it unnecessary. The oddest thing in the book is Dr Moore's judgment on this possible use of force by the Commonwealth government to uphold the law – 'the real threat to "law and order" emanated from Australia's most respectable address: "The Lodge", Canberra'.

Dr Moore always puts law and order in quotation marks to indicate that the term does not have his endorsement. He has no respect for liberal democracy. He announces he will not berate the Old Guard for endangering it by organising a private army, for liberal democracy is simply a system of class rule. His own position appears to be that the working class would have benefited from a communist take-over in the 1930s.

This is an unusual position. On the left now the more common view is that the Communist Party's ideology and methods were totally inappropriate for the Australian democracy – and yet they still berate the past opponents of Australian communism. Donald Horne was one of the victims of this. Firmly progressive, he once reported that he was still regarded with suspicion because he was anti-communist in the 1950s. And yet, he lamented, he was only saying then about the communists what his left friends were saying now. It's wisdom after the event that is honoured.

The position of those who still complain about the strength of the anti-communist campaign seems to be this: communism had no prospect of success in Australia, the response was out of all proportion to the threat. A steamroller was being used to crack a nut. Such a view misunderstands the dynamics of the body we're discussing – an open, democratic society. If an organised group of people assume positions of prominence and influence, which the trade unions and the Labor Party allowed the communists to do, and proclaim that they aim to overthrow the existing form of society; if they tell a Christian people that in the new order there will be no religion; if they tell the large number of property-holders there will be no private property; if they offer the dictatorship of the proletariat in place of cherished human rights; if they tell the party of reform they will control or supplant it in the cause of the revolution – then there will be outrage, denunciation, clamour, virulence and counter organisation. This strong feeling, like all others, will be enhanced and exploited for a variety of purposes, like selling newspapers or winning elections. This is how society demonstrates that what is being offered is totally inappropriate to its needs – which is what the left now acknowledges communism was. There is no other way. Free societies are expressive bodies. Because they are open-ended, no-one can speak with full authority on their behalf; they have to make their own declarations. Because a threatening opinion cannot be silenced, it must be shouted down. There may even be some hysteria and paranoia. If you want quiet, measured, economical treatment of unwelcome opinion, choose a society with a well-developed apparatus of repression. If you want a society where there is not only freedom of expression, but a calm and rational assessment of all views, try a debating club.

The left historians cannot put out of their minds the vision of social justice which communism offered and the decency and dedication of individual communists. They also have to face the fact that the vision and decency were vitiated by the madcap scheme, sold in Moscow as scientific, of reaching justice and equality through violence and terror. So far, from that tension we are getting only tortured apologetics. The tragedy still awaits its historian.

1990

WAS CURTIN THE BEST
PRIME MINISTER?

B Y COMMON CONSENT JOHN CURTIN HAS BEEN AUSTRALIA'S best prime minister. There are a few doubters, the most prominent being Paul Keating, who declared that Curtin was just 'a trier'. At the time he made this judgment Keating was angling for the top job, which he had been denied because Bob Hawke had reneged on a deal to resign in his favour. Hawke was a great admirer of Curtin and Keating's impiety helped to convince him that he would never resign in Keating's favour.

Keating's judgment on Curtin was given in a free-ranging speech on leadership to the National Press Club. He lamented that Australia had never had a leader in the top rank, no one like Washington, Lincoln or Roosevelt. To the objection that Australia's population was much smaller than that of the United States he had a ready reply: 'There weren't 230 million people when Thomas Jefferson was sitting in a house he designed for himself in a paddock at the back end of Virginia writing the words "Life, liberty and the pursuit of happiness."' If we had no other evidence, we would still know that this was a speech Keating wrote himself: 'a paddock at the back end of Virginia'! In fact it was delivered impromptu and was meant to be off the record.

Curtin himself thought he was ill-fitted for the job and would not have quarrelled with Keating's 'trier' label, which explains why he was so much loved and which makes criticising him a difficult task. Like most other people, I have been a great admirer of Curtin; I've held him close since I first heard at university how for nights he could not sleep when the Seventh Division of the Australian Imperial Force (AIF), torn from Churchill's grasp, was coming home across the Indian Ocean with inadequate escort. But now I agree with Keating that he has been much overrated. I also agree with Keating that there have been no great Australian prime ministers – and Keating, for all his aspiration and his understanding of transformative leadership, did not himself become a great prime minister. However, there has been one great prime ministership, the partnership of two men who disagreed over Curtin and came to hate each other: Hawke and Keating.

Templates to assess the qualities of prime ministers – achievements, longevity, administrative capacity, and so on – are designed to judge them all against all the criteria and so underestimate the extraordinary. Barton is not usually rated highly as a prime minister, but this omits from the assessment his part in creating the federal government that he first led. Whitlam is rightly downgraded for the chaos of his administration, but he does not get the credit for his unparalleled achievement in Opposition, when he reconstituted his party and its program. Hawke and Keating are credited with the major achievement of freeing up the economy from government control and ownership, but this was no ordinary 'achievement' because it reversed settled national policy of eighty years and was contrary to the ideology of the party they led. It was truly an amazing piece of statecraft; they simultaneously secured the economic future of the country and destroyed their party as a critic of capitalism.

Curtin faced extraordinary circumstances in leading the nation at war. The test of his quality is admittedly different from the rest: it is how well he coped with the war and what he made of the war for Australia. But if he is to retain his rank as the best prime minister, we would have to find in him something of the order of the transformative work of Hawke and Keating.

*

Because he was scared of flying, Curtin turned down all opportunities but one to consult with allied leaders overseas about the war: he did agree to attend the Commonwealth Prime Ministers' Conference in London in 1944. Among the honours he received in Britain was the freedom of the City of London. In his speech in reply at the Guildhall, he showed that he fully understood the importance of the struggle against Nazi Germany:

he said that Germany's attack on Poland was 'as much Australia's business as if Sydney itself had been bombarded by the Nazis.'

At the time of the invasion of Poland, however, his response was very different. As leader of the Labor Opposition he did not oppose Menzies' declaration that Australia was at war but he insisted that Australia do no fighting. No men should be sent overseas to the war and there should be no conscription. Australia should look after its own defence and could best serve the wider cause by providing wheat and wool. By 1944 he had come a long way – but had he? Leading Australia in a world war, the old pacifist and isolationist kept breaking through. This is evident in his public deeds and statements and more alarmingly in his off-the-record remarks to journalists, now published under the title *Backroom Briefings: John Curtin's War*.

When he became Opposition leader in 1935, Curtin devoted himself to uniting the party and making it electable after its splits and collapse in the Depression. Soon that meant finding a credible defence policy. The United Australia Party government insisted that only the British navy could defend Australia. It directed most of the defence budget to the Australian navy, which would cooperate with Britain's in time of war. The empire's defence strategy in the East was to rely on the naval base at Singapore, built in fits and starts between the wars. The British had no fleet based at Singapore, but in event of war they promised to send one – as soon as they could, given the other calls upon them.

The non-Labor governments had doubts about these assurances, since they kept asking for them to be renewed. Curtin openly questioned them. If Britain were hard pressed in Europe, no fleet or only an inadequate fleet would be sent. Australia would have to face its likely Asian enemy, Japan, alone. Hence it should build up its land and air defences against invasion and spend proportionally less on its navy. There was no chance that Labor in office would have spent heavily on defence of any sort, and Labor's ability to create a strong army was compromised by its opposition to conscription even for training, even to meet an invasion of the country. However, Curtin's policy pleased the Labor faithful, who wanted at all costs to keep Australia from what Curtin himself described as the 'quagmire' of European conflicts. Curtin took encouragement for his policy from certain army officers, jealous of the pre-eminence given to the navy and ready with explanations as to why the Singapore strategy would fail.

The United Australia Party denounced Curtin's policy as disloyal and dangerous, cutting Australia off from the great power pledged to protect it. To the charge of disloyalty Curtin replied that Australians' first duty was the defence of Australia. The fallacy of this approach was that Australia could not defend itself against a great power; hence the defence of Australia could not properly be conceived as standing apart from the battles between the great powers and their outcome.

The government of Robert Menzies had its doubts about joining the war in Europe since Japan might seize the occasion to threaten Australia. But after receiving another British assurance about the defence of Singapore, it moved to contribute to the war in a way absolutely contrary to the principles of the Labor Opposition. Volunteers were called for and were sent away as the Second Australian Imperial Force (without the referendum that Labor insisted must precede any deployment of troops outside the continent). Conscription was applied so that men had to train and serve in the militia for home defence. A national register of employment was created (which Labor feared would lead to industrial conscription).

Labor opposed all these measures on their introduction but, by painful manoeuvres, came to accept them. Curtin did the nursing and cajoling to ensure that Labor was not going to be caught as an opponent of the war. His aim was to keep the Labor Party together so that its great project of remaking the economic and social order would not be imperilled. He did his work so well that Labor became a more united party than the United Australia Party that was running the war and he a more commanding leader than his opponents could provide. In the elections of 1940 Labor made significant gains and it held as many seats in the House of Representatives as the United Australia Party and Country Party combined. Two independents held the balance of power and kept Menzies in office. Menzies had enemies undermining him within his party and he seemed unable to gain the popular support that a wartime leader needed. He resigned and Arthur Fadden, the leader of the Country Party, briefly became prime minister. The instability within the governing ranks continued so that in October 1941 the two independents decided to switch allegiance and install a more stable administration.

So Labor, initially opposed to all the measures that had shaped Australia's war effort, now assumed responsibility for it. This represented an abject failure of the parties that understood much better than Labor why the safety of Australia depended on the British empire prevailing against Germany. But Curtin, in his first statement as prime minister, made a good fist of linking Labor to this war: 'Labor stands for Australia; Australia stands for and with the Empire; the Empire stands and fights for liberty and freedom wherever liberty and freedom are in danger.'

Curtin saw himself as a man of destiny and he had been treated as such by his close Labor colleagues, who gave him emotional support and protected him when he was crippled by alcoholism and depression. He lamented that the labour movement had descended into humdrum politics and the pursuit merely of better wages and conditions, but he still hoped that fate might deliver the circumstances in which Labor, with him as its leader, could remake the world. His moment of destiny seemed to have arrived in 1941, but the fates had given him the wrong task. He did not want Labor to run the war; he wanted Labor not to be damaged by it. He doubted his own capacity as a war leader. His followers by contrast wanted to seize the chance that the war had brought and some wanted to start implementing the Labor program under cover of war. Curtin knew that his authority as a war leader would depend on his not pursuing the Labor program – which, in any case, would be difficult to do in a hung parliament. But when everyone said that he was the man – even Menzies and Fadden acknowledged his fitness – it would be damaging to Labor not to take the responsibility that had been presented to him.

He found very quickly that he could do the job; he was decisive, convincing and reassuring in a time of danger. He had the authority and determination to impose the restrictions and discipline of total war on the community. He was able to keep united a more than usually fractious Labor Party. But one part of the job he could not do. Six weeks after he became prime minister, the *Sydney* was sunk with all hands off the coast of Western Australia. Curtin could scarcely bring himself to make the announcement of this loss, knowing what suffering he was about to cause the relatives of the men who had died. In his distress he had to be comforted and supported by the governor-general. He blamed himself for the disaster because if he had been more forceful with the striking wharfies who had delayed the ship's departure, it would not have met the German *Kormoran* which sank her. How could a man so constituted be a wartime prime minister and send men to battle? He could not; Curtin left the decisions about deployment of troops totally to his generals, which after March 1942 meant to the American general Douglas MacArthur, the results of which we will examine later. Curtin admitted that he did not have the head for war; he did not have the stomach for it either. In this matter he wanted not to be responsible.

When Curtin met Churchill in London in 1944, he formed the impression that 'Churchill fires every shot and suffers every wound.' No one but Curtin discovered this sensitivity in the British bulldog. Curtin alone of the Commonwealth prime ministers declined Churchill's invitation to visit the D-Day headquarters in England. Curtin was opposed to the landing in Normandy; he thought the casualties would be too high and that the allies would be better to send their armies to support the Russians in the east. This madcap idea he got from MacArthur. His high sensitivity to casualties went beyond what was proper in a conscientious general: he told journalists off the record, 'I wouldn't like to be among the poor bastards who will undertake it.' While it was honest of the prime minister to acknowledge his own cowardice, the comment shows how incapable he was of thinking about any military campaign. Cowardice, physical cowardice, is a grave charge. One of Curtin's approving biographers, Lloyd Ross, is prepared to use the term and Curtin's daughter, Elsie, reports that her father was terrified of what the Japanese would do to him should he fall into their hands.

*

Menzies' solution to the hung parliament of 1940 had been that a national government should be formed, as had been done in Britain. But it was a Labor principle not to cooperate in office with any other party. Curtin gave voice to the party's view: 'I refuse to desert the great body of Labor to prop up political parties of reaction and capitalism.' But Curtin himself was more responsible and did not believe that Labor should never cooperate with the class enemy, even at the expense of the nation's war effort. He proposed to Menzies that an advisory war council be established, composed of the leading men of both parties. Menzies agreed and so before he became prime minister, Curtin had been privy to the diplomatic cables flowing between Australia and Britain concerning the war in the Middle East and the preparations, or lack of them, for the likely war against Japan.

Curtin distinguished himself on the council by his close concern for the defence of Singapore and his urgings that Britain send a fleet as it had promised to do. This seems odd for a man who was notorious as a critic of the Singapore strategy, but it was the government's policy that had been followed and not his own. It is more puzzling that when Churchill said in September 1941 that there would be a force of capital ships placed in the Indian Ocean before the end of the year, Curtin immediately assumed that it would happen and that it would work as a deterrent to the Japanese. He recommended a reduction in the number of men called up into the militia and the period of their training. Men taken out of the army could make munitions. Curtin was never happier than when it seemed Australia's role in the war was to grow food and make munitions.

Curtin was so desperate to protect Australia and to have other people do the fighting that he could lose all judgment. While still Opposition leader he tried to negotiate a deal with the Japanese envoy: in the coming war, Japan would spare Australia in return for Australia supplying it with iron ore. (To appease was not unusual; a separate peace for Australia was.) As prime minister after the war with Japan had begun, Curtin urged Churchill to encourage Russia to attack Japan by agreeing to all Stalin's territorial claims in Eastern Europe, Iran and the Far East. Churchill reminded him that the forcible transfer of people was against the principles of the Atlantic Charter.

Against Admiralty advice, Churchill did send to Singapore, not a fleet, but two capital ships, the *Prince of Wales* and the *Repulse*. Sadly the aircraft carrier that was to protect them did not come too. Three days after Pearl Harbor, Japanese planes sank them from the air. That ended Singapore's career as a naval base, but Curtin and his ministers sent more Australian troops there and redoubled their efforts to get Churchill to reinforce it, though its function was now symbolic only. Churchill sent the Eighteenth British Division, which he would rather have sent to Burma. The convoy carrying them was attacked by the Japanese from the air – so much was this a lost cause. Then the Australian government learnt from Earle Page, its minister in London, that there was talk of evacuating soldiers from Singapore, as the Japanese drive down the Malayan peninsula could not be halted. The Australian government was incensed and replied that this would be 'an inexcusable betrayal'. These words came from Evatt, the foreign minister, not Curtin. The prime minister, as often happened in a crisis, had become ill and had retreated to his home in Perth. Churchill switched tack and gave the order that Singapore must be defended. He was worried about giving up the fight when the Americans were defending to the last in the Philippines and because the Australians were pressing him to stay, but in his words, 'There is no doubt what a purely military decision should have been.' So thousands of British and Australian soldiers went into captivity.

Curtin is credited with being prescient about the fall of Singapore, but when the event was in prospect he showed no sign of independent thought. Churchill considered getting the troops out so that they could fight another day; Curtin could not. When the Singapore strategy had failed (as he had predicted), Curtin wanted the British to stick to it because that is what they had promised – and so he helped make the disaster more complete. This is not to say that any other Australian leader would have reacted differently. They had all been involved in pressing Britain to defend Singapore and had a huge emotional commitment to its survival. It is to say that Curtin had no more thrown off the mind-set of colonial entitlement than the rest. He suffered deeply for it; the fate of the prisoners of war was always in his mind.

With the fall of Singapore Curtin announced that the 'Battle for Australia' was about to begin. The recurring nightmare of an enraged yellow nation taking vengeance on white Australia was about to be realised. Except that the Japanese were not intending to invade Australia. They wanted the rubber, tin and oil in South-East Asia. It was hard for Curtin and his ministers to accept that Australia was not the goal despite Churchill, Roosevelt and MacArthur telling them it was most unlikely.

Of course, if there was a doubt they could not lay the prospect aside, but this fear was beyond the reach of military appraisals.

The Japanese advanced so quickly through South-East Asia that, briefly, elements in their navy advocated an invasion of Australia. The army quickly had this plan rejected; bogged down in its war in China, it did not want another difficult campaign. The strategy remained to isolate and harass Australia but not invade it. The advance along the Kokoda Track in the direction of Port Moresby was not intended as an advance into Australia, which is how it was popularly seen at the time and since. It was to extend and secure the southern perimeter of the Co-Prosperity Sphere.

The official war historian Lionel Wigmore says the leaders of the Australian army were not thrown by the collapse of Singapore because this is what they had predicted. But the situation at the fall of Singapore was very different from the scenarios they had entertained. When Japan moved south, it had another war on its hands in China, where most of its army remained. When the British failed at Singapore, Australia was not alone. The United States was in the war; it had already been planning joint operations with the British for twelve months and Roosevelt was pledged to the defence of Australia. All this they knew; they could not know at first that the Japanese were not intent on invasion, but even if that was the aim, the other factors in play made that threat very different from what they had envisaged. Australians fighting alone on their own soil against the yellow hordes was an image not readily erased. The view of army leaders is important, for the army chief of staff, Vernon Sturdee, was advising Curtin in the first months after Pearl Harbor.

The myths about Curtin are so strong that it might still be believed that he had to fight Churchill to get the soldiers of the AIF returned from the Middle East to defend Australia against the Japanese. Churchill himself proposed the move; two divisions, the Sixth and Seventh, left the Middle East early in 1942, with Curtin agreeing that the Ninth Division could remain. The dispute was over where best the returning divisions could be deployed against the Japanese. On its way across the Indian Ocean, Churchill proposed that the Seventh Division could best be used to defend Rangoon in Burma. With all the outer defences of Australia falling, Sturdee urged that the troops must come home and threatened to resign if they did not. Curtin was happy to follow the advice; it chimed with his own view that the defence of Australia was his first duty and, after another near mental collapse, he told Churchill that the men must come to Australia. Roosevelt, at Churchill's urging, put pressure on Curtin to change his mind. The president offered to send American troops to Australia in place of those diverted to Burma and tried to calm Curtin by saying that despite the rapid Japanese advance the vital centres of Australia were not in danger.

Churchill and Roosevelt regarded the war as one and since finding ships to move troops was always a problem, the troops, of whatever nation, nearest to the action should do the job. The reason they were so keen to prevent a Japanese takeover in Burma was that the so-called Burma Road could then be kept open, by which the allies were supplying China with the materials of war.

The dispute went on for days and was referred to the Advisory War Council, where Menzies and Fadden urged that Churchill's request be granted. Curtin stood firm. Meanwhile Churchill, assuming that Curtin could not resist the pressure, ordered the ships to sail to Rangoon. All the Australian leaders were properly outraged at this and when Curtin insisted, Churchill of course complied – and became more deeply hostile to the Australians who had pushed him the wrong way on Singapore.

Today the Museum of Australian Democracy in Canberra stages re-enactments of this dispute in the Cabinet Room at Old Parliament House and visitors then decide who was in the right. Museum staff report that Australians always take Curtin's part. This is not surprising since even such an eminent historian as Geoffrey Serle, who wrote the entry on Curtin in the *Australian Dictionary of Biography*, did not understand the issues at stake. He conceives the dispute as between British imperial and Australian interests. British imperial! – when the United States' president was urging Curtin to agree. And not in Australian interests! – what country had a greater interest than Australia in keeping China in the war and so reducing the capacity of Japan to move south?

Military historians today say that Curtin's decision was the correct one. It was too late to save Rangoon. Churchill believed that if the British

Eighteenth Division had been sent there – and not to Singapore – there would have been a chance, so the Australians were doubly responsible for its loss. If the Australians had been landed at Rangoon, they would have taken some time to be in battle order because their ships were not 'tactically loaded'; that is, men and their equipment were not in the same ships. Only late in the controversy did Curtin put this point to Churchill. His first and strongest point was that the defence of Australia had to be carried on in Australia, which was also the best base for the counter attack against the Japanese. Throughout the controversy, he never acknowledged that keeping China in the war against Japan was in Australia's interests. So if Curtin was right in this dispute, it was for the wrong reason.

Curtin's chief claim to a place in Australian history has been that he was responsible for Australia turning away from Britain towards America as its great power defender. The key words he used, which were part of a New Year's message in the Melbourne *Herald* of 27 December 1941, were:

> Without any inhibitions of any kind, I make it quite clear that Australia looks to America, free of any pangs as to our traditional links or kinship with the United Kingdom.

This is taken to be a bold and original concept, beyond the reach of Labor's opponents, bound more closely to the British empire. But everyone concerned with victory against Germany had been looking to America. Churchill was from the time he took office. Menzies made a private appeal to Roosevelt to save Britain and the cause of liberty when France looked sure to fall. When Menzies visited Washington in May 1941 on his way home from Britain, Roosevelt assured him that the United States would defend Australia against Japan. On his return to Australia, Menzies gave a major speech in the Sydney Town Hall that was broadcast nationally, in which he said:

> Now you and I are looking more and more to the east, to the great democracy of the United States of America. It is a good thing that we should look there, and I believe that we do not look there in vain.

This declaration elicited no particular notice because Menzies did not associate it with a downplaying of the British connection; indeed most of the speech was devoted to a very moving account of how the people of Britain were standing up to Hitler.

It had long been a commonplace in Australian defence thinking that if the British were unable to defend Australia then Australia would have to make an appeal to America and hope to God that the ties of blood won out against American isolationism. Churchill himself had said as much before World War I. Curtin referred to this when, the next day, he defended his statement to his chief defence advisor, Frederick Shedden. But it was not the looking to America that caused surprise and dismay to the British people of Australia, but the 'free of any pangs'. Shedden told Curtin that as an ardent advocate of the British Commonwealth he should have said 'without any lessening of bonds with the United Kingdom.'

Curtin immediately corrected 'free of any pangs' and his retractions, clarifications and loyal affirmations went on for weeks. Curtin declared that 'Our loyalty to His Majesty the King goes to the very core of national life' and the 'indissolubility of Empire' was the foundation of the Labor program. With 'free of any pangs' dropped (though not from the history books), Curtin thereafter gave as his rationale for looking to America that Britain was too hard-pressed to help Australia.

The statement enraged Churchill, who had just sacrificed the *Prince of Wales* and the *Repulse* to the defence of Australia, and Roosevelt, to whom it seemed to be directed, thought it smacked of panic and disloyalty. Not a clever move to put offside the two men who were the ultimate guarantors of Australia's safety! Churchill was in America conferring with Roosevelt when Curtin's statement appeared. The two great allied powers were planning an unprecedented integration of their command structure: joint chiefs of staff and allied commanders working together in the various zones into which the world was to be divided. While all this was in train, the panic merchant from the Antipodes declares that he prefers one power to another. How crass Curtin must have seemed!

Curtin was simply unlucky. His press secretary wrote the statement – though he approved it – and it was not addressed to the two allied leaders.

It was addressed to the Australian people as a report of what was in train and the challenges ahead. It was destined for the magazine section in the back of the paper until the acting editor saw its news value and high-lighted it with a 'pointer' on the front page. 'Free of any pangs' was then flashed around the world to the dismay of Roosevelt and Churchill and the delight of the propaganda outfits in Berlin and Tokyo, who had a story about Australia deserting Britain.

Curtin was well informed of the meeting between Roosevelt and Churchill by cables from Richard Casey, the Australian minister in Washington. Curtin sent identical cable messages to the two leaders, devoted solely to the need for reinforcements at Singapore and the region. He knew enough not to communicate with them through the pages of an afternoon newspaper in Melbourne.

Before his New Year message was issued, Curtin knew that the United States was to spearhead the counter attack against Japan and that Mac-Arthur was Roosevelt's chosen commander for this region. The president preferred that an invitation come from Australia, which had duly been sent. There were already American troops in the country. Australia's 'turn to America' had been arranged by Churchill and Roosevelt. Curtin and his New Year message had nothing to do with it.

The famous message looks increasingly problematic as an achieve-ment. It was, however, a great achievement for Curtin in domestic politics and with the historians. Because of the controversy that 'free of any pangs' aroused, the message with its call to America became well known. When American troops arrived, followed soon after by MacArthur, they seemed to have come at Curtin's bidding. Curtin and his supporters milked this for all it was worth. Admiring historians and biographers then took these claims at face value, to the great enhancement of Curtin's reputation.

Australia's ANZUS treaty with the United States was secured by the Liberal government of Robert Menzies in 1951. Periodically Labor has been attacked as not sufficiently loyal to the alliance, to which Labor's reply has been that it created the alliance under John Curtin with his 'turn to America' statement. The falsity of that claim should now be evi-dent. In fact, Curtin did attempt to secure an alliance of some sort with the United States and was rebuffed.

Shedden, who guided Curtin on defence strategy, thought that through MacArthur Australia might be able to have more influence on allied defence policy than it had had with Churchill. With the men of the AIF back in Australia, they would constitute for a time the major part of MacArthur's best troops and so MacArthur would be beholden to Australia. MacArthur was not at all disposed to acknowledge this debt; he systematically hid the fact that his troops were Australian and it was MacArthur who told Curtin and Shedden that they would continue to have more 'pull' with Britain than the United States. Shedden himself recorded the general's blighting of his hopes because he took the minutes of the meetings between MacArthur, Curtin and himself, which were styled the 'Prime Minister's War Conference':

> The Commander-in-Chief desired to point out the distinctions between the United States and the United Kingdom in their relations and responsibilities to Australia. Australia was part of the British Empire and it was related to Britain and the other Dominions by ties of blood, sentiment and allegiance to the Crown. The United States was an ally whose aim was to win the war, and it had no sovereign interest in the integrity of Australia. Its interest in Australia was from the strategical aspect of the utility of Australia as a base from which to attack and defeat the Japanese. As the British Empire was a Commonwealth of Nations, he presumed that one of its principal purposes was jointly to protect any part that might be threatened. The failure of the United Kingdom and U.S.A. Governments to support Australia therefore had to be viewed from different angles.

Such a comprehensive put-down suggests the Australians had been angling for some formal recognition of their needs. The other evidence for this comes from the reports of Gerald Wilkinson, who was Churchill's liaison officer-cum-spy at MacArthur's headquarters. MacArthur told Wilkinson that on his arrival in Australia Curtin indicated that 'Australia was ready to shift over to the US away from the British Empire, but that he (MacArthur) had refused to listen to any such talk ...' Wilkinson himself thought MacArthur was probably exaggerating Curtin's remark, but there was plainly some discussion. Churchill knew of it, for when Wilkinson met him in London he was able to say with a chuckle what the Americans' response to Australia's overtures had been: 'They told them they would not have them.'

Having been rebuffed, and seeing that in its post-war planning in the Pacific America was very much looking after itself, Curtin turned back to Britain. At the 1944 Prime Ministers' Conference he tried and failed to strengthen the Commonwealth by the creation of a permanent secretariat. He appointed the king's brother, the Duke of Gloucester, as governor-general. These are not the moves recognised in the Labor legend about Curtin, which claims him as the prime minister who cut ties with Britain.

*

Curtin was much happier fighting against Japan than participating in the war in Europe and the Middle East. He depicted the Pacific War as a new war. The difficulty with this formulation was that the other protagonists did not see it this way. Japan's latest move continued its expansion, begun in 1937 when it attacked China. It now moved south because Russia, its chief enemy in Asia, was fully stretched repulsing the Germans in the 'old' war. Hitler, the instigator of the 'old' war, immediately joined the 'new' by declaring war on the United States. This made Roosevelt's task easier because, having been drawn into the 'new' war by Japan, he wanted to devote most of his efforts at first to the 'old' war in Europe. That was what Churchill had been angling for ever since the 'old' war began. Curtin was properly concerned that Japan's entry into the war directly threatened Australia, but it was panicky or purblind in the Australian leader to think that everyone else would now divide the world war in two to recognise that fact.

Before Japan attacked in the Pacific, Roosevelt and Churchill had decided to run a holding war against Japan and concentrate their efforts on beating Hitler. The danger to Australia of the 'beat Hitler first' strategy was that the 'holding line' against Japan might not hold to the north of Australia and the country would be invaded. By mid-1942, after the

American victories in the naval battles of the Coral Sea and Midway, it was clear that any danger of invasion had passed. It was at this time that Labor ministers first learnt of the 'beat Hitler first' strategy, which is something of a puzzle since it was scarcely top secret and could be read from the actions of the allied leadership. But though Australia was safe, Curtin railed against the strategy. He was encouraged in this by MacArthur, who did not want to run a holding war in the Pacific. Curtin supported his pleas for men and resources from the allied leadership without recognising that MacArthur's wish to return to the Philippines as soon as possible and make a name for himself was a different matter from the safety of Australia.

Curtin's off-the-record complaints about the allied 'neglect' of Australia make sorry reading.

> Curtin said it was useless addressing questions to Churchill and Roosevelt … he was fed up with the way these two men played ball with one another, quite regardless of the world at large.

There were still Australian forces fighting in the 'old ' war – airmen in Britain and the Ninth Division in the Middle East – which Curtin thought strengthened his claim to attention:

> Russia, which was fighting nowhere outside Russia, was getting more planes in a week than we got in almost a year.

This remark was delivered on 2 February 1943, just as the Russians turned the tide against Hitler at Stalingrad, the western half of European Russia having been invaded. Curtin's correction later in the session scarcely improved matters:

> He realised that Russia and China had probably stronger claims than Australia. On the other hand we were the only white race in the southern hemisphere, and almost the only Empire [he meant 'Dominion'] country doing anything.

Taking a broader view, he blamed Australia itself for the allied neglect:

> Curtin said it was the proper fate of any country which did not build its own defences and therefore could not logically look to anybody else. It was also the proper fate for a country that thought it could fight anybody's war before it made its own position safe.

Anybody's war! That's what the 'old' war was. Nothing to do with Australia! So much for Australia standing for freedom and liberty against the Nazi assault, which was how the prime minister publicly represented the war when he took office in October 1941 and in his speech at the Guildhall in 1944. What a noble pedigree 'other people's wars' has!

The greatest contribution of Australian troops to allied victory in the war was the Ninth Division's participation in the battle of El Alamein in North Africa in October–November 1942, which was the first victory against German forces. Curtin came close to denying Australia this honour. He regretted having left the Ninth Division in the Middle East when the other two AIF divisions came home. He had been signalling he wanted its return and then insisted on its return just as the second decisive El Alamein battle was about to commence. Bruce, the high commissioner in London, learnt from General Alexander that of all the formations under his command the Ninth Australian Division was the one he could least afford to lose. That did not move Curtin; why had they been made pivotal, he asked, when they were meant to be coming home? But Bruce held off conveying Curtin's instruction for its immediate return. The Australians performed magnificently, spearheading the attack; Churchill sent glowing measures of appreciation. When journalists asked Curtin whether he would follow Churchill in ordering church bells to be rung to celebrate the victory, he replied that he would not; the churches could please themselves. He did not like the word 'Victory'; he preferred 'Thanksgiving'. Privately to journalists he asked why the Australians were being used as 'the chopping block' when there were 900,000 other troops in the Middle East. That Australians might suffer higher casualties because they were used as shock troops stirred no pride in him. Though Curtin wished that Australian troops had not been there,

El Alamein became part of the national memory.

Labor had adjusted its policy to support Australia's involvement in the 'old' war and to conscript men for the defence of Australian territory. However, there had been no change to the policy of no conscription for service overseas, even though the enemy was now in the seas immediately to the north of the continent. Having two armies – the conscript militia for Australian territories and the volunteer AIF able to serve anywhere – was highly inefficient and damaging to morale. Since the AIF was the elite force, every militia unit was suspect. Militia men could transfer into the AIF but were sometimes prohibited from doing so to preserve militia units and some AIF officers suffered the indignity of being transferred to the militia to stiffen the ranks. The Opposition and the press had been calling for one army since Japan entered the war, but Curtin was unmoved. The problem of one part of the armed forces not being able to leave Australian territory was not yet acute; it might become so when the holding war was over.

The problem did become acute late in 1942 because the American press began to complain that while American conscripts were defending Australia, Australian conscripts could not leave their homeland. MacArthur, ever alert to anything that could damage his claims to more support, told Curtin that the militia policy would have to change. So Curtin told the Labor Party organisation that it would have to give up its sacred anti-conscription policy, for which Curtin himself in World War I had been the great champion, and create one army. It refused to do so; the most it would agree to – and this only by the narrowest of margins – was a temporary extension to the area in which the militia could serve. This did not extend to Japan or even to the boundaries of MacArthur's South-West Pacific zone. Its northern border was the equator, so in the southern half of Borneo the militia could fight but not in the northern.

This change to Labor's policy is regarded as one of Curtin's great achievements. Despite its absurdities it did achieve its purpose, since the criticism from America ceased. But notice that Curtin was unable to effect a fundamental change in Labor's thinking. Though the Japanese bombing of Darwin from Timor had shown the folly of thinking that an 'overseas' war was somehow a lesser threat, Labor's traditional policy was reinstated after the war: only volunteers, specially recruited, for service abroad and conscription only for home defence. It was left to the second Menzies government in 1950 to insist that when you joined the army you were agreeing to serve anywhere. Perhaps given how obscurantist Labor was on this matter, Curtin's achievement was substantial, though prompted to it by an American general. He almost certainly would have preferred to leave the old policy undisturbed, accepting that the war would be won by the conscripts of other nations being obliged to fight anywhere.

During the debate on the government's militia proposal early in 1943 and in the election later in the year, Menzies emerged as a severe critic of Curtin's 'parochial' approach to the war. Menzies was something of freelance; the United Australia Party, which he had led, was in its death throes, nicely symbolised by its leadership being in the hands of Billy Hughes, aged eighty. Menzies wanted one army able to serve anywhere and a defence policy governed by this principle:

> We must have a world conception of this war, in which we see Australia taking her rightful place, and not an Australian conception of the war in which we regard other Allied countries as incidental to our defence.

Or as Earle Page, the former Country Party leader, put it:

> We must abandon the view that it is only our skins that matter.

Curtin fully justified their critique in his policy speech for the 1943 election, when he accused the Menzies government of having neglected the defence of Australia by sending men to 'far-flung battlefields'; that is, to help Britain defeat Nazi Germany. Curtin talked of the crisis Australia faced soon after he came to office in 1941; Menzies said the greatest crisis for Australia and the world was when Britain looked as if it might be defeated in 1940.

Curtin had a lot going for him in this election: he had saved Australia from invasion (though that had not been the Japanese aim); he had brought MacArthur and the Americans (though they were sent, not bidden); he had run a united and effective government which had mobilised the nation for war (that much was true). Whatever the merits of his broader view of the war, Menzies and the shambolic United Australia Party could not provide an alternative government. It had to be Curtin and, as the Labor ads asserted, 'If you want Curtin you must vote Labor.' Labor won in a landside but that does not mean that Curtin's view of the war prevailed. During the election the allied invasion of Italy began and Mussolini was deposed. The battlefields were 'far-flung' but the newspapers were full of accounts of them, greatly overshadowing the news of the election. No Australians were involved in these battles but newspaper readers knew that the fate of Australia and the rest of the world hung on their outcome. Curtin did not like Australians taking too much interest in the war in Europe for fear that it would detract from their commitment to the war in the Pacific. In 1945 he discouraged the celebration of VE Day.

In the last stages of World War I Australian troops were in the thick of the fighting and scored notable victories. In the last stages of the war in the Pacific Australian troops were involved in side-shows and mopping-up operations. Even in his 'new' war Curtin could not arrange for Australian troops to play a significant part in final victory – and as always with Curtin the doubt remains whether he really minded.

On several occasions, MacArthur undertook to take AIF divisions with him to the Philippines long after he was determined to do no such thing. When it was clear that the AIF was not to be part of this advance, Curtin made no protest. He was absolutely in thrall to MacArthur, supporting his claims and protecting him from any threats to his control. He had allocated all Australian forces in the South-West Pacific to his command. Doing what the general wanted made defence policy easy. But what if there are two generals? General Blamey was head of the Australian army and officially commander of all land forces under MacArthur's command. MacArthur sidelined him from this latter role in line with his determination to have no Australians in the American limelight. Blamey was naturally jealous of MacArthur and anxious to carve out a role for himself.

Curtin's response to this conundrum was to do nothing. He was unwilling to contest MacArthur's wish that only Americans fight under him in the battles that mattered nor Blamey's wish that Australian troops be kept together and fight under his command. Since Curtin wanted the troops to be fighting somewhere, the result of his lassitude was that in the last year of the war Australian troops fought under Blamey in battles that did not matter.

Government control of the use of Australian troops disappeared. Blamey, left in charge of troops doing garrison duty in New Guinea, decided to go on the offensive against the Japanese, who had been by-passed by MacArthur in his drive northwards. When this policy was criticised in Australia as a waste of lives, Curtin asked MacArthur, as commander-in-chief, whether he was happy with it. MacArthur said it was being conducted well. But had he actually authorised it? Blamey said that MacArthur had provided landing craft so he must be in favour. When this was put to MacArthur, he said this provisioning was mere routine and he thought there was no need to go on the offensive. Chifley, the new prime minister, rebuked MacArthur for embarrassing the government, which had used his name to answer the criticism of the offensive policy. A rebuke! It had never happened under Curtin. Reading the record as Chifley took over and the plans for Australia's part in the occupation of Japan were finalised, you feel that Australia had acquired a government again.

Defenders of Curtin's relationship with MacArthur argue that a small power has not much chance of influencing a great-power ally. What is disturbing in Curtin is that he made no attempt to test the boundaries. He did actually have some pull over MacArthur for MacArthur needed him to advocate the needs of his sector and if a quarrel with MacArthur had been carried to President Roosevelt, MacArthur might not have prevailed since he was a likely Republican Party contender for the president's job. But Curtin was content to be abject.

*

The best biographer of Curtin sadly left his work unfinished or, to speak plainly, he had scarcely begun it when he died. This biography-in-the-making is held in the John Curtin Prime Ministerial Library, an excellent facility at Curtin University in Perth. The biographer was the journalist and editor of *Nation*, Tom Fitzgerald. The data collected and the work unfinished bear out the old saying: 'Anyone can attempt to collect all the facts; only a historian knows how few facts are needed to make a history.' But fortunately Fitzgerald stopped collecting on occasion and started drafting. Here is his key to the understanding of Curtin:

> Curtin's innate high personal sensitivity to physical danger would naturally (and properly) have strengthened his abhorrence of war and militarism as a young man. In his years as prime minister, the dominant moral and emotional concern and the continuing pressure on his consciousness was the sacrifice of their lives that thousands of Australians were making on behalf of others, including himself and his kin, sacrifices that he may have felt would possibly have been beyond his own physical capacity to make.

As you read and listen to Curtin's speeches, you sense the correctness of this. The constant trope in his pleas for Australians to give up more for the war effort is the contrast between soldiers sacrificing their lives and the comfort of those at home, even with all the restrictions that war imposed. That this was deeply felt in himself is evident in the stridency and hectoring of his speeches; he blamed himself for not being able to persuade everyone to strip inessentials away and follow him in Spartan dedication. He was told – by Menzies, by the press, by his own PR people – that most people were making sacrifices for the war effort and the tiny minority who weren't were not going to be persuaded by more badgering or bribes. But he would not cease from scolding.

The trade unionists who continued to strike properly worried him. The coalminers drove him to distraction; neither pleas nor benefits nor punishment made a difference. Again he blamed their intransigence on himself and once offered to resign as prime minister if they would dig more coal. Curtin never visited the coalminers, just as he never visited the troops in the field. Had he done so they both may have become more human in his eyes, the miners less wicked and the soldiers less noble. They remained an appalling contrast locked in his mind, a recurring symbol of the failure of humankind and his own.

Curtin mounted an extraordinary attack on the people's pleasures. In Britain production of beer was maintained at pre-war levels and the government accepted that the morale of the British working man depended on his being able to get his pint, and not any pint: the one he was used to having. Curtin cut production of beer by one third. There were always shortages of beer and much time was wasted in searching out a pub with beer or a blackmarketeer who could supply it. The restriction probably damaged the war effort more than assisting it. Gambling on the horses distressed Curtin even more than drinking. He declared Raceless Saturdays, one in every month, and spent a great deal of time organising other restrictions and limitations and then defending them to outraged deputations. If race meetings could not be banned outright, he wanted to ensure that people could not get the information to follow the races off the course, which of course SP bookmaking required. But money spent on gambling continued to rise.

One looks in vain in Curtin's speeches for the memorable phrase; speech-making was one of his great strengths but you had to be there. His pithy remarks occur in his denunciations of pleasure:

> I am utterly unconcerned if there is not enough beer.
> Betting is the canker of Australia.
> Brains and brawn are better than bets and beer.

These remarks were on the record; the last was used in government advertisements. Off the record he said 'he couldn't understand the mentality of the Australian people. One day they were in a panic and the next they wanted more race meetings.' Putting people in a panic was one of Curtin's ploys to stimulate the war effort. That he could not understand why people might still want diversions in a war – not more race meetings; just the ones he had banned – showed how warped his understanding had become. 'I regard it as ridiculous,' he pontificated, 'to suggest that a man ministers to his personal comfort by hanging around betting shops on Saturday afternoons.'

In August 1942, when he had been assured that the danger of invasion had passed, Curtin took to cabinet a series of draconian proposals.

Among them were:

- Beer production to be cut by one half, instead of by one third
- The Commonwealth to take over from the states the policing of pubs with loss of licence and salutary sentences for offenders
- No drinks to be served with meals
- Race meetings to be reduced by 50 per cent
- 'Press to eliminate glamour from sporting reports'; that is, only the bare information of fixtures to be held and results to be published, which would see the demise of the *Sportsman* and the *Sporting Globe*
- 'Press to eliminate all mention in Social Pages of any person or function engaged in any activity not connected with the war effort'
- Businesses or persons who offend against regulations to have their premises or homes placarded
- 'Power to take over for a period, with loss of profit, any business firms that offend any regulation'

The prime minister was out of control. The cabinet rejected all these measures.

Despairing of the continuing selfishness of his people, Curtin moved to establish 'Austerity' as a state religion. There were Austerity Sundays of self-examination, when the people were to think of the men fighting 'a seven-day-a-week death struggle for us' and then 'how they can strip themselves for total war.' There was a six-part Austerity Pledge that Curtin wanted all Australians to take, which like his speeches was a little wordy. Point three was the shortest: 'We shall cut from our lives every luxury, every relaxation, every temptation to slack.' The press carried stories of how the Curtins at home were living Austerity. In 1944 on the prime minister's birthday, Mrs Curtin, by their mutual desire, did not give him a birthday present and there was no cake. The Protestant cast of the Austerity rituals intrigued Fitzgerald, since Curtin was brought up a Catholic. He posed the question – Was Curtin an instinctive Protestant? – and opened a file.

Curtin became promoter and patron of the Moral Re-Armament movement as the priesthood of the Austerity religion. Their musical tableau *The Battle for Australia*, whose message was cooperation and unselfishness, was performed in Sydney and Melbourne and Curtin had travel restrictions lifted so that some of the cast from both cities could perform for members in the dining room at Parliament House. Afterwards Curtin discussed with the producer how to get the show to six million Australians.

The ordinary purpose of Austerity was to reduce consumption and encourage savings, which could then be directed into war loans. Curtin turned it first into a mode of making himself and the people worthy of the soldiers and then into a preparation for socialism. The government had its own program for post-war reconstruction, but Curtin knew that unless men's hearts were changed, a gentler cooperative society was impossible (Fitzgerald had a file on Curtin's interest in human perfectibility). The war would jolt people out of their selfish trivial concerns and engender new bonds of brotherhood. All conflict would be quietened, including that between bosses and workers. One of the songs in *The Battle for Australia* was explicit in rejecting post-war planning:

> They ask us our war aims, they ask us our plan,
> They ask what's the new world to be,
> And what sort of Australia the ordinary man
> For the future most wishes to see.
>
> Now the problem before us, we've go to face facts,
> Is selfishness, grousing and greed;
> So we don't want new systems, new treaties, new pacts –
> It's new men and women we need.

At the parliamentary lunch for the cast of *The Battle for Australia*, John Dedman, one of Curtin's ministers, quietly disowned the message of the show and his boss. He said that a beginning has to be made at a personal level, but that society's institutional structure had to change.

The approach of victory in the war brought not satisfaction to Curtin but disillusion and despair. Even in the special circumstances of total war, the people had shown they did not have the spirit that a new social order would require. Worst of all, the labour movement, which was to manage the transition to a new order, contained trade unionists who would not work for the common cause and parliamentarians who undermined him. (Curtin was unusually sensitive to criticism from within his party. A normally ambitious man expects others to block and undermine him; Curtin, seeing himself as ambitious only for the cause, took criticism as a reflection on his purity.)

From the time of his death, it has been said that Curtin was a casualty of the war if ever there was one. This is correct so long as it is properly understood. It was not the burden of the war that killed Curtin; it was the burden of being John Curtin in the war. There has never been such an awkward and contrived prime ministership. The pacifist war leader burdened with guilt that finally unbalanced him. The socialist who was discovering that socialism was not possible. The ideas man who had to abandon or suppress nearly all his past positions. Fitzgerald lamented how little we know of the process by which, in the last ten years of his life, Curtin changed his views on so many matters. As we have seen, his public pronouncements could be different from his private views, which were still very much the old – or rather the young – Curtin. We have to allow the possibility that Curtin did not change his views much at all and that the whole prime ministership was a contrivance. He put himself through it all so that the Labor Party could fulfil its role – and then the Labor Party failed him.

Of course contrivance is a regular part of politics, but Curtin's spirit was antipathetic to his core responsibility of governing Australia in a world war. As he said, 'I was not trained to be a war lord. Yet fate pushed on to me at least the appearance of being one.' He could do the big performances – 'the man of peace putting on the vestments of the warrior chief' – and he adjusted himself and his party to do the job which did not turn out to be particularly demanding: he had to provide stable government for this base of American operations. But adjustment to events is different from understanding and commanding them. The war as a world war was beyond him; he put no Australian mark on it. Had the danger to Australia been greater, Curtin's poor standing in London and

Washington may have handicapped Australia's defence. His isolationism has too often been called statesmanship by simple-minded patriots. He yielded responsibility over where Australians fought to his generals. Even in command of the home front, where he operated more effectively, he was at odds with the people he had to lead and had to be saved by his cabinet from turning austerity into tyranny.

*

In calling for a reassessment of Curtin I have inevitably highlighted his short-comings and limitations. But the picture I have presented is true to the character that his intimates knew: commanding on the platform and in parliament, conciliatory within the party, but otherwise frequently moody, withdrawn, anxious and self-doubting. Chifley, his mainstay in the cabinet, was so different: calm, well grounded, unperturbed by criticism, but lacking the passion that Curtin could bring to public performances.

Though I cannot rate Curtin a great prime minister, I can well understand the admiration for him. The more unsuited and wayward he is found to be, the more he is admired for managing as well as he did in very difficult circumstances. He provided the nation with stable government when no one else could and from the unpromising materials that the Labor Party then afforded. I myself would not want to downgrade him far in the ranking of prime ministers. But admiration for overcoming incapacity cannot be the basis for a claim to greatness.

Egalitarian Australians loved Curtin for his personal qualities, which Geoff Serle lists as 'unassuming dignity, simplicity, sincerity, straightforwardness, absence of vanity, and refusal of any privilege' – so unusual in a politician. But these too should not be mistaken for greatness. Hawke and Keating were not nearly as nice.

2010

A REPUBLICAN MANIFESTO

USTRALIA WAS BORN IN CHAINS AND IS NOT YET FULLY FREE. We are an old dependency of the British crown which has not stirred itself to claim complete independence. But surely, you will say, we are a sovereign independent state? Not quite. We depend on Britain to provide us with our head of state. The queen may be called the Queen of Australia, but she is not Made in Australia.

If for any reason there ceased to be a monarch of Britain, our constitution would seize up. When the present governor-general retired or died, there would be no mechanism to replace him. Without a governor-general, ministers could not be appointed, bills could not be passed into law, parliament could not be summoned, and elections could not be held. Australia does not have a self-sufficient constitution.

At every stage in our gradual separation from Britain we have cut one tie and comforted ourselves that others remained. We became self-governing in internal affairs and Britain still defended us from external enemies. We appointed our own judges and appeals to the Privy Council in Britain survived. We became responsible for defence and foreign policy and the British monarch remained as our head of state. At no time have we said: 'Now we can manage fully on our own.'

And what would happen if we cut the last tie and created our own head of state? The monarchists say that we would fall into chaos and ruin. It turns out that our long history of self-government and our pioneering in democracy have taught us nothing. Our success in governing ourselves depends absolutely on our retaining the British monarch as our head of state. At this late stage in our dealings with Britain, the republican debate has flushed out living specimens of the colonial cringe – people who distrust the locals, including themselves. There are many reasons for supporting a republic, but as the debate continues one reason becomes more and more compelling. Under a republic there would be no more monarchists. We will cease to have as fellow citizens those who say that we cannot be citizens unless there is a British monarch on an Australian throne.

Of course under a republic monarchists will not be suppressed. They will simply lapse into silence and forget their old attachment. This is what happened to those who said we had to keep British governors and the British national anthem and British knighthoods. Once we have established Australian symbols, no patriot can advocate a return to British ones. But these people are slow learners. They sing 'Advance Australia Fair' and would be outraged at the appointment of a British governor-general, but they declare that the next step away from Britain is sure to bring the disaster which mysteriously did not follow from all the previous ones.

We need to break finally with Britain, not because Britain has served us badly but because she has served us too well. We have gained our independence with scarcely a struggle. The Americans and the Canadians fought the British for independence – so Britain in the mid-nineteenth century readily granted Australians the right to internal self-government. In the twentieth century Ireland and South Africa demanded the right to control foreign affairs and defence and in yielding to them Britain granted the same right to Australia as well. For ten years Australia refused the offer.

No one would wish away our peaceful severance from Britain. Few would deny that the benign supervision of the evolution of the Australian colonies into nationhood was one of the great triumphs of British statecraft. But there has been a cost. There has never been a moment when we have attached ourselves to our political system as the embodiment of our nation.

The yobbo who yells 'Go home!' to the Poms at the cricket is happy to borrow a Pom as his queen. This is not because he has been schooled by Australians for a Constitutional Monarchy to think of her as Queen of Australia. It is because he does not think of his Australianness as having any connection to politics.

Our critics are right to say that Australia does not need to become a republic to acquire a distinctive identity. Australians have a very well-developed sense of who they are, but it relates almost solely to their social being. We are free and easy, egalitarian, not snobby, and not class conscious: we are not Poms. We think little of ourselves as fellow citizens of the Commonwealth of Australia. Politics is simply there. We appear sometimes to believe that we have politics only because a few egomaniacs want to be politicians. To be suspicious of politicians may be no bad thing. To be suspicious of politics is unhealthy for a free people. A republican people is proud of its sovereignty and its status as citizens. Republicans are challenging the Australian people to take their citizenship seriously and make their political system wholly Australian. There is something irresponsible in relying on another state to provide part of our constitutional machinery. It is only a small step to a republic, but it is the first step into full maturity.

*

The monarchists ask why we concern ourselves so much with the queen when she interferes so little in Australian affairs. All she does is appoint the governor-general on the recommendation of the prime minister. Exactly so. That is all she does. She does not do – she cannot do – the chief part of her job, which is to serve as the symbol of the Australian nation.

There was a time when she did. When we thought of ourselves as British as well as Australian, when our chief trade and defence ties were with Britain, when we valued our membership of the British empire and Commonwealth, then a British monarch of Australia was no anomaly. But that world has gone. We are no longer a British people. Britain no longer has an empire and offers us nothing in trade or defence. Britain turned its back on the lands that shared her queen and entered Europe. Whole communities in rural Australia which had come into existence by supplying the British market were told to find other markets or dissolve. I do not blame the British. I wish we were as hard-headed. We are not abashed to queue as foreigners to enter the land of our queen.

The queen herself has been to Strasbourg to give her sanction to British membership of the European Community. On the produce from her own farms she receives the subsidies paid under the common agricultural policy which does such damage to Australian agricultural exports.

The queen of Australia is one of the enemies of rural Australia. Such are the consequences of our keeping the British monarch after our commonality of interest with Britain has ended.

For Australians of the pioneering age the monarch became a symbol of home and of empire and they forgot those aspects of the monarch which were at odds with all they believed in. It was a hereditary position and they wanted a society where birth could claim no privilege. The monarch was head of the established church and the thing they were most passionate about was that the state should favour no one religion over another. As the other reasons for keeping the monarch weaken, the contradiction between the queen and the Australia she represents becomes more glaring. Here is democratic, egalitarian Australia maintaining a hereditary head of state. A land which early separated church and state accepts that its monarch will head the Anglican Church and that she cannot become a Catholic. Is this the best symbol we can get of the Australian nation?

The number of Australians who will honour this symbol is declining rapidly. The erosion of loyalty to the queen is not to be measured by opinion-poll figures on support for the republic. The monarchists may scare people about the republic, but that is not the same as reviving the queen. For Australians to return to their near unanimous loyalty of the 1950s, history would have to run backwards.

There is something absurd in the monarchists' defence of the queen. As soon as she has to be defended, she has ceased to be a symbol of national unity. Monarchists are not upholding a living symbol, but a piece of constitutional machinery.

We are told that no matter how we arrange the election of a republican head of state, we will never get a president to command the respect that the queen enjoys, or rather once enjoyed. That is so. Under a republic the sacred object will not be the person of the president, but the bond which unites the citizens. We will pledge our allegiance to each other and the ideals and institutions which sustain our democracy. Let us say:

I will be a true citizen of the Commonwealth of Australia.
I will uphold its constitution as adopted and amended by
the people.

I will grant to all my fellow citizens, without distinction,
     equality of rights, opportunity and respect.

Do not think of the republic as loss; our monarchical words of allegiance are already dead. The republic will revive our civic culture.

*

Are we denying our past in becoming a republic? No. All that we honour now we keep – Shakespeare, two-up, Anzac, Mozart, *The Magic Pudding*. The only thing we jettison is our colonial selves. To become a republic we are keeping the institutions of government we have adapted from Britain and the United States – parliament, cabinet, the rule of law, the separation of powers, federalism. In becoming a republic we are claiming that part of our heritage which honours a people who govern themselves. Republicanism is part of our past, which is as large as the course of Western civilisation. I confess we are not innovators. Republicanism began in Rome in the fifth century BC. The monarchists are the true innovators – they plan for one state to use in perpetuity the monarch of another. The maintenance of such an arrangement, despite time and circumstance and the indifference, not to say hostility, of the nation supplying the monarch to the nation borrowing the monarch, has no parallel in the annals of humankind.

The paradox of being a colony is that you become more like the mother country as you move away from it. We were first ruled by governors, with no one having a vote: a most un-British regime. We became more like Britain when we acquired our own parliaments. The likeness grew stronger when we took responsibility for our foreign affairs and defence. We were then a sovereign state as Britain is. The likeness will be stronger still when we create our own head of state. Britain does not have a foreigner as its head of state. The presidency will not be a hereditary position but the occupant of this office will in effect be an elected 'constitutional monarch', someone who reigns but does not rule, a perpetual tribute to the British original.

We are asked what republic we wish to imitate. None. We will be imitating ourselves for our aim is to preserve our existing system of government and create an elected head of state to do what the governor-general now does. If you want constitutional excitement, look elsewhere. The best guide to the behaviour of our future republic is not any other republic, but our own past. Our future will be as stable and democratic as our past has been.

Of course there are difficulties in creating a republic. But while monarchists boast of our incapacity to solve them, republicans will not. It is not after all so difficult a task: larger than changing the national anthem, but much smaller than the establishment of the constitution in the first place. In the 1890s our political leaders drew up the constitution of 128 clauses and against determined opposition the people voted 'Yes' at referendums to endorse it. Now we are told that it is too difficult to create an Australian head of state. We will not believe it.

Let those who love the queen be treated with respect as the queen herself should be. Let us save our contempt for those who want to keep the queen because they don't think Australians could manage on their own.

1994

AUSTRALIA'S ABSURD HISTORY

MULTICULTURALISM, WITH CONTRADICTION AT ITS HEART, has a great capacity for the absurd. Its exponents are now developing an absurdist history of Australia. This is how it runs: Once upon a time there was a small, inward looking, intolerant, racist Anglo-Celtic nation. It began to take migrants from Europe and then Asia. The migration program was an outstanding success. The nation turned into a diverse, open, tolerant society. The new migrants created the tolerance.

Where is the absurdity in this? That a nation which hated 'wogs' invited hundreds of thousands of Italians and Greeks to come to its shores? No, nations, like individuals, may under urgent necessity do what is distasteful to them. The rationale for the migration policy was to boost Australia's population and economy as a defence against a renewed threat from the north. Better the dark-skinned Greek than the Japanese. No, the absurdity lies in the claim that the migrants created the tolerance. The more benighted and bigoted we make the Australian people of the 1940s, the less likely it is that the migration program would have had a successful outcome. If the Anglo-Celts were so bad – and in the current demonology there is no-one worse than an Anglo-Celt circa 1940 – why did they not savagely oppress and permanently marginalise the incoming strangers, a process all too common and very easy to accomplish?

But if the strangers are numerous and carry with them a very different value system, could they then not have a transforming effect on the host society? The migrants were certainly numerous and over a short time constituted a reasonably high proportion of the old population, but they were not of one sort; they came from a number of different countries and were notoriously intolerant of each other. If Greeks and Turks, Serbs and Croats, Arabs and Jews live in peace in Australia, it is not because they brought tolerance with them. Let us abandon absurdity and explore a commonsense hypothesis: that the migration scheme has been a success because the roots of the tolerance lay in the society which invited the migrants to join it.

Multiculturalism makes ethnic origin into destiny. So at the last census Australians were asked about their ancestry and encouraged not to answer 'Australian'. Even those whose families have been here for four or six generations were meant to declare a European ancestry. As with individuals, so with society. In the eyes of multiculturalists Australian society of the 1940s, 150 years after first settlement, is adequately described as Anglo-Celtic. At least this acknowledges that the people of Australia were Irish and Scots as well as English, but it has nothing more substantial than a hyphen joining them. In fact a distinct new culture had been formed. English, Scots and Irish had formed a common identity – first of all British and then gradually Australian as well. In the 1930s the historian W. K. Hancock could aptly describe them as Independent Australian Britons.

To say that the Australians were more British than the British carries more of the truth than is usually realised. Britishness was not a very strong identity in Great Britain itself. The heartland of the United Kingdom was England and the English thought of themselves as English and only on the rare occasions when they wanted to be polite to the Scots did they use the term 'British'. In Australia the pressure of the Scots and especially of the Irish forced the abandonment of 'English' as the identity of the colonies in favour of 'British'. The Irish of course could still bridle at a British identity even when it included them as equals. In time, with the passing of the first generation born in Ireland and the growth of a distinctively Australian interpretation of Britishness, they were prepared to accept it. The Irish had done well in Australia and saw the adoption of self-government within the empire as the solution to the Irish problem at home, the system which had worked so well in the colonies.

Multiculturalists pride themselves on their respect for the identity people give themselves. They tell us that if Greeks want to call themselves Greeks, they should be referred to as such and not as Greek-Australians, still less as New Australians. In calling Australians of the 1940s and their descendants 'Anglo-Celts' multiculturalists depart from their own rule. This term has not been used by these people to describe themselves.

They were proud that they had constrained particular ethnic identities and subsumed them into the broader terms of British and Australian. The imposition of 'Anglo-Celt' is the tyrannical arm of multiculturalism. I find the term offensive.

The Irish were present in large numbers from the beginning of European settlement in Australia. Hence Australian society as it was forming had to accommodate the antagonism of Catholic and Protestant which had torn Europe apart and still poisoned relations between England and Ireland. If the Church of England, established by law and funded by compulsory contributions from all, was transferred intact to Australia, the old battles would begin again. We owe it to a liberal governor of New South Wales, a Protestant Irishman, that they did not. In 1836 Governor Bourke decided if there were to be established churches, all three of the great divisions of Christianity within Britain should be established. He would allot public funds on the same terms to the Church of England, the Catholic Church and the Presbyterians. This amazing measure was the clearest signal to the Irish that life in Australia was to be truly a new dispensation. A British government was financing the Roman heresy. The system worked well and was expanded to include any who wanted to join it – even Jews. It lasted in New South Wales until 1862, in Victoria until 1870. Those colonies then adopted the more orthodox liberal principle of complete separation of church and state which had been pioneered in this country by South Australia. Under either system the state was strictly neutral on an issue which could and did bitterly divide its people. This neutrality was policed with an eagle eye. All other distinctions between churches having been removed, the colonists argued bitterly over whether the Anglican bishop should take precedence at a government house levee over his Catholic brother.

Unlike in the United States and Canada, the English, Scots and Irish did not form separate enclaves. There was a remarkably even intermingling. This in itself suggests a high degree of toleration which was advanced further by the determination to keep sectarian rivalry out of community organisations. In the nineteenth century, hospitals, charities of all sorts, trade unions, friendly societies, sporting clubs, the mechanics institutes and the schools of arts which ran the libraries and the public halls – all these had Catholics and Protestants on their boards and among their members and clients and worked to keep them together. This was not easy. There was always low-level tension and sometimes spectacular brawls. Separate community organisations for Protestants and Catholics would have avoided this dissension, but threatened much worse.

In society at large public feuding between Protestant and Catholic occurred regularly and was sometimes savage. Historians who search mindlessly for conflict latch on to such episodes as if they have discovered a Belfast or a Beirut. But this public feuding did not lead to polarisation at community level or residential segregation and it encouraged people of goodwill on both sides to redouble their efforts to neutralise the conflict. The commitment to avoid old-world divisions was much stronger than the desire to perpetuate them.

The worst sectarian violence in our history occurred in Melbourne in 1846 when Catholic and Protestant mobs fired on each other on the anniversary of the Battle of the Boyne. But note the response. The colony's mini-parliament immediately passed a law banning processions held to commemorate festivals, anniversaries, or political events related to any religious or political differences between Her Majesty's subjects. Banners and music calculated to provoke animosity were forbidden. The poisonous cycle of demonstration and counter demonstration by which Northern Ireland keeps alive its troubled past was nipped in the bud. But all that colour gone from the streets! A disappointing outcome according to true multiculturalists who appear to believe that no social differences can be damaging, no matter how acute or passionately held they are – so long, of course, as all participating parties have access to a regularly-updated multicultural policy statement.

The liberal hope for education was that children of all religions could come together in schools run by the state. Religion would still be taught. Either the regular teachers would teach a common Christianity – the essentials of the faith to be agreed on by all the churches – or clergymen of the different churches would be allowed to come to the schools to instruct their own children. The opponents of these schemes were the churches, or more precisely the clergy. The laity in general supported them. The only church finally which could sustain its opposition to these schemes was the one where clergy had most power over the laity – the Catholic. Here old world antagonisms could not be kept at bay.

The Catholic bishops and priests were Irish and judging by their Irish experience thought any state scheme of education must be designed to undermine their faith. They could not see that the governments of the British colonies of Australia were different from the Protestant English state which oppressed Ireland. The Catholics were a large minority, but not large enough to stop the liberal schemes of education. The Catholic opposition to these schemes made state education into a Protestant cause. This issue became the most divisive in nineteenth-century Australia. The Catholic clergy set out to build their own schools and demanded that government money be granted to them. This was fiercely resisted. On the other hand the state rejected pressure to adopt some Protestant forms of instruction and worship in its schools. The state schools remained strictly neutral. Some Catholic children continued to attend them.

This battle confirmed the widely held view, stronger probably among Protestants than Catholics, that the clergy were a grave threat to the development of a tolerant society in Australia. They had an interest in exaggerating the virtues of their own faith and the shortcomings of others. In some colonies clergy were prohibited from becoming members of parliament to reduce their opportunities for sowing discord. In community organisations it was impossible to have a single clergyman participating; there had to be representatives of all major denominations. The usual practice was to have none. To isolate the divisive force of religion was relatively easy since no one church had ever established its pre-eminence. Much more than in England, Ireland, Scotland or Wales the clergy were confined to their churches.

Class differences which became significant from the 1880s were accommodated in a similar way to religious differences. At first sight Australia seems an unlikely place for strong class feeling to take root. In the late nineteenth century most of industry was still small-scale, living standards were the highest in the world, and workers did not experience the hauteur of an aristocracy or stigmatisation from a solid bourgeoisie. But doctrines of liberation galvanise best those who are more than half liberated already. Because the working class was better off and more self-confident they adopted more eagerly the new doctrines of social-ism and aggressive trade unionism. These did not so much lead working men to concentrate a new hatred on their class enemies – for these seemed inconsequential – as encourage them to think that an improve-ment in their own lot and the transformation of society could be readily accomplished. This heady optimism was rapidly punctured. The largest employers – ship owners, mine owners and pastoralists – quickly devel-oped their own organisations and when the unions blundered into a national strike in 1890 they were decisively defeated. During this strug-gle and the more desperate shearers' strikes of 1891 and 1894, employers were totally intransigent, police and troops were deployed by govern-ments, on occasions strikers used or threatened violence, and some strike leaders were gaoled.

There was widespread dismay that social disruption and hatred of an old-world intensity had broken out in the new. This was the mood in which the distinctively Australian response to class conflict emerged – the establishment of an arbitration court which would compulsorily settle industrial disputes. This did not end class conflict, but it insti-tutionalised it at a distance. The new disruption, which threatened so much, was declared to be amenable to the time-honoured procedure for dispute-settling, the law. Trade unionists accepted this regime because they were weakened by strikes and depression and because the rapid suc-cess of their new Labor Party gave them some guarantee that the state would not be used against them. The left has criticised them ever since for transferring industrial conflict, which is meant to be the growth point of socialism, to the tribunals of the capitalist state. But it was a capitalist state of a special sort which enhanced the status of workers by treating them as litigants of equal standing with employers and made their wages and conditions a matter of regular official concern.

Class differences were ameliorated in another way. In face-to-face encounters Australians gradually dropped old-world formality and defer-ence and spoke to each other as equals. This is an egalitarianism on which Australians have come to set great store. So far their historians have told them very little about how it came about. We know that complete equal-ity in form of address was first practised on the goldfields when men of all conditions were dressed in working man's clothes and doing hard manual labour. Everyone was 'mate'. We do not know how long it took for this practice to spread to the rest of society. It is hard to imagine it proceeding any further than the point it has now reached where given names are used not only in casual but in formal encounters.

The success of the Labor Party depended on its ability to keep Protestant and Catholic working men together. Since the Irish were overwhelmingly working class, the numbers of Catholics and Protestants in the party were close to being equal, which made it very different from any other public body. From the beginning it committed itself unequivocally against taking sides in any religious matter. Despite the high proportion of Catholics among its members, it refused to take up the Catholic cause of funding for church schools. Following the split in the party over conscription during World War I, the Catholics became even more prominent. The church began to think it could pressure the party to deliver on funding for its schools. The Catholic parliamentarians resisted. A Catholic party contested the New South Wales 1920 election to teach the Labor Party the lesson that it could not have Catholic votes if it ignored Catholic causes – and failed disastrously. Catholic voters and parliamentarians had refused to be diverted from the main cause, the improvement of workers' conditions, and this involved working with people of other faiths or no faith.

The other great Australian institution of the twentieth century, the RSL, had to discipline itself closely if it were to keep the old soldiers together. It had to avoid any party political or religious alignment. It could not take the easy option of ignoring religion altogether since it wanted a religious service to conclude the annual Anzac Day march. This was drawn up as a non-denominational service but the Catholic Church forbade its members to attend it which was its practice regarding any service not conducted according to its own rites. Conscientious Catholics accordingly dropped out from the march toward its end. This always rankled with the RSL whose animating spirit was the desire to retain the camaraderie of war which had made all the differences of civilian life seem irrelevant. In 1938 the Victorian RSL faced up to the problem of bringing the religiously divided together, the theme of so much of our history. It was an extremely tricky issue: to win Catholic participation the service must be completely non-religious, but to drop all references to God at the behest of Catholics would outrage Protestants. The League devised a new civic service, but to show it was not anti-religion it encouraged churches to hold their own services on Anzac Day and the civic service itself was left open for religious use. There was to be a two-minute silence – in which soldiers could pray according to their lights. There was even a hymn, 'Lead Kindly Light', a cunning choice this, written by a Catholic and not actually mentioning God. There were loud complaints from Protestant clergy at these changes, but they don't seem to have affected participation in the service. The Catholic Archbishop, Daniel Mannix, gave the new service his blessing and thanked the RSL for its consideration. For the first time Catholics and Protestants remembered their dead together.

*

It is true that British Australia before World War II was intolerant of non-British migration, but it was expert in the modes of toleration. The old dinner party rule that religion and politics should not be discussed had been the principle on which the formation of civil society had proceeded. Matters which were known to be divisive had to be kept at a distance or subject to strict local quarantine. Civil society should not be shaped by religion or politics, but preserved against them. This explains both the decencies of our private and community life and the vacuousness of our public discourse. The contrast with the United States is complete. There religious and ethnic differences have firmly shaped community life and the commitment to equality and toleration is made in public discourse: the noble words of the Declaration of Independence and the Constitution.

The reasons for the success of the migration program should now be apparent. Migrants had to suffer personal abuse and suspicion, but Australian society, except in its treatment of Aborigines, is uneasy with sustained and systematic social exclusion. Its instincts are inclusive. As one migrant reports, 'Australians did not especially like "foreigners" but they disliked drawing attention to themselves by being nasty to people more than they disliked foreigners.' It should not be forgotten that assimilation, now criticised for its cultural arrogance, was a welcoming attitude. And it demanded less than its latter day critics imagined. There was not a homogeneous society insisting on complete conformity. Migrants were not being asked to abandon everything; rather they were not to make a public display of difference; they were to 'mix in' and live among Australians and not in their own enclaves. That is, these new differences were to be handled like the old Protestant–Catholic differences had been.

The Australian ethos, as I have outlined it, was concerned not to obliterate difference but to overlook it. It is best caught by Henry Lawson:

> They tramp in mateship side by side
> The Protestant and Roman
> They call no biped Lord or Sir
> And touch their hat to no man

This is not envisaging a world where there will not be Protestants and Catholics or employers and employees. It insists that person with person, face to face, these differences are not to count. Much ink has been wasted by social scientists 'proving' that Australian society is not egalitarian because it has quite distinct differences of class and status. Our egalitarianism is rather the means by which we live more comfortably with those differences; it makes them less disruptive and demeaning.

Now, to leave differences out of account, as D. H. Lawrence observed in *Kangaroo*, can make for very superficial encounters. I can well understand migrants' complaints that Australians were passionless, offhand, and even when most polite, strangely indifferent to their background and experience. We are not looking for reasons why migrants were comfortable or contented – for migration must always be more or less traumatic – but to the general social circumstances which allowed for the accommodation and melding of peoples to proceed relatively smoothly. The process would have been different if the Australian people had been more divided socially among themselves and less concerned to bridge barriers.

Nearly all migrants entered the Australian economy as workers. It is often said that migrants were exploited because they had to take the lowest paid jobs which Australians thankfully left. But the trade union movement only agreed to the admission of migrants as long as they were to be paid award wages. Unskilled migrants, knowing no English and with no experience of trade unions, came under the protection of the arbitration court. This put a severe limit to their 'exploitation'. The unions' historic opposition to migration had arisen because they feared that migrants, especially those with low expectations and less ability to defend themselves, would drive wages down. They had to be assured that this would not happen before they would support the post-war scheme.

Some Australians were disappointed that migrants did not mix in readily and that they formed, temporarily as it turned out, their own residential enclaves. But the freedoms of a free society are real. Freedom of movement, of residence, of speech and publication, of association, of business enterprise could not be denied the migrants. The commitment to an open society means that we agree to live with what is unusual, distasteful or even threatening. It is a great act of faith and easy enough to think it foolhardy. However, if liberalism has its dangers, it also has it unexpected rewards. Modern Australia is one of them. In the space which an open and tolerant society gave them migrants found security, prosperity and self-confidence and transformed the society in ways which their hosts had not intended. They have made it a much more diverse, lively and exciting place. Because the outcome was unintended, Australians can take no great credit for it, though the commitment to openness and tolerance was theirs. Since liberalism's achievements depend on self-restraint, it is easy to overlook its outstanding practitioners.

The children and grandchildren of southern European peasants are now flocking into Australian universities. If they choose to study sociology, there is a good chance they will be taught that migrants are a badly treated minority. They might well have as their textbook Professor J. S. Western's very popular *Social Inequality in Australian Society* which declares that the history of migration 'has, in many important aspects, been a history of economic deprivation'. This amazing conclusion is reached by surveying the population twenty or thirty years after the migration program has begun and 'discovering' that migrants are over-represented in the ranks of unskilled labour and under-represented in the professions and boardrooms.

How, you might ask, would a just society have treated these migrants? (This is not a question Professor Western asks: enough for him that every difference is an inequality.) Is it seriously being suggested that Australian society should have contrived to have these migrants distributed evenly through the hierarchies of skill and wealth in the first generation, even though so many of them arrived without skill, capital and knowledge of the language? What a piece of social engineering that would have been. The immigration officer at the foot of the gangway as the ship from Italy berths: 'All those from Calabria will be brain surgeons.' Given the mind-lessness of these statistical surveys one wonders why they do not examine the migrants at the point of arrival. Then they could 'discover' that *all* migrants were unemployed and owned little or nothing and hence pro-nounce even more decisively on the inequalities of Australian society. But to remind us that migrants had little or nothing to begin with would spoil the story of 'deprivation'.

We would need to be worried about the position of migrants in Australia if we did not believe that after two or three generations their descendants would be fairly evenly distributed through the economy and society. The signs are looking good. Already the statistical information on the first wave of southern European migrants – the Italians and Greeks – confirm what old Australians have long known: the migrants are doing very well. Italians and Greeks are more likely to own their own home, less likely to be unemployed, and more likely to keep their children on at school than the rest of the population.

Migrants have had to work hard to do well. They have experienced great difficulties in coming to terms with a culture very different from their own. These aspects of the migrant experience are brought forward in Professor Western's account not to lead us to admire the migrants or to understand better their difficulties, but as a further sign of the *inequality* of Australian society. This is the final absurdity. Try to imagine a society in which outsiders, ignorant of its mores and language, would not be handicapped and have to make special efforts to succeed.

In Professor Western's eyes to think of migrants, even the most recent, as outsiders is illegitimate. He criticises us for demanding that migrants become naturalised before they can join the public service, hold certain public offices and practise law. All this is discrimination!

We have reached the heart of the multicultural outlook: the denial of any superior legitimacy to the host culture. Insofar as multiculturalism makes what it calls 'Anglo-Celts' the equivalent of Italians and Turks, it denies the very notion of a host. We are all immigrants of many cultures, contributing to a multicultural society. This may serve the needs of ethnic politics. As serious historical or sociological analysis it is nonsense. To found policy on it may be perilous.

I say 'may' because there are grounds for believing that multiculturalism has made little difference to the way migrants and the host culture interact. Migrants face a cruel dilemma – to get on and succeed they must adapt to the host culture (of whose existence they have no doubts); as strangers they are anxious to hold on to the culture they have brought with them. When our policy was assimilation the migrants held onto more of their culture than the policy-makers wished. Now when multiculturalism encourages them to keep their culture they are probably assimilating at the usual rate.

Many Australians appear to have interpreted 'multiculturalism' as a new name for the traditional toleration of difference and the willingness to accept migrants into their lives. When John Howard as leader of the Opposition attacked multiculturalism they thought he was a bigot, planning to close down Italian restaurants or prohibit the speaking of the Italian language. The Prime Minister, Bob Hawke, defended multiculturalism but then launched a citizenship campaign and began to stress what must be the common elements of our culture: the English language, parliamentary democracy, the rule of law, tolerance, the fair-go, – all of course 'Anglo-Celtic' which it seems is *not* to be just one among many cultures.

Multiculturalism interpreted in this way, a diverse society united by core institutions and values, is unexceptionable. But the institutional legacy of a more separatist multiculturalism is still with us: public funding of migrant organisations so they can maintain their culture. This has two dangers. Firstly, the obvious one that migrant cultures contain elements antagonistic to the core values. If you fund Greek schools, will you breed intolerance of Macedonians? If you fund Muslim schools, are you undermining the policy of equality for women? The second, indirect danger is that the support of migrant culture smacks of official favouritism. Nothing could more endanger the standing of migrants in this society; it is offensive to the liberal and egalitarian elements in our culture, the same elements which have been so important hitherto in the success of the migration program. No wonder, as the Fitzgerald Committee reported, the majority of Australians are puzzled and annoyed at multiculturalism. The multiculturalists of course see migrants as a disadvantaged group and so worthy of state assistance. Ordinary people, with a much better nose for these things, know that while new migrants might need help the Italians and Greeks are now a long way from being underdogs.

How could policy-makers be so obtuse as to push the migrant cause against the grain of this society? Perhaps because they have no knowledge of or respect for old Australia, which they label 'Anglo-Celtic, intolerant'. Let them suspend operations until they learn what sort of people we are.

1990

WHERE BEST TO LOOK?
THE FIRST XI BOOKS

ARE THE FINEST GUIDES TO AUSTRALIAN HISTORY ALWAYS those written by historians? Asked to name the best history books on Australia, I find my mind wanders to works that are not history proper. Is this because our historians have been poor, or because Australia doesn't yield its secrets when the usual methods are applied?

At the 2006 'summit' called by the Howard government to discuss the teaching of Australian history in schools, I signed up to the proposition that children should, among other things, know 'significant public events and developments'. But is knowing *them* the way one comes to know Australia? In the United States or England, the public events of the past still definitely shape the nation's sense of itself. Americans are, as their Declaration of Independence avers, committed to liberty and the pursuit of happiness. The English are proud of creating the mother of parliaments and the protections of the common law. And in France, for a long time, a person's attitude to the Revolution determined which of the town's chess clubs they would join. Our history hasn't worked like this.

Two days after the history summit, I went to see my football team play at the Melbourne Cricket Ground. I rode by escalator up to a seat in the newest stand. In large handwriting on the walls surrounding me were the first rules of the Australian game, drawn up by the Melbourne Club in 1859. It was, of course, not the original document; I am not sure even whether the handwriting was a blown-up version of the original, but I felt that frisson of awe and attachment which sustains museums and which Americans feel when they look at the original Declaration of Independence under glass.

It might not be history, but there is a sporting lore in this country:

names, dates, records, rules, triumphs and near misses. Remember Wayne Harmes sliding across the wet ground to keep the ball in play in the 1979 Grand Final, giving Carlton the opportunity to kick the goal that defeated Collingwood? And is it true that the boundary umpire who did not call the ball out of bounds was Harmes's cousin? We have no equivalent lore of our public life. Everyone knows that Don Bradman kept up the nation's spirits during the Great Depression, but how many know the name of Joe Lyons, who left the Labor Party during the Depression and became prime minister on the other side? If children are to be taught 'public events and developments', they will be learning what their elders do not know and seemingly don't need to know.

So let us begin privately, in a small dining room in an English county town. The guests have just left and the host and hostess are quarrelling. The hostess is about to utter the Australian declaration of independence. The talk of these two was created by the novelist Henry Handel Richardson in *The Fortunes of Richard Mahony* (1930). Richard Mahony had made money as a doctor in gold-rush Ballarat; his wife Mary had only very reluctantly gone 'Home' with him to Buddlecombe. Her first supper party there was a disaster, for she had put on a slap-up Australian spread and her guests had no more than toyed with it. She should have served just biscuits and sherry.

Her husband upbraids her for this terrible *faux pas*, to which she responds with a denunciation of the restrictions of English social life:

To remember I mustn't shake hands here or even bow there. That in some quarters I must only say 'Good afternoon' and not 'How do you do?' – and then the other way around as well. That nice Mrs Perkes is not the thing and ought to be cold-shouldered; and when I have company I am not to give them anything to eat. Oh, Richard, it all seems to me such fudge! How grown-up people can spend their lives being so silly, I don't know. Out there, you had to forget what a person's outside was like – I mean his table-manners and whether he could say his aitches – as long as he was capable ... or rich. But here it's always: 'Who is he? How far back can he trace his pedigree?'

The Fortunes of Richard Mahony becomes a somewhat turgid saga, but its description of society out *there*, of Victoria after the gold rush, has not been bettered.

*

Politics, which must be a large part of 'public events and developments', scarcely appears in the books of Geoffrey Blainey, the most prolific and popular of our historians. He is an economic historian, though of a unique sort: he is interested in 'all trades, their gear and tackle and trim', and the tradesmen, too; in the economy, that is, close to the ground as well as in the broad. Economic historians used to think that they could ignore politics, but they are now more aware of the importance of political stability for economic growth, and they may be interested even in culture as the matrix in which economic life occurs. Blainey can take as given political stability in Australia, since government has never broken down and had to be reconstituted. No one criticises Blainey for ignoring politics, and he goes on capturing much of the life of the country without it.

I limit myself to naming one of his books, confident that readers who try it won't need my recommendation to read more. The title of *The Tyranny of Distance* (1966) has passed into the language, despite my own efforts to argue that the book does not justify its title. What the book *does* do is to give, in a very palatable form, an account of the development of the Australian economy with, as always, some shrewd comments about social life as well. It is a tribute to the vividness of Blainey's imagination and the magic of his simple prose that he can make economic life so interesting.

*

David Denholm had a sense of the reclusive nature of Australian history. In the preface to *The Colonial Australians* (1979), he offers a mild rebuke to the established historians who have asked 'large questions', to which they have given 'large answers'. He announces that he will deal with small questions, mere trifles, and he immediately takes the reader deeper into Australian society than the usual histories. He is interested in how quickly guns fired, why surveyors were so attached to straight lines, how many people rode horses, how church architecture related to belief, the fate of the gentry who were meant to have disappeared. Though starting small, he also links Australia most tellingly to the civilisation from which it came.

In the gem of the book, an essay prompted by Francis Greenway's church at Windsor, he identifies the origins of the building in this way:

> The church that rose on the knoll at Windsor came from the ancient Greeks and their command of straight-line geometry; from the fifteenth-century Italian Renaissance which captured the Greek feeling for proportion in the shaping of things; from the seventeenth-century civilisation of Holland (brought into England by William of Orange) with its Flemish technique of securing bricks one upon another; from eighteenth-century Georgian England's love of functional simplicity, order, symmetry and restraint; and from the early nineteenth-century provincial training of the ex-convict who put it all together. St Matthew's came, through Greenway's mind, from all the ages of the West.

*

Politics and economics are central in the classic short history *Australia* (1930), written by Keith Hancock. He traces how the concern for 'fair and reasonable' conditions led to a distinctive Australian political economy, with its ever-widening controls on wages, imports and prices and ever-growing subsidies through the provision of government services. So powerful were these impulses that Hancock feared they would strangle the economy and hence the opportunity to provide a good living for all. *Australia* is a bold and brilliant characterisation, and Hancock's deft and witty formulations have been landmarks for all subsequent scholars.

The book is now very dated, since the old controls and supports have been de-regulated away – except that Hancock finds the origins of the country's political economy in the character of the Australian people;

in their generous, perhaps naïve commitment to 'fair and reasonable' conditions for all. This formulation cannot be caught by the usual categories of political philosophy. Its modern manifestation is the belief in the 'fair go'. Whether it has any residual force against the disciplines of a global economy, we will soon discover.

*

If character is what must be understood, we cannot go past *The Broken Years* (1974), Bill Gammage's account of soldiers in World War I. Gammage is a worthy successor to the great Charles Bean, the official historian of Australia's part in the war, and follows him in believing that the character of the soldiers was important for their battlefield success, and that a distinctive Australian character was distilled in its soldiers.

Gammage uses the soldiers' diaries and letters to trace how their attitudes changed as the war progressed. His description of their mindset during the last campaigns in France is almost as eloquent as Bean's famous words at the close of his Gallipoli volumes in the *Official History*. Gammage writes:

They lived in a world apart, a new world, scarcely remembering their homes and country, and grieving little at the deaths of mates they loved more than anything on this earth, because they knew that only time kept them from the 'great majority' who had already died ... So they continued, grim, mocking, defiant, brave, and careless, free from common toils and woes, into a perpetual present ...

*

Keith Hancock controversially described the Labor Party as the creative initiating force in politics (against the evidence of much of his book). There have been many books written on the Labor Party, mostly by people who take this view of it. The one that best conveys the spirit of the early party and the devotion of its supporters was written by Billy Hughes, whom the Labor faithful consider a rat. *Crusts and Crusades*

(1947) is a series of reminiscences, not a history proper. I have lectured to students on the Labor Party with most success when I have merely read extracts from it.

Hughes's vivid account of his own preselection in 1894 shows that branch-stacking was present at the party's birth. The oddity of the Labor Party in New South Wales – so different from the British model – was its ability to win seats in the country. The first steps, however, were not always encouraging. Hughes describes how he was refused all service in a country town where he hoped to found a branch. There was no sign of the shearer whom he had enlisted outback, who was meant to chair his meeting. Outside the meeting hall, the minuscule Labor blow-in got into an argument with the town blacksmith, who was about to annihilate him when a band of shearers rode up. Their leader knocked out the blacksmith, took the stage still dripping with blood, and opened the meeting thus:

> 'Look 'ere, us blokes have organised this 'ere meeting to 'ear this bloke – and by cripes we're going to 'ear 'im. The first one of you Rockley blokes as opens 'is mouth will get it in the neck. Now then,' he said, turning to me. 'Let 'er go.'

*

Richmond, the industrial inner suburb of Melbourne, was pure Labor, but in Janet McCalman's *Struggletown* (1984) the Party is somewhat distant; she deals with houses, marriages, family and work, and gives the best account we have of working-class life and particularly of the gap between the respectable and the rough. The book deals with Richmond in the first half of the twentieth century and is based on interviews with old Richmond people, whose words are given plenty of space. We get to know them as characters.

The book runs against feminist orthodoxy in discovering that within the home, the wives were commonly in charge: they were strong and determined individuals who often barely tolerated their feckless husbands. As far as I know, this claim of domestic matriarchy has simply been ignored by those who take a contrary view of women's place in

Australian history. History writing does not always proceed by careful assessment of new evidence; sometimes it simply proceeds.

*

Women receive little attention in Hancock's *Australia*; they feature prominently in the best modern successor to Hancock, John Rickard's *Australia: A Cultural History* (1988). He uses 'cultural' in the anthropological sense, to mean the whole way of life of a people. As a good modern he does not have Hancock's confidence that a single Australian character can be identified; he highlights the differences between men and women, Catholics and Protestants (totally ignored by Hancock), bosses and workers, Anglos and the 'inferior' races. But unlike so many moderns, he does not think his work is complete when he has divided society by race, class and gender. What makes the place distinctive? His answer lies in establishing an Australian style of dealing with or accommodating difference. This is a very fruitful notion.

*

When Hancock wrote of the pursuit of the fair and reasonable, there was another, very different society on Australian soil, one that was cruel, chaotic and exploitative. Xavier Herbert's historical novel *Capricornia* (1938) gives us the other Australia of the Northern Territory, of white Australia lording it over the Aborigines and fucking them as well. The savagery of Herbert's depictions makes this an 'unbalanced' history – Ann McGrath has given us a different view of Aborigines in the cattle industry – but the power of this portrait is irresistible, and the book can be treated as history-making in itself, a shouting of what had been hidden.

*

If you prefer a calmer tone and the economy of Greek tragedy to a saga's sprawl, read Katharine Prichard's novel *Coonardoo* (1929). Like *Capricornia*, it deals with the taboo of sex across the racial divide, in this case on a cattle station in northern Western Australia. That the decent white man will not have sex with the Aboriginal woman he loves, which leads to the undoing of them both – this is the myth that reconciliation needs. *Coonardoo* should be taught in schools, if we followed John Carroll's advice and gave schoolchildren myths rather than history. Certainly no historian has brought together so compellingly the land itself and the two peoples who have inhabited it.

*

So far the most recent history book I have cited was published in 1988. Is this because our historians have been poor? It is not a pleasant thought; but we can set it aside because, in 2003, Inga Clendinnen published *Dancing with Strangers* and revealed new capacities in the craft of history. As an ethnographic historian, her skill is in deciphering cultures that have left few, if any, records. She finds meaning by interpreting action as it was described by outsiders hostile to or puzzled by what they were seeing. In *Dancing with Strangers*, she brings these skills to the study of the encounters between Aborigines and Europeans in the first settlement at Sydney Cove. She develops startlingly new views of the spearing of Governor Phillip and his ordering of the first punitive expedition against the Aborigines. She calls her reinterpretations hypotheses or even guesses, but they are so dazzling that we are left groping to offer alternatives. All previous accounts are now in question.

Her book opens with Aborigines and Europeans dancing together. It ends with two peoples moving apart into indifference and hostility, and concludes with these words:

> There remains a final mystery. Despite our long alienation, despite our merely adjacent histories, and through processes I do not yet understand, we are now more like each other than we are like any other people. We even share something of the same style of humour, which is a subtle but far-reaching affinity.

This brings us to the opposite pole from 'significant public events and developments'. If Clendinnen plans to crack this mystery, she will serve us well.

2006

THE DISTINCTIVENESS OF
AUSTRALIAN DEMOCRACY

DEMOCRATIC COUNTRIES HAVE THEIR DEMOCRACY IN common, but how democracy works and what it means to the people differ from country to country. The society in which democracy operates is different in each country and each country has its own history of democracy: how it came about and what came before it.

France became a democracy suddenly when a movement to reform the royal government turned into a revolution in 1789. The first democratic parliament was elected in 1792. It supported a dictatorial government that kept itself in power by executing thousands of its opponents.

Britain became a democracy very slowly and peacefully. The violence in England took place in the seventeenth century when the parliament made itself supreme over the king. That parliament was elected and controlled by landowners. The franchise was first widened 150 years later in 1832 but it took a hundred years to establish full democracy. Since there was no payment of members until 1911, the rich landowners, their friends and relations continued for a long time to be the largest group elected to parliament.

The United States became a separate country by rebelling against Britain. It proclaimed that all men were created equal and set up a new republican form of government. To belong to this new nation was to believe in certain political principles. At first the United States was not democratic. It became so quite soon and without violence. Democracy became identified with America, the natural result of the principles of equality with which the nation had begun.

The Australian colonies became democracies suddenly (like France), peacefully (like Britain) and while remaining colonies (unlike the United States). These three circumstances, as we shall see, had a great effect on what sort of democracy it was and how the people related to it.

The democracies established in the Australian states are now almost 150 years old. The central democracy, the Commonwealth of Australia, is over a hundred years old. They are among the oldest and most stable democracies in the world.

This should be one of the things Australians are proud about, but Australians do not think of their political record when they think of what sort of people they are. Society itself in Australia is very democratic, but Australians have little regard for their democratic government. How this strange gap came about and how government works well despite it, are the questions we will now try to answer.

*

The answer begins with origins. Democracy – manhood suffrage for the Legislative Assemblies – was established rapidly in the 1850s immediately after the grant of self-government. There was no large-scale movement in support of it. British thinking on constitutional matters was orthodoxy with that extra tightness produced in a dependent society. Democracy was a dirty word.

Two factors nevertheless made for democracy. In 1850 the House of Lords was tricked into halving the qualifications for the franchise in Australia. It was told that under the existing rules rich ex-convicts got the vote and free working men recently arrived did not. A respectable electorate required a low qualification. The low qualification then set was made worthless by the inflation caused by the gold rush which began in 1851. The tenant of any hovel in Sydney and Melbourne got the vote. The franchise had become so wide without any change in the law that conservatives, who were in charge of drawing up the constitutions for self-government, added new qualifications based on salary rather than property and rent in order to give the vote to their household servants, clerks and managers. It was a desperate ploy: to stave off full democracy they were giving more people the vote. When manhood suffrage was introduced (with a residential qualification) it gave the vote to very few new people compared with the huge increases that had occurred under the processes I have just outlined.

South Australia was rather different. Manhood suffrage was established early – in the constitution for self-government. The great book on South Australia's early history, *Paradise of Dissent* (1957) by Douglas Pike, spoke of a democratic triumph and of democrats. If Pike was justified in using these terms my argument is wrong for South Australia. Pike's footnotes direct the reader to a press report of a meeting of democrats who formed an association to watch over the debates on the constitution. This was fifty working men in an Adelaide pub. They certainly had a very democratic program. Mr Morris outlined it in his speech: manhood suffrage (for both houses), vote by ballot, House of Assembly elected for three years with equal electorates, upper house to be elected by the whole colony, members to serve for six years. Mr Morris concluded his speech with these words:

> This association is not a Chartist, Radical, or Democratic one, or one
> to be called by any of those ugly names, but an association which
> must watch over the formation of a constitution which will secure
> prosperity and civil and religious liberty to us and our children.

Here too *democracy* was a dirty word.

To understand this founding movement properly we need to discredit an alternative explanation for the easy triumph of democracy. It runs like this:

The first settlers came from very unequal societies where inferior people had to show respect to superior people. Most of the migrants to Australia did not come from the superior upper classes; they were middle class or working people. They wanted to get rid of old-world distinctions and create in the colonies a world in which people did not have to know their place. Anyone in Australia who tried to pretend they were upper class was just laughed at. The old distinctions simply could not be re-established in the new land. People began to treat each other as equals and so democracy was the only form of government that would suit them.

This is very misleading. Society was not democratised first and then politics. It was the other way about. Politics was democratised long before society was.

It is true that the migrants rejected some aspects of the old society: they did not want position to depend on birth or education or knowing the right people. But those who came to the colonies to better themselves wanted to show off their success in the old ways. What other signs did they know; what other signs would be recognised?

The migrants did not want dukes or lords in Australia, but successful migrants claimed the title of gentleman. Gentleman was an English rank which proved to be an excellent import for the colonies. It was not quite definite; the qualifications were elastic and could be stretched. They were stretched a long way. The test for not being involved in business was easily dropped. Even true gentlemen in Australia – and there were some – were very closely involved in money-making. So that made it acceptable for others to be making money. But the test was not dropped altogether. It was shifted. If you made money as a merchant, that was all right; if you ran a shop and served the public, you could not be a gentleman. As to good breeding, the new gentlemen in Australia pushed their ancestors as far up the social scale as they dared.

The final result was that in Australia most men who had made money could be gentlemen. This was a huge change in the rules and it was not reached without great social turmoil, but the category of gentleman did not implode. The one definite test for a new gentleman in Australia was that he had to be wealthy and a wealthy man could look like a gentleman once he had a large house and a carriage and dressed like a gentleman with top hat and tails.

The first partly-elected legislatures in Australia were made up of land-owners and squatters along with a few merchants and lawyers. They thought of themselves as gentlemen and were treated as such. They could appear as the local equivalent of the gathering of gentlemen at Westminster.

All this changed with the rapid move to democracy in the 1850s. The rich found it hard to get elected and were forced to retreat to the upper houses. Poor men of little education replaced them. Members heaped vulgar abuse on each other and some were only in parliament to benefit themselves.

Parliamentarians still dressed as gentlemen and hoped to be treated as gentlemen, but now there was an implosion: no-one believed that parliamentarians were gentlemen. The new democratic institution did not dress itself in its own clothes; it set itself up for a fall by putting on a distinctly undemocratic uniform.

Rich and educated people now regarded politicians as a low-class bunch of incompetents. They made fun of those who could not speak or write properly, who had done lowly work before they became MPs, and who had wives who could never be accepted into good society. If a rich and well-educated man did get into parliament, he was always apologising for keeping such low company. It did give him a lot of good stories to shock and amuse his friends.

These very ordinary parliamentarians had been elected by the votes of ordinary people. Their votes gave them the opportunity to show that they did not want parliamentarians to be just the rich and the well-educated. They elected parliamentarians who could not look down on them and whom they did not have to look up to. But they had not got rid of the idea that parliament was a place they should be able to respect. By their votes they had produced parliaments that they too despised.

Respect for parliament evaporated very quickly. In the Supreme Court in Sydney in 1861 the chief justice at the top of society and a criminal at the bottom shared a joke at the politicians' expense. The criminal was being tried for escaping from jail. Before the case began he asked that he be given another judge because it was the chief justice who had given him the harsh sentence that had put him in jail. The criminal said the chief justice might have 'prejudicial feelings' against him. The judge, thinking he had said 'political feelings', replied, 'Why should I have political feelings against you. Are you a member of parliament?' To which the criminal replied, 'Not yet.'

When the parliaments acted to protect their reputation, they discovered how little respect they enjoyed. The big man behind the bribing of the Victorian parliament in the 1860s was the squatter Hugh Glass. When the parliament committed him to prison, he became a popular hero. The Supreme Court set him free and the parliament took no further action. The most corrupt member of parliament was C. E. Jones, the member for Ballarat. While he was a minister, he took money to organise opposition to his own government. When this was discovered, the parliament expelled him, but Ballarat re-elected him.

The Ballarat voters thought he was no worse than the men who had expelled him, so they were not going to see him punished. A vicious cycle had set in. Parliament was despised, but voters continued to elect men who kept its reputation low.

In recent years, it is said, the reputation of politicians has fallen. If this is true, the change has been very small compared to the catastrophic collapse that can be dated precisely to the introduction of democracy in the 1850s.

*

So these are the inauspicious beginnings: a democracy ashamed to speak its name run by politicians who are held in contempt. But it need not have remained so. I consider a number of forces which elsewhere helped to attach citizens to the democratic state but which did not have that effect in Australia.

First is nationalism; it brought little credit to the state for reasons that are obvious. The independence of the state was readily granted by the metropolitan power and did not have to be struggled for. The Australian admiration for Britain increased after it had allowed self-government to the colonies in the 1850s and had encouraged the formation of the colonies into a nation in the 1890s. Australian nationality was formed in opposition to Britain but in other spheres – by the boasting about a more open society, by beating England at cricket, by producing superior soldiers. Australians are completely indifferent to the state as the symbol of their independence, as those who have tried to pluck this string for the republican cause have discovered.

One of the attractions of democracy for the common people of Britain and Europe was that it would give them the status of citizens rather than that of being the poor or the lower orders. In Australia, however, the common man was living well without needing to show deference to his betters before democratic politics began. Democracy was not needed to establish his dignity.

In the 1850s skilled building workers in Melbourne established the eight-hour day, the symbol of the higher status and rewards open to working men in this country. Soon afterwards all men acquired the vote, but it was the eight-hour victory that was celebrated annually by a public holiday, procession, picnic and sports, not the achievement of manhood suffrage, which had no heroes or heroics to commemorate. Working men used their vote to protect and extend their gains – to demand for instance that the state legislate for the eight-hour day or impose it on state contractors. With the collapse in living standards in the 1890s depression, working men used the Labor Party in an effort to get the state to guarantee what they had enjoyed previously. The institutional guarantor of a living wage became the arbitration system. Here was an attachment to the state, but not of a civic sort: the state was the guarantor of the living wage.

By the end of the nineteenth century there was a democratic movement openly proclaiming a democratic ideology. Its leaders were the progressive liberals who were committed to getting rid of the non-democratic elements in the colonial constitutions – like restricted upper houses and plural voting – who supported female suffrage, and who planned to establish the new Commonwealth of Australia on a democratic basis.

The progressive liberals gave serious attention for the first time to the concept of citizenship, the term that gives the people a civic identity; in the 1850s the term could not be used because the colonists were then unquestionably subjects of the Queen. The progressive liberals tried and failed to write a citizenship clause into the new federal constitution. The difficulty was that the starting point for the definition of citizenship was the status British subject – but you could not say that all British subjects in the Commonwealth were to be citizens because that would confer citizenship on Chinese born in Hong Kong and Indians. Against these people the colonies had enacted discriminatory laws and the new Commonwealth might well want to do the same. Safer then to do nothing. So for all its democratic elements the Commonwealth constitution was silent on citizenship – as it still is.

Early in the twentieth century support for Labor rose at an astonishing rate and by 1910 the Labor Party had squeezed out the progressive liberals and had taken the progressive mantle to itself. It was not overly interested in citizenship, for how could men and women under capitalism be considered equals until the Labor platform had been implemented? Those who were interested in citizenship regarded Labor's demand that members vote at the direction of a caucus as the antithesis of the independent judgment that a responsible citizen should exercise.

The new group that took citizenship seriously was the women's movement. Unlike men, women had had to struggle to get the vote and they based their case in part on the claim that they were already citizens, involved as they were in the care of children and the running of charities. After they got the vote the obligation of citizenship was their warrant for maintaining their own organisations and attacking the party politics of men. The women presented themselves as the more responsible sex, the true citizens, concerned for the common good rather than partisan advantage. The effort was heroic, but the women did not break the mould of party politics. Most women voted along the same lines as their men.

In the early Commonwealth progressive liberal governments introduced compulsory military training for boys and young men. Citizenship and soldiering were firmly linked. The name of the army for which they were being trained was the Citizen Military Forces. Billy Hughes in the Labor Party was a firm supporter of a citizens' army and with some difficulty he persuaded his party to accept it. Labor in office after 1910 implemented the policy of compulsory training.

In World War I, Hughes as prime minister tried to get his party to support conscription for service overseas. He argued that Labor had accepted in principle that all should contribute to the nation's defence; when the nation's fate was being decided in France conscription was the fair and efficient way to reinforce the Australian forces. The party organisation would not accept this and the party split. The Labor anti-conscriptionists were not, at least in public, opposed to the war; that would have been fatal. They had to develop a principled argument against conscription that would apply in any circumstances. The argument became that no more profound threat to individual liberty could be devised than making a man fight against his will. Conscription was undemocratic because it took away human freedom – an argument which has had no purchase in any other democracy since 1916–17. It remained a great force in this democracy. Labor took its argument seriously and after the war its platform declared against conscription in all circumstances, not only for service overseas but even for the defence of the continent against invasion. In this matter the socialist Labor Party was the defender of voluntarism. It was their opponents who stressed communal obligation and preached against selfishness.

Labor people still honour their party's defeat of conscription in World War I. I regard it as a disaster on several grounds: it was damaging to the cause of progressive social reform, to civic life, to a coherent defence policy – in World War II, Australia had to have two armies, a volunteer army that could serve anywhere, and a conscripted one to defend Australian territory. And the effect most pertinent to our theme: it separated soldiering and citizenship. In the years since some men have volunteered to fight; others have been conscripted, but only for limited purposes. Australia has a strong military tradition but it is not a tradition associated with the state; it brings no lustre to democratic government.

*

The attitude of the Labor Party was also responsible for another of the dissociations that distinguish our polity: the welfare system is not a universal one based on the contributions of the people. The non-Labor parties planned such schemes between the wars and came close to implementing them. Labor was opposed to contributions for welfare: it wanted the rich to pay for the welfare of the poor. In office during World War II, Labor introduced welfare benefits paid for from general revenue – and so kept true to the party platform; but it began to subject the workers to income tax – which was against the platform. This has remained the Australian way of welfare. Here the welfare system does not bind citizens together as equals. It is a system where some people pay, somewhat reluctantly, for the welfare of others. The exception is Medicare to which all contribute according to their means and from which all benefit. The strong support for Medicare gives us an inkling of what we have lost by running the rest of welfare on other principles.

A similar situation has developed with schools. In some democracies – France, Germany, Sweden, the United States – government schools take children of all backgrounds and teach them that they are future citizens of the one country. The government schools symbolise a common citizenship. That hasn't happened in Australia because private schools have been strong and are getting stronger. The reasons for this can be given very briefly: the Catholic Church stymied the plan to have a common primary school system and until it was too late the Labor Party was not interested enough in secondary education to challenge the dominance of the private and church schools in that sector.

Australians of course don't see private schools as an anomaly. A visiting American educational expert in the 1950s saw it as highly anomalous: he wrote that he was always being told what a democratic egalitarian society Australia was. If that was so, he wondered, why did the private schools hold such a strong place in the education system?

Well might he ask. His mistake, though, was to think that egalitarianism is genuine only if it shows itself in formal institutions like schools. That is not the Australian way. Australians treat each other as equals. This is the egalitarianism they have perfected. Australian democracy is first of all a democracy of manners.

Some people claim that Australian society is not egalitarian because there are wide differences of income, which may now be getting wider. This misses the point of Australian egalitarianism. It is the way Australians blot out differences when people meet face to face. They talk to each other as if they are equals and they will put down anyone claiming social superiority. It is the feel of Australian society that is so markedly egalitarian, not its social structure. The democracy of manners was established when differences in income were much greater than they are now.

The democracy of manners developed slowly – and for most of its history it was a relationship among men; only recently have women been part of this equality. The democracy of manners owes nothing to democratic politics, but it has implications for politics. Politics is necessarily about power, about inequality. In democracies those who exercise power gain their authority by the votes of the people. That inequality Australians are reluctant to recognise. Their egalitarianism is a bond of equals, in part directed against the disruption of authority. Australians will recognise that a boss or a military officer must have power, though they will respect him only if he exercises power properly. But politicians have no excuse for wanting power; they have wilfully put themselves above the rest. They will have trouble therefore in gaining respect, no matter who they are or what they do. Many Australians seem to think politics exists only because there are a few egomaniacs wanting to be politicians.

The democracy of manners is a precious achievement. One of the reasons people fought for democracy was that they wanted respect for ordinary people, that they should not be humiliated and scorned. Australians achieved that outside politics and their egalitarianism is more deep-seated and genuine because it is not a political doctrine. But so that all men can be equal, politicians have to be dishonoured.

*

It is time to look to the other side of my original question: why does the democracy work well despite the people having no strong attachment to it?

The European settlers of Australia were very diverse. There were people from three nations – the English, Scots and Irish – and they followed two faiths – Catholic and Protestant. The Australian colonies inherited their history of mutual suspicion, prejudice and bitterness.

From the first the different people lived amongst each other. Unlike North America, there were no localities which were solely Scotch or solely Catholic. In the United States the Irish came late to a settled society and crowded into ghettos in the cities. In Australia the Irish were part of the founding population and settled throughout the country with everyone else.

When different people live in their own areas and maintain their own culture and faith, it is hard for them to agree to belong to the one country. They need some idea or principle or feeling to bind them together. If this does not happen the country might split up.

In Australia the people of the three nations and two faiths were thrown together from the beginning. The oddity of Australia for the new settlers was not simply the physical environment; it was having so many half-foreigners as neighbours. They all had to make their lives in this new, strange mixture. They created a harmonious society by setting their differences aside and being good neighbours, or workmates or committee men. Australian society was integrated from the bottom up rather than from the top down. It did not need politics to unite it; sometimes politics was a destructive force.

From the earliest times there was a widespread determination to stop old-world hatreds from taking root here. Of course there were some who wanted to keep them alive. The ministers of the churches and their closest followers believed their faith was the true one and were ready to denounce the others as false. But even people who took their own religion seriously might not want to join in open warfare with others – unless something happened to reignite the old fears they usually kept under control. Fortunately, for the cause of social harmony, there were large numbers of people who did not take their religion too seriously.

Liberalism was a strong force in nineteenth-century Australia and it underpinned the task of keeping religion from disturbing the peace. But something much more positive was at work in Australian society: people actively worked to keep the peace by making sure that in community organisations there were representatives from all backgrounds and faiths. So there were Protestants and Catholics, English, Irish and Scots, on the boards and managing committees of hospitals and charities, friendly societies, sporting clubs and mechanics institutes.

This desire for social peace was not a political doctrine; it was not, as the political scientists would say, an acceptance of pluralism. The colonists accepted that there were differences between people that were not going to disappear, but they did not want simply to tolerate differences and live apart from each other. They wanted to find ways to come together; they thought the peace would not be secure unless this happened.

Behind this desire was a shared memory of how much bitterness had been caused by religious and ethnic differences in the countries from which they had come:

Our children shall, upon this new-won shore –
Warned by all sorrows that have gone before –
Build up the glory of a grand new World.

—John Farrell, 1883

In politics it was harder to maintain harmony. Election campaigns often turned into battles between Catholics and Protestants. On a committee or in a parade, all groups could be represented, but elections were inevitably a contest. If a Catholic ran for parliament all Catholics were encouraged to vote for him. Protestants then became alarmed that Catholics – urged on, they were sure, by their priests – were attempting to take over the country. They tried to rally all Protestants to oppose the Catholic candidate. This could happen without there being a policy division between Catholic and Protestant. From the 1870s of course there was – a bitter division over policy on education.

I think historians have been too ready to read back from sectarian disputes in politics to deep division within society. Australian cities did not turn into a Beirut or Belfast where the two warring sides have their own areas. The conflict in politics and public life remained at a distance from the community. It did not so much reflect community division as save the community from division.

Protestants and Catholics still lived amongst each other. They interacted in the neighbourhood, at work and in playing and following sport. They interacted in the unions and the Labor Party. Intermarriage continued despite the opposition of the priests. There were still many people on both sides wanting to set aside their differences. The Australian style of dealing with difference did not disappear. It is the social foundation of the peacefulness and decency of Australian democracy.

The divide between Catholic and Protestant ceased to be important in the 1960s. It had no deep roots in the structure of society, so when both sides decided to treat each other as fellow Christians, the dispute disappeared.

*

After World War II, Australian society had to deal with new differences on a vast scale. A mass migration program began which brought to this British society non-English-speaking people, at first from Europe, later from Asia and Africa, the Middle East and Latin America. Australians applied to this new challenge the formula which had brought peace to their mixed society. The government, supported by the people, wanted the new migrants to mix in with the old population and not form separate enclaves. The government knew that this would happen only if migrants were welcomed. It told the Australian people to call the migrants New Australians and it set up the Good Neighbour Council which arranged for old Australians to help the New Australians settle in.

Old Australians were suspicious of the newcomers and a few were openly hostile, but on the whole Australians accepted them. If the newcomers wanted to make a go of it here and did not make a nuisance of themselves, they could be Australians. Migrants found that Australians were generally friendly, but they were puzzled that Australians were not interested in their culture and experience. They were encountering the Australian style of mixing where people remain friendly by not exploring differences.

The migrants did not mix in as rapidly as the government had hoped. In the inner cities they did form something like enclaves. But within ten years they were buying houses in the suburbs and scattering themselves widely in the process. After twenty years their children were marrying old Australians. Australian society was again being rapidly integrated from the bottom up.

*

Almond and Verba in their famous study, *The Civic Culture: Political Attitudes and Democracy in Five Nations* (1963) identify three orientations towards the state – the participant, the subject, and the parochial. Participants believe they can influence government; subjects accept government authority; parochials don't understand government but act to get what they want from it. A good civic culture requires a balance of participant and subject orientations. Almond and Verba judge the UK as strong, perhaps too strong, on the orientation as subject. They explain this British attitude by the survival of deference to a ruling class. My take on Australia is that, as in Britain, the subject orientation is strong, but the British reason for this can't obtain here. So how can egalitarians be compliant subjects?

Australians think of themselves as anti-authority. It is not true. Australians are suspicious of persons in authority, but towards impersonal authority they are very obedient.

This is the country which for a long time closed its pubs at 6 p.m. and which pioneered the compulsory wearing of seatbelts in cars. Its people since 1924 have accepted the compulsion to vote. Its anti-smoking legislation is so tough that smoking is prohibited in its largest sporting stadium, the Melbourne Cricket Ground, though it is open to the skies. At an Australian Rules football match, the fans yell obscenities at the umpire and then at half-time walk quietly outside to have a smoke.

Australian government was not created in Australia. The government came off the boat, in the person of the governor and his officials, carrying all the authority of the government in Britain. With only one exception settlers never had to come together and form a government. The authority which secured to them the benefits of their pioneering was not of their making.

Melbourne was the exception; it alone of the colonial capitals was an unauthorised settlement. For a few months the settlers did govern themselves. Then the governor in Sydney visited and installed a magistrate responsible to him.

The founding governments of the Australian colonies had the virtues of the British government that created them; they provided a secure world in which all people enjoyed protection of their property and liberty. The convicts of course did not have their liberty, but they were deprived of it by the law, which also set the term for their release and protected the property and persons of ex-convicts as if they had always been free.

The early Australian governments were actually better than the British. The British government was run by the aristocracy and gentry who rewarded their followers with government jobs. The job might pay well but have no duties. If the job did have duties, the holder was not obliged to perform them himself. He hired a deputy to do the work, but kept most of the proceeds for himself. Jobs frequently did not have salaries; the holder made his money by the collection of fees which he could manipulate to his own advantage.

This system was being reformed just as Australia was settled and so the new rules applied here from the beginning. All jobs had to be real jobs; the work could not be done by a deputy; the reward would be a fixed salary rather than fees. So the British officials who ruled under the governor's control were efficient and honest.

Government did not begin with taxation. The funds of the first governments came from the British taxpayer. The job of the Colonial Office was to get the governor to limit his spending and to raise money by local taxation. It was some time before the colonists in Australia were paying the full cost of their government. For the first hundred years they never really did that because their defence was provided free by the British navy. For most of human history defence spending has been the biggest item in government budgets. In the Australian colonies it was one of the smallest, which allowed government funds to be spent on the internal development of the colony.

Usually in empires, governors of colonies taxed the people and sent the proceeds back to the mother country. In the Australian colonies taxes were not sent to Britain. After the revolt of the American colonies Britain resolved not to tax its overseas settlers. Britain got its benefit from the colonies through the increase of its trade and the returns on the private funds invested in Australia. The governor's job was to promote the development of the economy, which would enable the colony to pay its way and bring more benefit to Britain. There was a basic harmony between what the British government wanted of the governors and what the settlers wanted.

Governors and their officials built roads and bridges, improved ports, encouraged exploration, surveyed land for settlement, and provided settlers with their labour force, at first convicts and later free immigrants. The British government which sent the governors did none of these things in its own country. So the function of government changed in Australia; it was not primarily to keep order within and defeat enemies without; it was a resource on which settlers could draw to make money.

The social character of the government changed too, or rather it did not have a social character. In Britain government was closely linked to the social order; the richest people were the great landowners and they and their friends ran the government. In Australia the government was one person, the governor, who was detached from, and superior to, all groups in the local society. Yet government was much more than the person of the governor; he embodied the full authority of the British government and was the representative of the monarch. So government was both more singular and more abstract.

Settlers of course attempted to influence the governor. The richer settlers had more influence than others and they occupied the positions in the early legislatures, which were at first appointed and then partly elected. But these bodies never controlled the governor, and the governors did not rule simply in the interests of the wealthy settlers. Several governors clashed with the wealthy settlers. The demand for self-government in New South Wales in the 1840s came from the rich squatters who objected to Governor Gipps attempting to make them pay more for their land.

In the mid-1850s governors and officials were replaced by premiers and ministers responsible to parliament. The transition was smooth. The public servants remained in place. The regular business of government remained the same: to provide the infrastructure for the development of the economy. Democratic government made it easier for more people to make demands for roads, bridges and local services. If people wanted something done, they went in a deputation to the minister, escorted by their local member. If the local member could not get results out of ministers, he lost his seat at the next election.

The democratic governments, like those run by the governors, were omni-competent; they took on everything. They ran the school system and the police, which in Britain and in many other countries were the business of local government. Local government in Australia was weak; it was established late and did not cover the whole country. Its chief job was the making of local roads and in the towns the collection of rubbish. Where there was no local government, the colonial government did all that was necessary. In most of the countryside of New South Wales there was no local government until 1906.

The colonial governments did all their work without imposing direct taxation. Until late in the nineteenth century there was no income tax and no company tax. All the money you earned you kept. Government was not a burden that you had to pay for; it was a magic pudding; you could cut slice after slice and there was always more.

The magic was performed by the government collecting its revenue from taxes that you were unaware of – duties collected on imported goods – and from the sale of crown lands – which was not a tax at all. Local government did not tax directly; its revenue came from rates collected on land. This was the chief reason why it did so little and why in many places it did not exist at all. No-one wanted to give local government more responsibilities because that would increase direct taxes.

The first government schools were built only if local people raised some of the cost of the building. That gave them some say in the running of the school. But from the 1870s the colonial governments, without raising any new taxation, were able to cover the full cost of school building. Local control of education disappeared. Who could quarrel with this when schools came for nothing?

The democratic governments were responsible for huge undertakings. The government railways were the largest businesses and biggest employers in colonial times. The provision of teachers and policemen throughout the colony and the sale and management of crown lands required large government departments.

Colonial politics did not look as if it would manage these large undertakings well. Members were concerned with getting benefits for their electorate and willing to trade their support to do so. Governments were short-lived and always had only a precarious hold on power.

But though politics was confused and unstable, administration was honest and efficient. Frequent changes of government did not matter much because there were no fundamental disagreements over what governments should be doing. The senior public servants had tenure and many of them were of outstanding quality. Ministers appointed public servants to reward supporters but incoming ministers did not sack existing public servants.

To their credit, politicians did not use politics to enrich themselves. A railway might be built to please constituents though there was little real need for it; a railway might even be built to run close to the property owned by members of parliament; but the money for railways did not go directly into MPs' pockets. The governor, still appointed from Britain, was a guarantor that proper standards were maintained.

Though the colonists had little respect for their politicians, their faith in government grew in the nineteenth century. In the twentieth century they created a national government which was meant to have limited powers, but quickly came to be used as an all-purpose facility like the colonial governments. It was to protect and foster industry and ensure workers received a living wage and that farmers got a good return for their crops.

*

Government in Australia has been continuous; it has never broken down and had to be reconstituted. Except in the treatment of Aborigines, government has never been an oppressive force, something that large numbers of people feared. Government has never been simply a means of fleecing people; it has always been a supplier of services that people wanted.

There has been strong government but no ruling class. When the governors ruled, the rich landowners and squatters thought they would take over when self-government was granted. But when self-government came they were quickly defeated and democratic politics began. The democratic politicians were a very mixed bag indeed, not identified with any one group in society, so distinct that they were a group in themselves – the despised politicians.

Government is without social character; it is an impersonal force. That makes it possible for Australian egalitarians to give it the great respect that its record deserves.

The most distinctive characteristic of the Australian political system is compulsory voting. Polls show that a clear majority of people is in favour of compulsory voting. If there were no compulsion, there would be a reasonable turnout. But Australians want to be compelled to vote.

Those who write and comment on politics are overwhelmingly in favour of compulsion. In defending compulsion, they make a distinctively Australian contribution of political philosophy. To the objection that compulsory voting is a denial of liberty, they argue that governments regularly make citizens do things – to serve on juries, to pay taxes, to fight in the defence of the country. Of course governments compel citizens, but compulsory voting relates to another issue altogether: how governments are themselves created. Are citizens to be forced to create governments?

This argument has been developed in a society where the value placed on personal liberty and the responsibilities of citizenship has shifted markedly from that in other English-speaking democracies. The existence of government is taken for granted and the people can be forced to be citizens.

*

Australian democracy is certainly distinctive. There has been strong opposition to military conscription, but not to compulsory voting. Egalitarianism has not led to a universal welfare system nor prohibited the growth of private schools. Politicians have been held in contempt, but governments have been omni-competent and efficient. The people have been scornful of British snobbishness, but loyal to a British monarch. Men have been keen about mateship, leaving women to take citizenship seriously. There are no grand Australian statements about democracy, but the values that underpin it flourish in society at large.

All these characteristics have their causes. Taken together they account for that strange gap, that lack of attachment, between a democratic society and its democratic institutions of government, with which our enquiry began.

Another way of approaching the matter is to say that the movements for political democracy were not strong enough to command the society and to set its ideals. Manhood suffrage was achieved in the mid-nineteenth century when the word *democracy* could not be safely uttered. Democratic practice thus began without a democratic ideology.

A democratic ideology was certainly present in the second democratic movement at the end of the nineteenth century. Its carriers were at first the progressive liberals. It looked for a time as if the Labor Party that supplanted them could carry forward their ideal of an enlightened, democratic people shaping a new social order. Labor projected itself as the true national party and boasted of its moves to give the nation a strong defence force and to support compulsory military training. But in the Great War those who wanted Labor to be a class party for the workers took control, threw out the parliamentary leaders and gave Labor the pyrrhic victory of anti-conscription. Labor now carried the tag of being the disloyal party.

Labor recovered and was able on several occasions to govern well, but only as one party in a two-party system. It was not the standard-bearer of a wider democratic movement as it had been before the war. Indeed, the party system came to discourage wider democratic involvement. The small women's movement tried valiantly to keep alive the ideal of good citizens acting outside the party system – and failed.

Australia still awaits the moment when its natural democrats will become self-conscious citizens.

2002

SOURCES

An earlier version of Frank Bongiorno's introduction appeared in *The Monthly* online, 16 February 2016.

Alex McDermott's introduction is previously unpublished.

An earlier version of Robert Manne's introduction was delivered at the Allan Martin Symposium, Australian National University, 11 May 2006.

'Changing My Mind' appeared in Stuart Macintyre ed., *The Historian's Conscience: Australian historians and the ethics of history*, Melbourne University Press, Melbourne, 2004.

'How Did a Penal Colony Change Peacefully to a Democracy?' appeared in *Australian History in 7 Questions*, Black Inc., Melbourne, 2016.

'Transformation on the Land' is an excerpt from 'La sociedad rural y la politica en Australia, 1950–1930' in J. Fogarty, E. Gallo, H. Dieguez eds, *Argentina y Australia*, Instituto Torcuato Di Tella, Buenos Aires, 1979.

'Distance in Australia – Was It a Tyrant?', *Historical Studies*, vol. 16, no. 64, 1975, pp. 435–447.

'Colonial Society' appeared as 'Keeping Colonial History Colonial: The Hartz Thesis Revisited', *Historical Studies*, vol. 21, no. 82, 1984, pp. 85–104.

'Egalitarianism', *Australian Cultural History*, no. 5 ('Myths and Cliches'), 1986, pp. 12–31. Reprinted in S. L. Goldberg and F. B. Smith eds, *Australian Cultural History*, Cambridge University Press, Melbourne, 1988.

'The Pioneer Legend', *Historical Studies*, vol. 18, no. 71, 1878, pp. 316–37. The shortened version in this collection appeared in J. Carroll ed., *Intruders in the Bush: The Australian Quest for Identity*, Oxford University Press, Melbourne, 1992.

'Nothing but Bad' appeared in *IPA Review*, vol. 32, no. 3, December–February, 1988/89.

'How Sorry Can We Be?' appeared in *Sense & Nonsense in Australian History*, Black Inc., Melbourne, 2005.

'The Convict Legacy' appeared as 'An Oddity from the Start: Convicts and the National Character' in *The Monthly*, July 2008.

'Federation: Destiny and Identity', in *For Peace, Order, and Good Government: Papers on Parliament*, no. 37, Department of the Senate, Canberra, 2001, which draws on chapters 1 and 2 of *The Sentimental Nation: The Making of the Australian Commonwealth*, Oxford University Press, Melbourne, 2000.

'Why Did the Australian Colonies Federate?' appeared in *Australian History in 7 Questions*, Black Inc., Melbourne, 2016.

'Boxing and Honour' appeared in *The World of Albert Facey*, Allen & Unwin, Sydney, 1992.

'Making Voting Compulsory' appeared as 'Voters' in *Australian Democracy: A Short History*, Allen & Unwin, Sydney, 2002.

'Labor's Part in Australian History: A Lament' was presented as the Australian National University's Allan Martin Lecture 2006 and published in that year by Pandanus Books.

'Deeds of Courage' appeared as 'Political Courage: Some Australian Examples' in *The Monthly*, July 2007.

'The Communist Threat' appeared as 'Communism and Australia's Historians', *Quadrant*, vol. 34, no. 4, April 1990, pp. 26–31.

'Was Curtin the Best Prime Minister?' appeared in *Looking for Australia*, Black Inc., Melbourne, 2010.

'A Republican Manifesto' appeared in *A Republican Manifesto*, Oxford University Press, Melbourne, 1994.

'Australia's Absurd History: A Critique of Multiculturalism', *Overland*, no. 117, February 1990, pp. 5–10

'Where Best to Look? The First XI Books' appeared as 'The First XI' in *The Monthly*, October 2006.

'The Distinctiveness of Australian Democracy', *Quadrant*, vol. 46, no. 12, December 2002, pp. 19–27, which summarises the chief arguments of *Australia's Democracy: A Short History*, Allen & Unwin, Sydney, 2002.

SELECT BIBLIOGRAPHY OF JOHN HIRST

Adelaide and the Country 1870–1917: Their Social and Political Relationships, Melbourne University Press, Carlton, 1973.

Convict Society and Its Enemies: A History of Early New South Wales, George Allen & Unwin, Sydney, 1983.

The Strange Birth of Colonial Democracy: New South Wales 1848–1884, George Allen & Unwin, Sydney, 1988.

The World of Albert Facey, Allen & Unwin, Sydney, 1992.

A Republican Manifesto, Oxford University Press, Melbourne, 1994.

The Oxford Companion to Australian History, Graeme Davison, John Hirst and Stuart Macintyre eds, Oxford University Press, Melbourne, 1998; revised edition 2001.

Discovering Democracy: A Guide to Government and Law in Australia, Curriculum Corporation, Melbourne, 1998.

The Sentimental Nation: The Making of the Australian Commonwealth, Oxford University Press, Melbourne, 2000.

Australia's Democracy: A Short History, Allen & Unwin, Sydney, 2002.

'Kangaroo Court': Family Law in Australia, Quarterly Essay no. 17, Black Inc., Melbourne, 2005.

Sense & Nonsense in Australian History, Black Inc., Melbourne, 2005.

Making Voting Secret, Victorian Electoral Commission, Melbourne, 2006.

The Australians, Black Inc., Melbourne, 2007.

Freedom on the Fatal Shore, Black Inc., Melbourne, 2008.

Building a Free Australia: Places of Democracy, Australian Heritage Council, Canberra, 2009.

The Shortest History of Europe, Black Inc., Melbourne, 2009.

Looking for Australia, Black Inc., Melbourne, 2010.

Australian History in 7 Questions, Black Inc., Carlton, 2016.

INDEX